Euthanasia:
The Good of the Patient,
the Good of Society

Robert I. Misbin

Frederick  Maryland

University Publishing Group Inc.
Frederick, Maryland 21701

ISBN 1-55572-017-X

durch Mitleid wissen

Contents

PART III
Do-Not-Resuscitate Orders

PART IV
Legal, Ethical, and Religious Issues

APPENDIX

Contributors

Fredrick R. Abrams, MD, is a Professor at the Center for Health Ethics and Politics, Graduate School of Public Health, University of Colorado, Denver.

Pieter V. Admiraal, MD, is an Anesthesiologist at the Reinier de Graaf Gasthuis, Delft, the Netherlands.

Peter Angelos, MD, is a Resident in the Department of Surgery, Northwestern University Medical School, Chicago.

D.J. Bakker, MD, PhD, is Associate Professor of Surgery at the University of Amsterdam Academic Medical Center, the Netherlands.

Margaret Pabst Battin, PhD, is a Professor of Philosophy at the University of Utah, Salt Lake City.

Else Borst-Eilers, MD, PhD, is Vice President of the Health Council of the Netherlands, the Hague.

Howard Brody, MD, PhD, is Professor at the Center for Ethics and Humanities in the Health Sciences, Michigan State University, East Lansing, Michigan.

Titia H.C. Bueller is a Nurse studying health law at the University of Amsterdam, the Netherlands.

Courtney S. Campbell, PhD, is an Assistant Professor in the Department of Religion, Oregon State University, Corvallis.

Clarke D. Forsythe, JD, is Vice President and General Counsel, Americans United For Life.

J.K.M. Gevers, JD, is Professor of Law at the University of Amsterdam, the Netherlands.

Edward Grant, JD, is former President and previous Washington Counsel for Americans United For Life.

Mitchell M. Handelsman, PhD, is an Assistant Professor in the Department of Psychology, University of Colorado, Denver.

Nanette B. Hoffman, MD, is a Geriatrician at the Veteran's Administration Medical Center, Gainesville, Florida.

Laurence B. McCullough, PhD, is a Professor of Medicine and Ethics at the Center for Bioethics, Medicine, and Public Issues, Baylor College of Medicine, Houston, Texas.

Robert I. Misbin, MD, is an Associate Professor of Medicine in the Division of Endocrinology at the University of Florida School of Medicine, Gainesville.

Edmund D. Pellegrino, MD, is Director of the Georgetown University Center for the Advanced Study of Ethics, Washington, DC.

Ronald F. White, PhD, is an Assistant Professor of Philosophy in the Humanities Department, Mount St. Joseph College, Mount St. Joseph, Ohio.

Preface

On 8 January 1988 the *Journal of the American Medical Association* published an article entitled "It's Over Debbie," recounting the story of a resident physician who killed a patient with ovarian cancer in order to end her suffering. The journal later published letters commenting on the article. The response from physicians was virtually universal condemnation for breaching the primary ethics of the medical profession, "Doctors must not kill." However, responses from the lay public were more sympathetic. Readers related personal accounts of relatives who suffered needlessly prolonged deaths.

How should physicians respond to discussions about euthanasia? Many believe it is a breach of professional responsibility for physicians to put their heads in the sand or attempt to shield themselves with righteous indignation. In order to facilitate discussion, members of the Medical Humanities faculty of the University of Florida hosted a conference from 14 to 16 February 1991, entitled "Controversies in the Care of Dying Patients." The conference was sponsored by the American Medical Association, the Society for Health and Human Values, and the Siegfried and Josephine Bieber Foundation, and was attended by 300 participants who came from thirty-seven states, in addition to Puerto Rico and the District of Columbia, and from three Canadian provinces and four countries outside of North America.

The Conference did not end in consensus. But that was not its purpose. Rather, we wanted to bring to practicing physicians the opportunity to discuss with colleagues and to explore within themselves how to best meet the challenge of dealing with patients who request euthanasia. To those who reject euthanasia falls the task of finding alternative ways to alleviate the suffering that patients fear as they approach death. To those who accept euthanasia falls the burden of knowing that by moving beyond the traditional role of physician as healer, they run the risk of allowing the profession to become the tool of those forces in our society that value expediency over compassion. And to those, like myself, who are undecided, falls the greatest task. We must prevent the medical profession from becoming hostage to those who talk the loudest and insist that only they know what is right.

Robert I. Misbin

Introduction

Robert I. Misbin

On 5 November 1991 the voters of Washington State rejected an initiative that would have legalized euthanasia and physician-assisted suicide. Had Initiative 119 passed, it would have amended the state's Natural Death Act to permit "physician aid in dying," which was defined as "a medical service provided in person by a physician that will end the life of a conscious and mentally competent qualified person in a dignified, painless, and humane manner when requested voluntarily by the patient through a written advance directive executed at the time the service is desired." The request for physician aid in dying would have to have been made by the patient in the presence of two independent witnesses. Two physicians who had each examined the patient would have had to certify in writing that the patient had a terminal illness likely to result in death within six months.[1]

Although a national poll conducted on 18 through 20 October 1991 and published in the *Boston Globe* on 3 November showed that 64 percent of those surveyed favored giving terminally ill patients the option of physician-assisted suicide,[2] the Washington initiative was defeated by a vote of 54 percent to 46 percent.[3] Despite this setback, supporters of euthanasia have gathered enough signatures to put an initiative on the ballot in California in 1992 and hope to have an initiative on the Oregon ballot in 1993.[4] The California initiative, Proposition 161, includes the requirement that health-care providers report the number of euthanasia cases annually, including the ages and illnesses of those who had died. It also requires that for residents of a nursing home to receive physician aid in dying, their request must be witnessed by a patient advocate appointed by the state for this purpose.[5] These two requirements were written into the California initiative in order to provide the procedural safeguards that were lacking in the Washington initiative.[6]

Although the question of euthanasia (literally, a "good death") has been discussed since antiquity, it is only recently that the issue has captured the attention of the American public. The cover story from *Newsweek* from 26 August 1991[7] described how the suicide manual *Final Exit,* written by Derek Humphrey of the Hemlock Society, appeared on the *New York Times* best seller list within a few weeks of its publication.

How should physicians respond to discussions about euthanasia and assisted suicide? Many believe that for physicians to intentionally kill patients is incompatible with their role as healers. Others believe that the ultimate duty of physicians is to relieve suffering, and that at times this can only be accomplished by the patient's death. The purpose of this book is to examine various aspects of the euthanasia controversy. In the first section are the views of three physician ethicists about participation in euthanasia. Peter Angelos, a surgeon at Northwestern University, examines the distinction between direct killing and allowing patients to die of their illnesses. He concludes that the morality of the act is determined by whether or not there was intent to do good and not by whether the death was caused by action or omission. Thus, he argues that physicians who accede to requests of dying patients to end their suffering by a lethal injection are on firmer moral ground than physicians who refuse requests, but allow patients to die an unpleasant death by withdrawing treatment. By contrast, Dr. Edmund Pellegrino of Georgetown University, believes that it is crucial to make the distinction between allowing to die and direct killing. Dr. Pellegrino argues that patients have a right to accept or refuse a treatment based on their perception of whether that treatment will benefit them. Thus, if patients refuse treatment and are "allowed to die" of their disease, it is the *disease* that kills the patient. However, if a physician gives the patient a lethal injection, it is the *physician* who "kills" the patient, not the disease. Moreover, Dr. Pellegrino worries that to allow a physician to kill a patient, even at the patient's request, would desensitize physicians to the value of human life and to the nature of suffering, and would contribute to the hubris of the medical profession that life and death are subservient to physicians. In the final chapter of this section, Dr. Fredrick Abrams argues that a beneficent physician should be willing to take a flexible stand in order to help a patient whose needs may be exceptional. He does not advocate legalization of euthanasia, but argues that under certain conditions mercy killing should be recognized as an appropriate defense against a charge of manslaughter or professional malpractice.

The second section describes the practice of euthanasia in the Netherlands. Although still illegal, euthanasia in not prosecuted if it is performed for beneficent motives and in accordance with certain procedures. Dr. Else Borst-Eilers of the Netherlands Health Council traces the history of the euthanasia movement in her country and presents data on current practice. She attempts to answer the "slippery slope" argument that voluntary euthanasia will ultimately jeopardize the care of severely ill patients because of desensitization of physicians to the value of human life. In the second chapter, Professor Gevers of the University of Amsterdam describes how Dutch law has evolved to a situation where physicians are permitted to perform euthanasia, even though it has never been legalized. Next come divergent views from two prominent Dutch physicians. Dr. Pieter Admiraal is an anesthesiologist in Delft and one of the first Dutch physicians to openly perform euthanasia. To him, it is the ultimate professional responsibility to grant the request for euthanasia from a patient whose suffering he cannot relieve by other means. To Derek Bakker, a surgeon from the University of Amsterdam, euthanasia is an abrogation of professional responsibility that will ultimately jeopardize the quality of care that is provided to the terminally ill. Both Dr. Admiraal and Dr. Bakker draw on their own clinical experience to support their views. Finally, Professor Margaret Pabst Battin of the University of Utah examines the differences in culture between the United States and the Netherlands and explains why the practice of euthanasia, which appears to work well for the Dutch, would probably lead to bad results if applied to the American system of health care.

The third section deals with ethical and legal issues surrounding do-not-resuscitate (DNR) orders. The technique of cardiopulmonary resuscitation was developed to prevent premature death, as, for instance, in a patient who has a cardiac arrest during an evolving myocardial infarction. By the mid 1970s, it became clear that attempts at resuscitation were being made on hospitalized patients who were dying from an underlying disease process that was irreversible. The result in many cases was only to prolong the process of dying and cause needless suffering for patients and their families. In order to remedy this problem, hospitals have been required to develop policies to identify those patients on whom cardiopulmonary resuscitation should not be attempted. It is now widely accepted that dying patients have the right to request not to be resuscitated, and that if they have lost decision-making capacity, their request can be made on their behalf through an advance directive or appropriate surrogate. What remains controversial is whether physicians should have the authority to withhold resuscitation in patients for whom they believe it would be medically futile, and if so, whether they must inform the patients and/or their family of the decision. In New York State, physicians are required by law to attempt resuscitation unless they have obtained specific consent from the patient or surrogate that resuscitation be withheld. In the first chapter of this section, the Ethics Group of the Memorial Sloane-Kettering Cancer Center gives the history of the New York State DNR law and presents data on how it has affected medical practice at the center. Next, Dr. Howard Brody of Michigan State University discusses whether patients have a right to demand resuscitation under conditions in which it is unlikely to offer them any genuine benefit. Dr. Nanette Hoffman of the University of Florida provides a review of the literature on the outcome of attempted resuscitation in various categories of illnesses. She notes, for example, that survival after cardiac arrest in patients with sepsis is virtually zero. Progressive systemic acidosis is also associated with abysmal survival. Based on these data, she argues that physicians are on strong ground not to attempt to resuscitate certain patients, regardless of whether there is consent from the patient or family. In the fourth chapter, Professor Laurence McCullough of Baylor University examines the philosophic basis for the claim made by Drs. Brody and Hoffman that physicians need not offer CPR to patients for whom it would be medically futile. He reasons that harm would be done to many patients in a system that allows an individual patient to demand futile resuscitation and argues that no one has the right to make a demand that would produce so much harm to others and be so wasteful of scarce resources.

The final section deals with the legal, ethical, and religious issues involved in euthanasia. Edward Grant and Clark Forsythe of Americans United for Life trace the legal history of the right-to-die movement in the United States. They note that courts have consistently held that the right to refuse life-sustaining treatment does not end when patients cease to have decision-making capacity, but can be exercised on their behalf through advance directives or through the substituted judgment of others. Thus, they argue that if the right to demand euthanasia became a legal option, courts would be likely to follow precedent and allow others to request that suffering patients be killed for their own good. Once this threshold is crossed, they fear that the next logical step would be involuntary killing of infants with severe birth defects and elderly patients with dementia. Next, Professor Courtney Campbell of the Religious Studies Department at Oregon State College summarizes the positions on euthanasia taken by most of the major American churches. He goes on to explain what role religious-based arguments should play in a diverse and secular society like the United States. Next, Titia Bueller of the University of Amsterdam reviews the political and religious history of the Netherlands and attempts to explain what is unique about Dutch society that accounts for the support of voluntary euthanasia by a large segment of the population. Professor Ronald White of Mt. St. Joseph's College examines the ethical issues involved in physician-assisted suicide. He believes that suicide is not an irrational response to an incurable debilitating illness, and that assistance by physicians in patients' suicides is part of their professional obligation to help patients avoid harm. In the final chapter, Professor Mitchell Handelsman of the University of Colorado discusses the legislative history that led to passage by Congress of the Patient Self-Determination Act. This act took effect 1 December 1991, and mandates that health-care facilities discuss advance directives with patients and inform them of their right to refuse life-sustaining treatment.

NOTES

1   R.I. Misbin, "Physician Aid in Dying," *New England Journal of Medicine* 325 (31 October 1991):1307-11.
2   "Euthanasia Favored in Poll," *New York Times,* 4 November 1991, A16.
3   "Voters Turn Down Mercy Killing Idea," *New York Times,* 7 November 1991, B16.
4   P. Steinfels, "In Cold Print, The Euthanasia Issues Can Take on Many Shades of Color," *New York Times,* 9 November 1991, L11.
5   The California Attorney General has prepared a fact sheet about Proposition 161 that will be distributed to voters. Appendix 1 is a summary based on this fact sheet, with samples of the patient's directive and statement of witnesses.
6   B.J. Crigge, "New California Initiative," *Hastings Center Report* 22 (March/April 1992):8.
7   K. Ames, L. Wilson, R. Sawhill, and P. King, "Last Rites," *Newsweek,* 26 August 1991, 40-41.

Part I

Euthanasia in the United States? Physicians' Responses

1

Physician Responsibility for Euthanasia

Peter Angelos

The recent controversy sparked by three well-publicized news items have revealed the ongoing debate over the appropriate role of physicians in active euthanasia. In January 1988, the article, "It's Over, Debbie," appeared in the *Journal of the American Medical Association*.[1] The article gave an account of a resident physician's response to a patient who had stated, "Let's get this over with." The physician gave the patient an overdose of pain medication, which resulted in death. The publication of this article led to responses that varied from threats of prosecution to whole-hearted support by some patients' rights groups.

More recently, Dr. Jack Kevorkian has provided doctor-assisted suicide to three patients. In June 1990, Kevorkian helped a woman diagnosed with Alzheimer's disease to die.[2] In this case, a competent person was given assistance in committing suicide by using an intravenous device built and connected to the person by Kevorkian. Then in October 1991, Kevorkian helped two more women, neither of whom had terminal diseases, to commit suicide. One woman, who had multiple sclerosis, used a device similar to the one Kevokian had used previously. The other woman, who suffered from a painful pelvic disease, was killed by carbon monoxide gas administered by face mask.[3] Again, the public response to these activities has been mixed. After the 1990 case, Kevorkian was charged with first-degree murder, but the charge was eventually dismissed.[4] After the 1991 cases, which were eventually ruled to be homicides, Kevorkian's medical license was suspended by the Michigan Board of Medicine.[5] Further legal action against Kevorkian is reportedly being considered.

Yet another example of the growing public debate concerning euthanasia is the case of Dr. Timothy E. Quill, who prescribed barbiturates to his patient

"Diane" knowing that she was planning to use them to commit suicide.[6] As a result of reporting this case of physician-assisted suicide, Quill received support from many in the medical community; however, he also risked criminal indictment for assisting suicide.[7]

There appears to be growing public support for euthanasia in the United States. In the fall of 1987, the Humane and Dignified Death Act was sponsored for the ballot in California, but it failed to receive sufficient signatures to be included as a referendum item on the ballot. In the fall of 1991, voters in the state of Washington narrowly defeated Initiative 119, which would have allowed physicians in certain circumstances to give lethal injections to patients who requested them.[8] The related topic of assisted suicide has also proved to have wide public interest, as shown by the rise of Derek Humphrey's suicide manual, *Final Exit*.[9] to the top of best-sellers lists. Thus, the question of the physician's role in euthanasia has a practical urgency in addition to its theoretical and philosophical debate.

BASIC TERMS

The term "euthanasia" is derived from the ancient Greek word for "good" or "merciful" death.[10] Its contemporary definition has become blurred by the controversy associated with the act of euthanasia. Euthanasia, as used in this paper, refers to the intentional termination of the life of a person to prevent his further suffering.[11]

There are two common distinctions: one distinction is among voluntary, involuntary, and nonvoluntary euthanasia; and the second distinction is between active and passive euthanasia. The distinction among voluntary, involuntary, and nonvoluntary euthanasia is based on the intentions of the patient. Voluntary euthanasia is when a competent person requests that his life be terminated. Involuntary euthanasia is when a patient's wish to continue his life is overridden by family or guardian. Because involuntary euthanasia is conceptually identical to murder, it has been categorically opposed even by those who accept voluntary euthanasia. Nonvoluntary euthanasia is when a person is not competent to communicate or to make a choice about his own death.

The distinction between active and passive euthanasia is commonly referred to as the difference between killing and letting die. It has been claimed by some that active euthanasia is always wrong, but that passive euthanasia is sometimes acceptable. For example, it is considered to be a form of active euthanasia to give a patient a lethal injection in order to hasten death deliberately. On the other hand, the decision not to treat medical problems or the decision to remove a patient from a respirator is usually considered passive euthanasia. On a fundamental level, this distinction has been based on the purported difference between actions (or commissions) and omissions.

In its most problematic form, the issue of euthanasia relates to active euthanasia, because many people already accept passive euthanasia. At the heart of the controversy is the physician's responsibility for responding to a patient's request for active euthanasia. In considering the issue of physician responsibility for active euthanasia, two questions must be answered. First, is there any moral impediment to physicians' acceding to the requests of terminally ill patients for active euthanasia? Second, if active euthanasia can be morally justified, are physicians morally bound to provide active euthanasia?

THE REALM OF PHYSICIAN RESPONSIBILITY

Before these questions can be answered, the notion of physician responsibility must be addressed. The term is used carelessly in many different contexts without recognition of its various connotations. Although different uses of the term "physician responsibility" are often not clearly distinguished, the fact that there are different uses reflects the ambiguity inherent in defining the scope of a physician's responsibility and in evaluating the issue of a physician's responsibility for euthanasia.

For the purposes of this paper, the term "physician responsibility" will refer to the realm over which a physician exercises appropriate concern and expertise. Thus, physician responsibility would include all actions relating to the well-being of patients, whether they be the actual treatment of physical and mental ailments, or the associated counseling involved in such treatment. The crucial question is whether a physician's acquiescence to a patient's request for euthanasia should be included in the realm of physician responsibility. In order to answer this question in the affirmative, it is necessary to show that there is nothing immoral when a physician agrees to fulfill a patient's request for euthanasia.

THE MORAL DISTINCTION BETWEEN ACTIVE
AND PASSIVE EUTHANASIA

Central to many arguments against active euthanasia is the putative moral distinction between active and passive euthanasia that the medical profession has traditionally acknowledged. Stating that there is a moral distinction between any two things is to suggest that there is a difference that is based on the standards of acceptable behavior. In other words, a moral distinction is based on some system of valuation of right and wrong.

Traditionally, passive euthanasia has been considered acceptable, whereas active euthanasia has been considered unacceptable. This position is exemplified in the statement accepted by the House of Delegates of the American Medical Association (AMA) in 1973:

> The intentional termination of the life of one human being by another --mercy killing--is contrary to that for which the medical profession stands and is contrary to the policy of the American Medical Association.

> The cessation of the employment of extraordinary means to prolong the
> life of the body when there is irrefutable evidence that biological death is
> imminent is the decision of the patient and/or his immediate family. The
> advice and judgment of the physician should be freely available to the
> patient and/or his immediate family.[12]

Clearly, this statement suggests that there is a moral difference between "mercy
killing" (active euthanasia) and "cessation of the employment of extraordinary
means to prolong the life of the body" (passive euthanasia).

The philosophical assumption underlying the AMA statement is that there
is a moral difference between actions and omissions. In certain situations, the
distinction between an omission and an action is ambiguous, and in such
situations, people are held legally and morally accountable for omissions as
much as for actions. For example, a parent's failure to feed a child could be seen
as an omission. This same case can be characterized as an action--a parent
starving a child. Regardless of whether the child's plight is described as the result
of an action or an omission by his parent, the parent would nevertheless be
blameworthy. This example illustrates the problem of grounding morality on the
distinction between actions and omissions.

Is there a moral difference between killing and letting die? Consider the
physician's role in the following two cases. In Case A, a sixty-seven-year-old man
suffering from terminal metastatic malignant melanoma is diagnosed with
pneumonia. He requests that he not be given antibiotics to treat his pneumonia
so that his tremendous pain and suffering may be ended. Without antibiotics, it
is assumed that this man will die of pneumonia. In Case B, yet another sixty-
seven-year-old man suffering from terminal metastatic malignant melanoma
requests that his physician give him a lethal injection so that his tremendous pain
and suffering may be ended. Despite the deliberate similarities between these
two cases, they differ. By acquiescing to the patient's request in Case A, the
physician is viewed merely as refraining from preventing the patient's death. In
Case B, however, the physician's granting of the patient's request is viewed as
killing the patient.

This seems to be an important difference because, according to the AMA
distinction, Case A is an acceptable request for a physician to meet, whereas
Case B is "contrary to that for which the medical profession stands." But what
are the differences between Case A and Case B that have such moral significance? In Case A, the physician--hoping to lessen the amount of pain and
suffering the patient will experience--goes along with the patient's request and
refrains from providing potentially life-prolonging antibiotics. Why would the
physician do such a thing? One could argue that the patient has a right to refuse
treatment, which the physician is legally bound to respect. But at a deeper level,
the physician would do such a thing because he and the patient agree that the
patient would be better off not living longer. Thus, the patient's life will be

shortened for his own benefit. However, Case B looks very similar to Case A. Out of a desire to lessen pain and suffering of the patient, the physician and the patient decide that the patient would be better off not having his life prolonged. As a result, the physician gives a lethal injection. In both cases, motives seem to be the same, and the ultimate result is the same--namely the patient dies sooner than he might otherwise have. The only difference seems to be that in Case B, the physician performed a physical action that resulted in the patient's death, whereas in Case A, the physician failed to intervene with antibiotics once the patient developed pneumonia. Thus, a physical action or bodily event seems to have led to a significant moral distinction.

The error of making a moral distinction based on the presence or absence of a physical act is more clearly illustrated by J. Rachels's two cases in *The End of Life:*

> In the first, Smith stands to gain a large inheritance if anything should happen to his six-year-old cousin. One evening while the child is taking his bath, Smith sneaks into the bathroom and drowns the child, and then arranges things so that it will look like an accident.
>
> In the second, Jones also stands to gain if anything should happen to his six-year-old cousin. Like Smith, Jones sneaks in planning to drown the child in his bath. However, just as he enters the bathroom Jones sees the child slip and hit his head, and fall face down in the water. Jones is delighted; he stands by, ready to push the child's head back under if it is necessary, but it is not necessary. With only a little thrashing about, the child drowns all by himself, "accidently," as Jones watches and does nothing.[13]

The only difference in these two cases is that in the first, Smith killed his cousin, whereas in the second, Jones let his cousin die.

To claim that there is a moral difference between these two cases implies that morality is dependent on the presence or absence of a physical act. Both Smith and Jones acted for the same motive, and in both cases the consequences are the same. But only Smith committed the physical act of holding his cousin's head underwater. If this were truly a valid basis for making a moral distinction, then Smith's action would be considered morally worse than Jones's inaction. Such is not the case, however. Jones's inaction of standing by and watching the child drown is just as morally reprehensible as Smith's active drowning of the child. Thus, morality does not turn on the absence or presence of a physical act. In fact, morality is in no way tied to a physical event. Therefore, it follows that if the only difference between killing and letting die is the presence or absence of a physical act, there is no moral difference.

As previously discussed in the examples involving the two sixty-seven-year-old men, active euthanasia is different from passive euthanasia only in that active euthanasia involves the presence of a physical act; the motivations and consequences are identical. Accordingly, attempts to find a significant moral distinction between active and passive euthanasia must fail. Moreover, if there is no moral difference between active and passive euthanasia, then any justifications that may be accepted for passive euthanasia can be equally applied to active euthanasia. Although the preceding arguments have shown the collapse of the distinction between active and passive euthanasia, many arguments are still posed in terms of the active-passive distinction. For this reason the terms "active" and "passive" cannot be entirely eliminated from the following discussion.

EUTHANASIA AND THE GOALS OF MEDICINE

Some commentators have attempted to preclude physician participation in euthanasia by arguing that it goes against the goals of medicine. However, the goals of medicine are not clearly defined and do not offer a clear argument against euthanasia in all cases. Naturalists such as Leon Kass have argued that the appropriate goals of medicine should be limited to those that aim at the healthy human being.[14] Health, according to the naturalist view, is defined as a level of well-functioning that compares favorably with a reference or standard. Naturalists argue that such reference or standard can be deduced from the conditions existing in nature, without regard for values imposed by man.

If this naturalistic concept of somatic health is used to define the appropriate role of physicians, then physicians ought not be servants of the desires or wishes of individual patients. Desires and wishes of patients are not relevant to the determination of their health. Rather, their health should be determined by species-specific standards. Procedures such as abortions, vasectomies, in vitro fertilization, and cosmetic surgery do not further the naturalists' view of health and, therefore, are not considered appropriate for a physician to perform. Similarly, naturalists consider it inappropriate for a physician to participate in active euthanasia, because it is contrary to their view of health.

There are weaknesses in the naturalists' view of health and in the way this view defines the goals of medicine. The purely naturalistic definition of health fails to realize that the concept of health cannot be divorced from human values even in the most clear cases where treatment seems appropriate. Consider someone with a broken leg seeking medical attention. According to the naturalist view, a broken leg no longer meets the minimum state of anatomical and physiological norms; therefore, the decision to seek treatment of the broken leg is value free. This conclusion is unfounded. In reality, the consistent response throughout different cultures to mend the broken leg simply is a reflection of the uniformity of values.[15] Underlying the general agreement that a broken leg should be treated is merely the consensus that such activities as walking, running, working, or playing have value.

In contrast to the naturalists, normativists define health in reference to human values. Whereas naturalists frame health in terms of *well-functioning* with respect to norms found in nature, normativists focus on *well-being*, which can only be determined based on what an individual considers to be of value to him. Because health is a social construct, which is based on personal desires and values, a healthy condition for one person may not be considered as such by another. Consider two women who discover they are pregnant. One woman has been trying for a number of years to have a child. Because she values the bearing of a child, she considers her condition to be healthy; that is, the pregnancy enhances her well-being. The other woman, for whatever reasons, does not want to have a child. For her, the pregnancy diminishes her well being and, thus, it is not a healthy condition.

Not only does the concept of health differ from one person to the next person, but also it is changeable over time as human values change. This phenomenon is illustrated by an oft-used example. In the 1800s, masturbation was regarded as an evil activity and came to be considered a disease for which people were treated.[16] Today, masturbation is no longer seen as a malady requiring treatment. This change in view reflects the fact that much of the social taboo of masturbation has dissipated.

Put simply, a healthy condition, according to the normativists, is one that is valued. Thus, the goals of medicine are determined largely by what is valued by persons. For example, a terminally ill patient who is suffering intolerable pain may desire to end her life. A normativist would not view a request by such a patient to terminate her life to mean that her life has no value. Rather, such a request would be considered an assertion of that person's value for autonomy in choosing death rather than continued existence in suffering. Because meeting such a request by a physician furthers a healthy (that is, valued) condition, it would be within the realm of medicine and, consequently, the realm of physician responsibility. Thus, the view of some that the definition of health necessarily precludes physician participation in active euthanasia does not address the valid points raised by the normativists.

The distinctions between the naturalists' and the normativists' views of health illustrate the complexity of the concept of health. Given the examples discussed above, it would appear that the naturalists' view of health is overly simplistic. Thus, one cannot preclude physician participation in euthanasia by claiming that it is not consistent with the goals of medicine.

PHYSICIAN RESPONSIBILITY FOR EUTHANASIA
AND THE HIPPOCRATIC OATH

A cluster of arguments against the participation of physicians in euthanasia is based on the supposed traditional rejection of euthanasia by physicians. The Hippocratic Oath has been the basis for many of these assertions. The relevant passage in the oath states: "I will neither give a deadly drug to anybody if asked for it, nor will I make a suggestion to this effect."[17] The long tradition of deference granted to the Hippocratic Oath by Western medicine is not sufficient basis for claiming that physicians should not participate in active euthanasia.

 ✗ Not all of the directives of the oath are consistently upheld by modern medicine. For instance, those who swear to the oath are prohibited from practicing surgery ("I will not use the knife"), and yet contemporary medical practice is not limited to nonsurgical specialties. Thus, it is not clear why the directive prohibiting euthanasia should be so adamantly upheld. Paul Carrick, a scholar on ancient medical ethics, suggests that the oath was not an important guide to medical practice, even in ancient Greece.[18] In fact, he is of the opinion that the Hippocratic Oath was simply a document describing the rules of a particular guild of practitioners of medicine in ancient Greece. Carrick's claim offers another reason for discounting the importance of the oath's prohibition of active euthanasia. Thus, not even ancient traditional medicine can support an argument against physician participation in euthanasia. ✗

A related argument raised against physician participation in active euthanasia is based on yet another Hippocratic phrase that physicians must "do no harm." This so-called principle of medical ethics is also based on the Hippocratic writings, although it is not specifically found in the oath. The phrase comes from one of the lesser known Hippocratic works, the *Epidemics*, and is found in the following context: "Declare the past, diagnose the present, foretell the future; practice these acts. As to diseases, make a habit of two things--to help or at least to do no harm."[19]

The difficulty in using this passage, or even the stronger versions that have developed from it, is that the notion of harm is ambiguous. It is not obvious that harm refers simply to physician harm or to the shortening of a patient's life. A more accurate interpretation of this passage requires the understanding that there are many different kinds of harm that should be avoided by a physician. These include emotional or psychological harm, as well as physical harm. When a suffering patient requests that his life be terminated in order to stop his pain, a physician would be harming the patient by not granting his request, unless the physician can stop the pain short of killing him.

Another set of arguments against physicians participating in active euthanasia is based on the belief that its practice will corrode the trust of patients in physicians. Some claim that killing is antithetical to the healing relationship that physicians must cultivate with their patients. Thus, once physicians start killing patients, irreparable damage will be done to the physician-patient relationship. Alexander Capron makes such a claim when he states:

 ✗ I never want to wonder whether the physician coming into my hospital room is wearing the white coat (or the green scrubs) of a healer--concerned only to relieve my pain and restore me to health--or the black hood of the executioner. Trust between patient and physician is simply too important and too fragile to be subjected to this unnecessary strain.[20]

The claim that euthanasia corrodes the physician-patient relationship might make sense if physicians were to start making secret decisions to kill certain of their patients. If this were to occur, certainly many patients would rapidly lose trust in their physicians, and thereby severely strain the relationship between physicians and patients. This concern, however, is misplaced in cases of voluntary euthanasia. The tact that a physician would respect a patient's request to "care" for him by providing a lethal injection seems scant evidence that trust between patient and physician will be lost. In fact, in the Netherlands, where euthanasia is practiced, no evidence has been gathered to suggest that there has been a deterioration of the trust between patients and their physicians. It is important to remember that the healing relationship also includes helping and caring for the patient. Sometimes the best that a physician can do is to end a patient's suffering.

PHYSICIAN PARTICIPATION IN EUTHANASIA
AND THE SLIPPERY SLOPE

Another group of arguments against euthanasia is based on the notion that by engaging in active euthanasia, physicians will start down the path toward the general degradation of human life. There are two types of these so-called slippery-slope or wedge arguments. As discussed below, neither of these arguments are valid in the current debate concerning physician participation in euthanasia.

The first version of the slippery-slope argument asserts that once the first steps toward a position are taken, one is in danger of taking all of the additional steps toward the final position. This final position tends to be a moral stance that is agreed by society to be undesirable. The problem with this argument is that exceptions to general principles are commonly made without necessarily negating the entire principle. For example, despite the belief in our society that killing is wrong, we accept killing in self-defense. As such, one who has killed in self-defense is not punished for his act. However, this exception has not led contemporary society to accept more widespread killing, such as killing in response to minor annoyances. Thus, it is the case that even though some killing is allowed, this does not necessarily lead to the acceptance of killing in all circumstances. Likewise, by virtue of allowing physicians to participate in voluntary euthanasia, one is not logically committed to permitting physicians to perform involuntary euthanasia.

The second and stronger version of the slippery-slope argument is the psychological version asserted by Philippa Foot: "Apart from the special repugnance doctors feel towards the idea of a lethal injection, it may be of the very greatest importance to keep a psychological barrier up against killing."[21] This argument focuses on the tendency of human nature to accept practices that are familiar. Thus, if a new practice is similar to one that has already gained widespread acceptance, it is argued that people will more readily accept the new practice regardless of the logical distinctions that may be present. As applied to physician participation in active euthanasia, it is argued that if such participation is accepted, we will have taken the first steps toward the general devaluation of human life.

The grounds for the psychological version of the slippery-slope argument are derived mainly from an interpretation of a particular historical event: the Nazi program of genocide during World War II. The first to use the Nazi atrocities to discredit proposals for euthanasia in the United States was Leo Alexander, a Boston psychiatrist who was an expert witness for the prosecution at the Nuremberg war trials.[22] Alexander, in a widely quoted *New England Journal of Medicine* article in 1949, asserted that the killing in Nazi death camps began as a limited program of euthanasia:

> The beginnings at first were merely a subtle shift in emphasis in the basic attitude of the physicians. It started with the acceptance of the attitude, basic in the euthanasia movement, that there is such a thing as life not worthy to be lived. This attitude in its early stages concerned itself merely with the severely and chronically sick. Gradually the sphere of those to be included in this category was enlarged to encompass the unwanted and finally all non-Germans. But it is important to realize that the infinitely small wedged-in lever from which this entire trend of mind received its impetus was the attitude toward the nonrehabilitable sick.[23]

This excerpt explicitly sets forth the psychological version of the slippery-slope argument. Alexander suggests that from the "subtle shift in emphasis in the basic attitude of the physicians" toward the severely and chronically ill came the ultimate atrocities of medical experimentation and mass exterminations.

✗ There is a basic problem in applying the progression taken by physicians in Nazi Germany to the present debate concerning euthanasia. In general, for any analogy to be effective, the comparison must be between two similar situations. Essential to the analogy with the Nazi situation is the assumption that the practices conducted under the label "euthanasia" in Nazi Germany are similar to the practices considered as euthanasia today. There is, however, significant evidence to suggest that these terms do not refer to similar practices. The Nazis' idea of euthanasia developed out of the "scientific racism" movement common in some European intellectual circles during the last decade of the nineteenth century. An important aspect of this line of thinking was the emphasis placed on the integrity of the organic body of the *Volk*, or the preservation of racial or cultural groups.[24] Proponents of scientific racism argued that on behalf of the good of the *Volk*, the state had the right to control the death of individuals. Thus, the Nazi term "euthanasia" grew out of a tradition that allowed state-sanctioned murder. ✗

While Nazis emphasized the benefit to the state, the contemporary use of the term "euthanasia" refers to the good or easy death in terms of the benefit rendered to an individual person as judged by the person himself. Although both usages of the term refer to practices that result in death, the justification of the practices is completely different. In Nazi Germany, people were killed supposedly "for their own good," yet this presumed benefit was determined by state officials rather than by the people who were actually going to die. Those who were killed were the ill, senile, or members of particular ethnic or cultural groups that the state considered undesirable. On the other hand, patients are killed or allowed to die today because they have requested euthanasia, and such requests are based on the patients' own determination that death would be beneficial. Thus, this major difference between the Nazis' use of the term "euthanasia" and the contemporary use of that same term makes it impossible to form an analogy between the Nazi situation and the current debate on euthanasia.

Moreover, it would appear that the Nazis purposely misused the term "euthanasia" to deter outrage that may have resulted from their atrocities. Lucy Dawidowicz, a distinguished historian of the Holocaust, has stated:

"Euthanasia," as the Nazis used the term, is not euthanasia in our terms. "Euthanasia" was only a code name which the Nazis used as both camouflage and euphemism for a program of murder--killing various categories of persons because they were regarded as racially "valueless."[25]

Not only does the Nazi experience lose its effectiveness as an analogy, it is historically irrelevant to the contemporary euthanasia debate because the Nazis never practiced euthanasia in our sense of the word. Accordingly, proponents of the psychological slippery-slope argument cannot use the progression of the physicians' role in Nazi Germany as an example of what would occur as a result of physicians' participation in active euthanasia in current times.

PHYSICIAN RESPONSIBILITY FOR EUTHANASIA
AND PATIENT AUTONOMY

An important argument in favor of physician participation in euthanasia is based on the importance of respecting the autonomy of competent persons. Traditionally, competent patients have been legally allowed to refuse treatments even if the refusal will lead to death. Physicians have allowed patients to choose death out of respect for patient autonomy. Numerous philosophical theories have emphasized the importance of respecting autonomy. In addition, autonomy is generally accepted as an important principle of medical ethics. For example, it is general practice to obtain informed consent from competent patients for any medical treatments they may receive. As a corollary, treatments are not given to patients who withhold consent.

X On the basis of the principle of autonomy, physicians have generally agreed that competent patients should make decisions concerning their own care. As noted in the discussion of active and passive euthanasia above, physicians, through the AMA, have endorsed the view that in certain circumstances, patients may decide to have treatments withdrawn or withheld, which would have prolonged their lives. As also discussed above, there is no moral distinction between omissions that result in death and physical actions that result in death. To be consistent, therefore, a patient's request for active euthanasia also should be respected. In other words, a competent patient's request that treatments for his terminal disease be withdrawn should be granted out of respect for the patient's autonomous choices. Likewise, that same patient's request to have his life terminated by active euthanasia should similarly be granted by his physician, because there is no clear moral difference between omissions that lead to death and actions that lead to death.

Some have tried to avoid the conclusions of this argument by redefining what is meant by an autonomous choice. They argue that patients cannot rationally and autonomously choose active euthanasia.[26] Further, they argue that the act of making such a choice is proof that the patient is no longer competent to make an autonomous decision. Thus, they conclude, the principle of autonomy should no longer apply to this patient. This line of argument fails because of the same inconsistences previously seen. If a patient can rationally and autonomously decide in favor of an omission that leads to death, there is no reason to suggest that a patient cannot also rationally and autonomously decide in favor of an action that leads to death. Thus, if one accepts the principle of autonomy, one must also accept physician participation in active euthanasia when requested by a competent patient.

Some critics of the arguments based on the principle of autonomy have argued that a patient's request for active euthanasia is not a manifestation of an autonomous decision. Rather, a patient's request for active euthanasia is a decision made out of desperation. Richard Fenigsen claims that active euthanasia is requested only when a patient is not provided adequate pain control medication or enough attention by physicians to alleviate suffering.[27] Implicit in Fenigsen's claim is the assumption that physicians are best able to judge the needs of patients. This veiled paternalism suggests that physicians can determine and meet all of the important needs of patients, despite what a patient might request. Fenigsen states of dying patients:

> They needed support, relief from pain, breathlessness, or nausea. Until their last conscious moments they needed to belong, to share with all of us our common destiny, fears, uncertainties, and hopes.[28]

Although these seem to be important aspects of a dying patient's condition that ought to be addressed by physicians, Fenigsen misses an essential point by ignoring a patient's need to exercise self-determination in making autonomous choices concerning his own death.

The acceptability of physician participation in active euthanasia is not based solely on the alleviation of patient's pain or suffering. Rather, such participation by physicians is acceptable because active euthanasia is appropriately part of a patient's autonomy. Requests for euthanasia should not be discounted because the physician believes that he has met all of the dying patient's needs. It is only by listening and respecting the patient's autonomy that the physician will understand what is necessary for the patient. X

PHYSICIAN RESPONSIBILITY FOR EUTHANASIA AND CONSEQUENTIAL CONSIDERATIONS

If we focus our attention on only the consequential differences between active and passive euthanasia, perhaps the strongest argument in favor of physician participation in active euthanasia becomes apparent. Consider the following case. A seventy-five-year-old woman with advanced, widely metastatic colon cancer is suffering constant pain from the disease itself, as well as from the numerous intravenous lines required for her care. She is competent, and in numerous discussions with her family and physician has stated that she does not want to continue living in her present circumstances. According to the data available, there is little hope for any alteration in the progressive downward course of this woman's condition.

Having decided that she does not consider her life to be worthy of being prolonged, this patient may request that no further treatments (such as antibiotics for pneumonia) be started, and that resuscitation efforts be withheld if she goes into cardiac arrest. Alternatively, she may request that active euthanasia be performed (such as a lethal injection). In both situations, her goal is to shorten the life that she finds unbearable.

X What are the likely consequences of either scenario? In the first situation, the woman's intolerable pain and suffering will continue until the occurrence of one of two likely events. Either she dies of a condition other than the colon cancer, such as pneumonia or cardiac arrest, or she dies of the progression of the colon cancer itself. In either case, the patient must endure the pain and suffering for whatever length of time is necessary until the terminal event occurs. By contrast, in the second situation, the patient's life will be ended at the time that she considers it to be no longer worth living. There is no necessity, in this second situation, for the patient to have her suffering prolonged while waiting for a terminal event. In terms of the consequences suffered by the patient, there seem to be more benefits from active euthanasia than from the withholding of treatment. Thus, based on the consequences for the patient, active euthanasia seems to be a better and more humane alternative. X

Underlying this consequentialist argument for physician participation in active euthanasia is the principle of beneficence. Stated in general terms, beneficence requires that one help others to obtain certain important and legitimate interests and abstain from harming such persons.[29] The principle of beneficence can be problematic when it is unclear whose interests we must promote and upon whom the obligation of promoting those interests falls.

However, in the case of a patient with whom a physician has a personal and sustained professional relationship, there is no doubt that the principle of beneficence requires the physician to advance the patient's best interests as much as possible. When a competent patient expresses a clear request that she be allowed to die so as to end intolerable suffering, as in the example above, the principle of beneficence requires her physician to try to end her suffering in as humane a manner as possible.

REQUIREMENTS OF PHYSICIAN PARTICIPATION IN EUTHANASIA

The foregoing discussion presents evidence that there is no moral impediment to physicians' acceding to patient requests for active euthanasia in certain circumstances and that active euthanasia is indeed within the realm of physician responsibility. Fundamentally, the accepted justifications for passive euthanasia, which are assumed for purposes of this paper to be uncontroversial, may be extended without deformity to active euthanasia. Furthermore, three of the most common arguments against physician participation in active euthanasia do not withstand careful analysis. First, due to the controversy surrounding the appropriate definition of health, one cannot claim that physician participation in active euthanasia is outside the aims of medicine. Second, there is no evidence that physician participation in euthanasia corrodes the character of medicine either through altering the traditional role of the physician or through diminishing patient trust in physicians. Third, the slippery-slope argument has been shown to be lacking in plausibility. Finally, based on the consequentialist view and the importance of autonomy and beneficence, arguments favoring physician participation in active euthanasia have been set forth.

Having shown that there are no moral impediments to physician participation in active euthanasia, the second question posed at the outset--the question of whether physicians should be morally bound to provide active euthanasia--must be addressed. If an action is morally acceptable, is a physician obligated to take such an action? In other words, if it is moral for a physician to participate in active euthanasia, is it immoral for a physician to refuse such an appropriate request? Although there has been little attention paid to this second question in the medical ethics literature, it is an important component to the entire euthanasia debate. The answer to this second question has a significant and practical impact on the practice of medicine.

Medical interventions fall into various categories. In some cases, physicians are bound to provide treatment regardless of personal beliefs. For example, if an otherwise healthy patient sustains a cardiopulmonary arrest in the hospital, unless there is a valid do-not-resuscitate order, the physicians present are bound to provide resuscitative treatment. Physician responsibility in such a circumstance requires the performance of certain medical interventions.

There are, however, cases in which a physician might provide a specific medical intervention even though there is no obligation to do so. For example, a physician might be requested to perform a first-trimester abortion because the mother believes that she is not psychologically prepared for motherhood. A physician might also be asked to provide a second breast-augmentation procedure for a woman who states that after the first procedure her agent felt that her breasts were not large enough to allow her to be hired for certain modeling jobs. In these last two examples, the physicians are asked to apply their medical knowledge to further their patients' interests. However, there are significant differences between these examples and the first example of providing resuscitative interventions. In the last two examples, physicians might have strong personal beliefs that the interventions requested are not appropriate for physicians to provide. In circumstances such as these, physicians must exercise personal judgment and act according to their consciences. If acceding to a patient's request conflicts with a physician's strongly held, personal ethical beliefs, then the physician ought simply to provide appropriate referrals.

Providing active euthanasia is more like the last two situations above than like the first. It is a legitimate medical intervention that might be appropriately requested and performed in certain situations. Although it is consistent with the goals of medicine to accede to such a request for active euthanasia, a physician ought not be required to provide active euthanasia. The principle of autonomy previously discussed is just as important when applied to the physician, for decreasing the physician's power to choose courses of action does not necessarily enhance patient autonomy.[30] Just as a patient's autonomy must be respected in choosing whether, for example, a particular treatment should be continued or withdrawn, a physician's autonomy must be respected in deciding how to respond to a request for active euthanasia.

Although there should be no specific injunction against the development of "euthanasia clinics," where patients might go to find physicians who would be willing to provide active euthanasia, such facilities would clearly subvert many potential benefits for patients. If a dying patient knows that his physician will be ready to help him throughout the difficulties of terminal illness even by going so far as to provide active euthanasia if pain becomes intolerable, much of the patient's fears of the last stages of life prior to death might be relieved. Such a situation would lead to greater trust within the physician-patient relationship, as patients who found the last stages of their lives to be unbearable would not be forced to end potentially important relationships with their physicians. Patients and physicians would then be able to fully explore all of the options at the end of life with honesty and candor.

Thus, active euthanasia can be justified on a number of ethical grounds. It is not inconsistent with the goals of medicine. It would not appear to lead to a breakdown in the relationship between physician and patient. Rather, it would seem to encourage further discussion between patient and physician of what interventions are available at the last stages of life. Furthermore, providing active euthanasia in certain circumstances when requested by patients is the most humane intervention possible. Active euthanasia is not, therefore, outside of the physician's responsibility. However, physicians ought not be morally bound to provide active euthanasia.

NOTES

1   "It's Over, Debbie" (anonymous letter to the editor), *Journal of the American Medical Association* 259 (1988):272.

2   N. Gibbs, "Dr. Death's Suicide Machine," *Time* (18 June 1990):69-70.

3   "Examiner Rules Homicide in 2 Deaths Assisted by Kevorkian," *Chicago Tribune*, 19 December 1991, 18.

4   D. Gianelli, "Murder Charge Filed against Dr. Kevorkian May Spur further Euthanasia Debate," *American Medical News* (14 December 1990):3,34.

5   M. Williams, "Dr. Kevorkian's Future without a License Is Uncertain," *American Medical News* (9 December 1991):9.

6   T.E. Quill, "A Case of Individualized Decision Making," *New England Journal of Medicine* 324 (1991):691-94.

7   W. Glaberson, "Doctor Who Aided Patient Suicide May Be Tried," *New York Times*, 22 July 1991, B12.

8   "Voters Turn Down Mercy Killing Idea," *New York Times,* 7 November 1991, B16.

9   D. Humphrey, *Final Exit* (Eugene, OR: Hemlock Society, 1991); and K. Ames, *et al.*, "Last Rights," *Newsweek,* 26 August 1991, cover story.

10   D.C. Thomasma," The Range of Euthanasia," *American College of Surgery Bulletin* 78 (1988):4-13.

11   For ease of reading, a singular pronoun ("his" or "her" instead of the more cumbersome "his or her") will be used throughout this chapter.

12   AMA, 4 December 1973, quoted in J. Rachels, "Active and Passive Euthanasia," in *Contemporary Issues in Bioethics*, 2d ed., ed. T.L. Beauchamp and L. Walters (Belmont, CA: Wadsworth Publishing, 1982), 313.

13   J. Rachels, "Active and Passive Euthanasia," 314.

14   L.R. Kass, *Toward a More Natural Science* (New York: Free Press, 1985).

15   H.T. Engelhardt, Jr., "The Roles of Values in the Discovery of Illnesses, Diseases and Disorders," in *Contemporary Issues in Bioethics*, 73-75.

16   H.T. Engelhardt, Jr., "The Disease of Masturbation: Values and the Concept of Disease," in *Contemporary Issues in Bioethics,* 59-63.

17   Hippocratic Oath, trans. L. Edelstein, in *Ancient Medicine: Selected Papers of Ludwig Edelstein,* ed. L.C. Temkin and O. Temkin (Baltimore: Johns Hopkins University Press, 1967), 6.

18   P. Carrick, *Medical Ethics in Antiquity* (Dordrecht, Holland: D. Reidel, 1985), 151-56.

19   *Epidemics* I.II, trans W.H.S. Jones, cited in Carrick, *Medical Ethics in Antiquity*, 156.

20   A.M. Capron, "Legal and Ethical Problems in Decisions for Death," *Law,*

Medicine & Health Care 14 (1986):144.

21 P. Foot, "Euthanasia," in *Ethical Issues Relating to Life and Death,* ed. J. Ladd (New York: Oxford University Press, 1979), 38.

22 T. Taylor, "Biomedical Ethics in the Shadow of Nazism," *Hastings Center Report* (August 1976, special supplement):3-6.

23 L. Alexander, "Medical Science under Dictatorship," *New England Journal of Medicine* 241 (1949):44 [emphasis added].

24 R.J. Lifton, *The Nazi Doctors* (New York: Basic Books, 1986), 46.

25 Taylor, "Biomedical Ethics in the Shadow of Nazism," 3.

26 H. Kuhse, "The Case for Active Voluntary Euthanasia," *Law, Medicine & Health Care* 14 (1986):147.

27 R. Fenigsen, "A Case against Dutch Euthanasia," *Hastings Center Report* 19 (1989, special supplement):27.

28 *Ibid.*

29 T.L. Beauchamp and L.B. McCullough, *Medical Ethics: The Moral Responsibilities of Physicians* (Englewood Cliffs, NJ: Prentice-Hall, 1984), 27-35.

30 T. Tomlinson and H. Brody, "Futility and the Ethics of Resuscitation," *Journal of the American Medical Association* 264 (1990):1280.

2

Doctors Must Not Kill

Edmund D. Pellegrino

He knew my objective to do good, though he did not believe in the good to be done.

Anthony Trollope, The Fixed Period

INTRODUCTION

Is it ever morally licit for physicians intentionally to kill a patient to relieve suffering even with the patient's request? Should the long-held proscription against active euthanasia be relaxed legally and ethically, as it has been in the Netherlands? Are physicians who oppose active euthanasia being unfaithful to their traditional duty of compassion? These questions are being debated in the United States and in several Western European countries. They are highlighted by the legal, ethical, and social tolerance for euthanasia in Holland and the growing public and professional sentiment elsewhere that favors the termination of life by physicians. How the medical profession, society, and the public answer these questions promises to have a profound effect on the moral quality of the physician-patient relationship and of the whole of society.

In this article, I shall argue that physicians should not kill, directly or indirectly, even out of compassion, for three reasons. First, the moral arguments favoring euthanasia are logically inadequate. Second, killing by physicians seriously distorts the healing relationship. And third, the grave social conse- quences of such killing are morally prohibitive.

Euthanasia literally means "good" or "gentle" death. No one can reasona- bly oppose a "good" death. But some construals of euthanasia are morally defensible; others are not.[1] It is crucial, therefore, to define the sense in which I shall use the term. I shall argue against what is called "active" euthanasia--the intentional killing of a patient by a physician, with the patient's consent (voluntary euthanasia), or without consent when consent is impossible (nonvoluntary euthanasia), or when consent is possible but not sought (involuntary euthanasia). To include in this definition such qualifiers as "good" or "gentle," and to evade the use of the term "killing," is to beg the central moral question--as Van der Meer does in his definition.[2] Van der Meer also manipulates the definition by including "in the patient's interests," so that involuntary euthanasia also can conveniently be accommodated. The ethical issue is too serious to permit its obfuscation by either euphemism or euphuism.

What is called "passive" euthanasia--allowing a patient with an incurable disease to die either by withholding or withdrawing life-sustaining support--will not be my concern in this essay. Nor will "mercy killing," which includes killing by family, friends, or someone designated by society to play this role. My focus is specifically on killing by physicians, for this is what many seek to legitimate today.

The line of argument I oppose can be summarized as follows. Active euthanasia is a beneficent and compassionate act because it relieves human suffering. Moreover, human beings should, on the principle of autonomy, have the right to end their lives when they wish to terminate their sufferings. Physicians, as agents of the patient's welfare, should assist either by directly killing the patient or by assisting the patient in suicide. Since physicians are best qualified to assist in dying, they should participate if the patient's "right to die" is to be actualized. Physicians already participate in passive euthanasia. Since there is no moral difference between killing and letting die, the opposition to active euthanasia is logically untenable.[3] In addition, the abuses envisioned in slippery-slope arguments can be prevented by legal guidelines and criteria, like those currently used in Holland.[4] No physician who is morally opposed need participate. Medical ethics should be updated to take account of the changed religious, moral, and political milieu. Because of all of these arguments, the proscriptions in law and ethics against physician killing must be relaxed.

I recognize the appeal of this line of argument in a pluralistic, democratic, and secular society. Nothing that follows is meant to impugn the sincerity or motives of the proponents of euthanasia. Their desire to spare human suffering is commendable. It is the *means* they use to this end that are morally unacceptable.

I will make my case without invoking what, for many, are still the two most powerful arguments against euthanasia: (1) the Jewish and Christian belief that humans are stewards and not the absolute masters of the gift of life, and (2) the Christian belief that even human suffering may have meaning. David Thomasma and I have enlarged on this perspective in a forthcoming volume.[5] The religious viewpoint is unpalatable to contemporary mores, but it still hovers in attenuated form over the debate and is not lightly dismissed. However, since these arguments involve faith commitments, they are rejected by those without a faith commitment. For this reason, I shall confine my argument solely to the philosophical objections. Even without recourse to religious beliefs, active euthanasia is morally untenable.

ADEQUACY OF THE ARGUMENTS

The burden of proof weighs heavily on those who would abolish a moral proscription so deeply rooted in public and professional morals and in so many cultural traditions. However, a review of the major arguments advanced in favor of euthanasia does not sustain the necessary burden of proof.

The Distinction Between Killing and Letting Die

Advocates of euthanasia reason that there is no moral distinction between killing the patient and letting the patient die by deliberate withdrawal or withholding of life support or lifesaving treatment. This argument ignores the fact that in euthanasia, the physician is the immediate cause of a death that she fully intends. This act differs from withholding or withdrawing treatment. When treatment is discontinued, it is the disease that kills the patient. In so-called passive euthanasia, we remove our intervention for good reasons (for example, it is no longer effective or beneficial and its burdens are disproportionate). To continue treatment would be unethical, since futile, burdensome, and expensive treatments would be forced on the patient in violation of the canons of good medicine and of the patient's best interests. Adherence to these canons is a primary professional obligation. The physician also violates this moral canon if she continues with unnecessary, burdensome, or futile treatment.

James Rachels, who makes the most extended case against the distinction between killing and letting die, admits that the general sentiment that favors such distinction has some weight. He argues that such intuitions should be distrusted, however, because the well-off members of society have more to fear from relaxing the prohibition against active euthanasia than letting people die.[6] This is an unconvincing argument that begs the question of interest.

When the patient is "overmastered by the disease," to use the Hippocratic phraseology, we have a moral obligation to stop treatment, since our interventions serve no beneficial purpose.[7] When we do so, the natural course of the disease supervenes. The disease, not the physician, kills the patient. As Daniel E. Callahan suggests, medical hubris has grown to such proportions that we think nature is totally subservient to us. We take responsibility for its operations as well as our own. However, the AIDS epidemic, the ubiquity of bacterial resistance to antibiotics, and Alzheimer's disease, Callahan reminds us, are physical causes of death we do not control.[8]

Proponents of euthanasia also argue that there is no distinction between euthanasia and giving a patient morphine to relieve pain that could end in death from respiratory depression. This is a specious argument, because under these circumstances the primary intention is not to kill the patient as in active euthanasia, but to relieve pain; if death occurs, it is the result of a side effect of a powerful drug. Physicians use hazardous drugs and perform many operations in precarious cases where the intent is to help. The risk of dangerous side effects is tolerable, if benefits can be achieved in no other way. The use of morphine would be euthanasia only if the dose were deliberately calculated to cause respiratory depression. Rather, the effort is to titrate the dose, so as to achieve the beneficial and avoid the harmful effect. This titration is not controllable by formula. It may be in error, but the risks of side effects are outweighed by the proportionate potential for pain relief.

Euthanasia and Patient Autonomy

X A second argument for euthanasia justifies it on grounds of respect for the moral right of autonomy and the dignity of the person. The logic of this assertion is suspect. When a patient opts for euthanasia, he uses his freedom to give up his freedom. In the name of autonomy, the patient chooses to eradicate life and consciousness, the indispensable conditions for the operation of autonomy. He loses control over a whole set of options, all of which cannot be foreseen and many of which would be of importance if life--the basis of freedom--had not been forgone. Moreover, if suffering is so intense that it limits all other options, and euthanasia is the only choice, then that choice is really not free. Seriously ill persons suffer commonly from alienation, guilt, and feelings of unworthiness. They often perceive themselves, and are perceived by others, as economic, social, and emotional burdens. They are exquisitely susceptible to even the most subtle suggestion by physician, nurse, or family member that reinforces their guilt, shame, or sense of unworthiness. It takes as much courage to resist these subliminal confirmations of alienation as to withstand the physical ravages of the disease. Much of the suffering of dying patients comes from being subtly treated as nonpersons. The decision to seek euthanasia is often an indictment against those who treat or care for the patient. If the emotional impediments to freedom and autonomy are removed, and pain is properly relieved, there is evidence that many would not choose euthanasia.[9]

Euthanasia is too often an act of desperation that physician, family, and friends can forestall. To do so, they must provide the understanding, support, and sharing that will assure the sick person that she is still very much a member of the human community going through an experience everyone will eventually share. X

Beneficence

The most powerful argument for euthanasia is based upon compassion, mercy, and beneficence. These are obligations intrinsic to medicine as a healing art. Even those who see meaning in suffering urge comfort and relief of pain for the dying. Compassion and mercy would seem to override all other considerations.

X The duty of beneficence indeed obliges the physician to help the patient to a good and gentle death. It is also compassionate and morally commendable to help a person to die well. A good death completes life with a finale befitting our true dignity as thinking, conscious, and social beings. The aim of medicine should be to facilitate a death that is as pain-free as possible but that is also a human experience. We can justify euthanasia for our pets precisely because they cannot possibly understand suffering or dying. They cannot die in a "human" way. But humans can grow morally even with negative experiences. A good death contributes something valuable to the whole human community. It enables us to assess our human relationships and to come to grips with the important and ultimate questions of human destiny, which believers and nonbelievers alike must confront. A good death is the last act of a drama, which euthanasia artificially terminates before the drama is really completed. X

Some might object that all of this can be achieved in preparation for euthanasia and, even more effectively, before suffering makes rational thought difficult. But is this really so? How much of the quality of our deaths is dependent on living through the experience as it presents itself? To cut off this experience abruptly is to abort what might be the most important experience of our lives and a contribution to the lives of family, friends, and those who attend us. Often we see ourselves most clearly at the hour of our death. We see what we have made of ourselves. Critical times force us to reveal and confront the inner self. Artifices and circumlocution are no longer acceptable. Euthanasia deprives us of these last insights into who and what we have been, and it closes the door on the final accounting we may want to make.

Finally, there is the illusion that a life that is free of all anxiety, suffering, or misfortune is the "good" life. But, such a life is devoid of opportunity for expression of some of our most characteristically human feelings--mercy, compassion, understanding, empathy, love, and giving of ourselves to others. To be sure, dying persons can teach us good and bad lessons. A "good" death helps all of us to become more humane--something we lose easily in the sanitized, atomistic, hedonistic world in which we live. Miguel de Unamuno may not have been entirely wrong when he wrote: "Suffering is the substance of life and the root of personality. Only suffering makes us persons."[10] This is not an argument for letting patients suffer, but it does suggest that inevitable suffering may serve some purposes that are not immediately apparent. The lives of many of the handicapped, the retarded, and the aged teach us much about courage and personal growth and give some substance to Unamuno's observation.

Beneficence and compassion remain the first principles of medical ethics. No one would seriously urge sadism or masochism. Especially to be avoided is the unnecessary suffering resulting from the inappropriate overuse of technology. But, a case can be made that beneficence requires not killing, but alleviation of physical and emotional suffering by optimum palliative care--the comprehensive physical, emotional, and community support that leaves more options to the patient than instant oblivion.

The Necessity of Euthanasia

From the medical point of view, even if euthanasia were morally licit, does it follow that it is necessary? The motivation for euthanasia arises principally from two worries: fear of intolerable pain, suffering, and anguish, and fear of becoming a victim of overzealous physicians and dehumanizing medical technologies. These are legitimate worries, but both are well within the power of medicine to remedy without resort to euthanasia. Improved measures for relief of pain and anxiety are already available. It still remains for physicians to use them effectively.[11] We must be unequivocal about physicians' duty to do so. The current trend to active euthanasia only underscores the moral obligations of physicians to practice competent analgesia, to understand why the patient requests death, and to deal with and remove those reasons in a program of palliative care.[12]

Hospice programs or palliative care offer comprehensive alternatives to euthanasia that are more respectful of beneficence and autonomy than killing. They relieve pain and anxiety, prepare the patient for the experience of dying, anticipate the need and value of advance directives, and establish understanding between patient and physician about which life-support measures are acceptable to the patient and which are not. These programs enlist the help of family and friends to make dying a communal experience, in which the dying person contributes something positive to those around her as well as to her own growth as a person. The physician's obligation to act beneficently and to show respect for the patient's dignity is better served by these measures than by killing the patient.

Plebiscite Ethics

Another line of argument relies on the fact that "polls" show that a majority of people favor legalizing euthanasia. Little is said about the notorious difficulties of conducting polls without contaminating the responses by the way the questions are posed. It is not clear how respondents interpret the question or what question they think they are answering. Many, for example, still confuse killing with letting a patient die when death is imminent and inevitable. Many may favor euthanasia because they think it is the only way to retain control over their dying or to prevent unnecessary overtreatment of terminal illnesses. Others are not aware of the alternatives to intolerable suffering--competent use of analgesics, hospice and palliative care, and changed social attitudes toward the terminally ill. Some among them may be personally opposed, but believe others should be free to choose euthanasia, and so favor legalization. It cannot be denied that public interest in euthanasia is considerable, judging by the number of people who have bought Derek Humphrey's book, *Final Exit*.[13] A few have already used it as a death manual to guide their own suicides.

From the ethical point of view, arguments based on the results of polls assume that a plebiscite, a majority opinion, or even true consensus can establish what is right and good. Equally specious is the argument that if a practice exists widely, it should become law so it can be regulated. Or, that what becomes legal is therefore moral. And what is no longer secret gains moral credibility by being exposed to the "light of day."

These arguments are seriously flawed. There have been too many instances in human history--past and present--of immoral laws (segregation, slavery, suppression of the rights of women and children, and so forth). There have also been morally distorted societies in which popular approval and law condoned serious violations of human rights (Nazi Germany, Stalinist Russia, and Fascist Spain and Italy, for example). Something more philosophically cogent than public opinion, national sentiment, or law is needed to make a cogent case for the moral acceptability of euthanasia.

DISTORTION OF THE HEALING RELATIONSHIP

Even if euthanasia did not have the deficiencies in moral reasoning I have outlined, it would be morally dubious in the light of the "internal morality" of medicine itself. By internal morality, I mean the moral obligations that devolve upon physicians by virtue of the nature of medical activity.[14] On this score, I am in agreement with Leon Kass[15] that euthanasia is a serious violation of the moral nature and purposes of medicine.

I have discussed my own philosophy of medicine elsewhere and will only summarize a few points here. Medicine is a healing relationship. Its long-term goal is restoration or cultivation of health; its more proximate goal is healing and helping a particular patient in a particular clinical situation. Medicine restores health when this is possible, and enables the patient to cope with disability and death when cure is not possible. The aims of medicine are positive, even when death is inevitable. Healing can occur even when cure is impossible. The patient can become "whole" again if the health-care professional helps him to live with a disability, to face dying, and to live as human a life as circumstances will allow.

Medicine is also ineradicably grounded in trust.[16] The physician invokes trust when she offers to help. The patient is forced to trust, because he is vulnerable and lacks the power to cure himself without help. The patient is dependent upon the physician's good will and character. The physician--to be faithful to the trust built into the relationship with the patient--must seek to heal, and not to remove the need for healing by killing the patient. When euthanasia is a possible option, this trust relationship is seriously distorted. Healing now includes killing. The already awesome powers of the doctor are expanded enormously. When cure is impossible, healing is displaced by killing. How can patients trust that the doctor will pursue every effective and beneficent measure when she can relieve herself of a difficult challenge by influencing the patient to choose death?

Uncertainty and mistrust are already too much a part of the healing relationship. Euthanasia magnifies these ordinary and natural anxieties. How will the patient know whether the physician is trying to heal or relinquishing the effort to cure or contain illness because she favors euthanasia, devalues the quality of the patient's life, or wants to conserve society's resources? The physician can easily divert attention from a good death by subtly leading the patient to believe that euthanasia is the only good or gentle death.

This is not a blanket indictment of the character of physicians. But the doctor is an ordinary human being called to perform extraordinary tasks. Her character is rarely faultless. We cannot simply say the "good" doctor would never abuse the privilege of euthanasia. Whose agent is the doctor when treatment becomes marginal and costs escalate? Will the physician's notion of benevolence to society become malevolent for the older patient? How can the aged be secure in the hands of younger physicians whose notion of a "quality" life may not include the gentler pleasures of aging that Cicero praised in the *De Senectute*? Can patients trust physicians when physicians arrogate to themselves the role of rationers of society's resources or are made to assume this role by societal policy? We already hear much talk of the social burdens imposed by chronically ill, handicapped, terminally ill adults and children and the necessity of rationing, with the physician as gatekeeper.[17]

Moreover, there are clinical imponderables that can undermine the physician's judgment. To define a pain as intolerable, to distinguish gradations of suffering, and to prognosticate accurately are difficult enough in themselves. These difficulties are easily compounded when the patient pleads for release or the physician is frustrated, emotionally spent, or inclined to impose his or her values on the patient. When the proscription against killing is eroded, trust in the doctor cannot survive. This is already apparent in Holland, that great social laboratory for euthanasia. According to some observers, older and handicapped people are fearful of entering Dutch hospitals and nursing homes.[18] Older Dutch physicians have confided to some of us their personal fears of being admitted to their own hospitals. There is anecdotal evidence of physicians falsifying data to justify euthanasia, making egregious mistakes in diagnosis and prognosis, entering into collusion with families, and ordering involuntary euthanasia.[19] These anecdotal impressions must be better documented. Further study of the Dutch experience is therefore crucial for any society contemplating euthanasia as public policy. Present evidence indicates that the slippery slope--conceptual and actual--is no ethical myth but a reality in Holland.[20] When the physician who traditionally had only the power to heal and to help can now also kill, the medical fiduciary relationship--one of the oldest in human history--cannot survive.

There is also the serious effect on the physician's own psyche of premeditated, socially sanctioned killing. To some degree, physicians are desensitized to loss of life by their experiences with the anatomy lab, autopsy operating rooms, and the performance of painful procedures. To carry out their duties, doctors must steel themselves against suffering and death to avoid being emotionally paralyzed in the actions they must take daily. Euthanasia reinforces this objectification of death and dying, and further desensitizes to killing. A "gentle" death, as Van der Veer wants to call it, is still a premeditated, efficiently executed death of a living human being.[21]

At this point, proponents of euthanasia may correctly point out that, historically, the prohibition against euthanasia was respected only by one group of physicians, the Hippocratics. Other physicians approved the practice of euthanasia as some physicians overtly and covertly do today. Paul Carrick makes clear that in antiquity, doctors were inconstant in their respect for the Hippocratic Oath.[22] This fact does not in any way weaken the argument I have been making based in the nature of the healing relationship. Medical codes are not self-justifying. They have only recently become the subject of critical examination. I would contend, for reasons stated briefly above, that a critical examination of the moral basis for medical practice must proscribe euthanasia because it contravenes the primary healing purposes of medical activity. Moreover it is capricious to argue that since some physicians in the past and some in the present practice euthanasia, it should be legalized. An immoral act does not become moral because it is common practice. Morality must have deeper roots than mere medical custom or even the code of medical ethics.

The medical profession is a moral community.[23] Its members have a collective moral responsibility to patients and society. For this reason, the whole profession must oppose the legalization of euthanasia as detrimental to the welfare of patients and the integrity of society. Individual physicians cannot abstain on grounds that they oppose euthanasia but believe in free choice. The social nature of the acts of dying and killing do not permit anyone to choose such a socially destructive option. This is why the American Medical Association and British Medical Association have recently reaffirmed the proscription against doctors killing patients under any circumstance.[24]

THE SOCIAL IMPACT OF EUTHANASIA

Much as libertarians would like to see euthanasia as an individual decision protected by an absolute privacy right, it is an event inescapably fraught with social significance. A society that sanctions killing must abandon the long-standing tradition of "state's interest" in human life.[25] This devalues all life but especially the lives of certain citizens--the chronically ill, the aged, and the handicapped. Those who do not take the easy exit that legalized euthanasia offers become selfish overconsumers of their neighbors' resources. The vaunted autonomy of the choice for euthanasia withers in the face of the subtle coercion of a social policy that suggests the incurably ill are a social, economic, and emotional burden. Few of us would not feel the pressure to do the "noble" thing and ask for euthanasia, especially if the physician is gently urging us to do so.

The social sanction of euthanasia presumes a responsibility to monitor the killing process to keep it within agreed upon constraints. Killing then becomes bureaucratized and standardized. But even with standardization of criteria, it is impossible to contain euthanasia within specified boundaries. Laws will not prevent abuses, despite the hopes of those who favor legalization in the United States. The Dutch experience shows that even when euthanasia is not legal but is tolerated, expansion of its boundaries--from voluntary to involuntary, from adults to children, from terminally ill to chronically ill, from intolerable suffering to dissatisfaction with the quality of life, from consent to contrived consent--is inevitable.[26] The ethical proscription against killing by doctors is a social sea wall. Once it is breached, it is impossible to avoid inundation. Literature often teaches ethics more effectively than moral philosophy. One needs only to read Trollope's *Fixed Period* to appreciate how the most benevolently generated and seemingly rational policy of euthanasia can corrode human relationships.[27]

Another imminent social danger is the real possibility that euthanasia will converge with the current trend toward rationing of health-care resources. It is a short way from the need to contain costs to covertly or overtly planned euthanasia for those members of our society who present the greatest economic burdens. At the beginning, some might suggest rationing needed care to retarded or handicapped infants, very old people, or those with fatal, incurable diseases like Alzheimer's. Once euthanasia, in any of its forms, is legalized, the temptation to encourage its use, tacitly or overtly, to alleviate one of our most socially vexing problems--the increasing scarcity of health-care dollars--will be strong. This could be the first slip on the slippery slope, which leads inexorably from voluntary to nonvoluntary and involuntary euthanasia. This is evident already in the recent Dutch government report on euthanasia in the Netherlands.[28]

Some of euthanasia's protagonists are so convinced of the individual and social benefits of killing that they believe it is unjust not to make them available to patients who cannot give consent--infants, anencephalics, the retarded, persons in a permanent vegetative state, and so forth. On this view, covert euthanasia--that is, killing patients who could consent but whom it is not deemed necessary to consult--would be permissible. These proponents of euthanasia argue that it is unjust to deny such patients the benefits of relief of suffering just because they cannot, or will not, give consent. Some argue that such patients impose unjust economic, social, emotional, and physical burdens on family, health professionals, and society and, thus, should be killed as a matter of medical duty.[29] Others in the name of "compassion" urge the involuntary killing of the handicapped and retarded, since there is no place on this earth where they can be "happy."[30] Here we have a conceptual slippery slope that prepares the way for the actual slippery slope and provides its rational justification. The horrendous nature of these conclusions requires more rebuttal than I can give in this chapter. Suffice it to say that the moral aberrancy of these conclusions is ample proof of the immorality of the premises from which they derive. This is precisely the kind of reasoning that led to German physicians' killing of the "unfit" and to the Holocaust.

In the United States, a model state law has been proposed in Iowa that would legitimate all the "abuses" of the slippery slope. The model sanctions euthanasia for children (with or without parental approval), includes an appeal mechanism enabling children to override parental objections, sanctions proxy consent on behalf of incompetent patients, and establishes a registry of people qualified to administer aid in dying. The aim of this law is to provide "quality control" in the termination of life and "a principled means of managing health care resources," thus dangerously conflating allocation decisions and euthanasia.[31]

Rachels chooses to rely on the "good sense of judges and juries" and the medical profession to prevent abuses. In any case, he argues, the good results will outweigh whatever abuses might occur.[32] But experience in Holland and in the current debate in the United States suggests that this may not be the case at all. Rachels is right when he says that the slippery slope is the "outstanding argument" against legalized euthanasia, and he is seriously wrong when he disposes of its reality so cavalierly.

The arguments for making assisted suicide a moral option, moral duty, or legal choice are equally indefensible.[33] The arguments adduced here against euthanasia apply as well to assisted suicide. Physicians are *de facto* moral accomplices in what happens to their patients. Even when they are moved by compassion, as was Dr. Timothy Quill (the physician who recently revealed his role in a euthanasia case in the *New England Journal of Medicine*), physicians cannot morally justify cooperation in terminating the patient's life.[34] They cannot excuse themselves by a professional "Pontius Pilate Act" if they provide the lethal drugs and the directions for their effective use. This is indefensible moral cooperation, in that it shares the patient's intent to commit suicide. Further, the doctor's cooperation is essential for the patient to achieve his or her purpose. For the same reasons, physicians cannot cooperate with socially "designated" killers, "obitiatrists" or "teliastrists."[35] Even though such cooperation is more remote than assisted suicide, the physician cannot remain at a distance. Someone will have to say this disease is "incurable"; this pain, "intolerable"; this patient is "competent" or "incompetent" to give consent. The proponents of euthanasia are right--legalization is impossible without cooperation of the medical profession. And for all the reasons I have given, physicians cannot cooperate in the killing of their patients directly or indirectly.

OBLIGATIONS OF PHYSICIANS WHO REJECT EUTHANASIA

What are the moral obligations of physicians who reject all forms of euthanasia? To begin with, we must accept responsibility for confronting the reality of pain and suffering--the fear and emotional traumata of the fatally ill and dying person and the legitimate desire for a good death. We must counter the destructive force of euthanasia with a constructive effort. If, as I have argued, killing is not a good death, what can we--indeed, what must we--as physicians do to help the patient achieve as good a death as possible without killing him? First of all, physicians must recognize that the request for euthanasia is a plea for help and an attempt to regain some measure of control over one's life that fatal illness seems to take away so forcibly. Why does this particular patient want to be killed? Is it pain, suffering, loss of dignity, depression? Is it a challenge to see whether the physician, family, and friends really do care? Is it a test to see if the family really regards the patient as a burden? Is it fear of bankrupting the family, fear of being kept alive artificially to no purpose, or a response to the doctor's attitude of futility or disinterest? There are many reasons for the request to be killed and many remedies once we know the reason.

Clearly, the physician has a moral obligation to ascertain these reasons and to spend the time necessary with the patient to learn about the factors specific to the situation. Too many physicians are still fearful of talking about death. Physicians must engage the help of nurses, social workers, pastoral counselors, family, and friends in discerning the reasons for a patient's request. They must mobilize the forces necessary to remove or ameliorate these causes. Physicians must work out with each patient that patient's definition of a good death, and determine--before a crisis comes on--what life-support measures will and will not be acceptable to the patient.

We must assure patients that they can control the starting and stopping of life-sustaining measures by advance directives when they lose their competence to do so as the disease progresses. Physicians should dispose of their own anxiety about making patients into addicts. Pain relief competently applied is a moral obligation, as are all other supportive measures. Addiction in the last weeks of life and even death as an unintended side effect of analgesia are morally defensible. Physicians unable or unwilling to make the investment of time and emotion required for comprehensive palliative care should not care for patients who need such care. They would be better placed in specialties that do not often confront terminal illness. Physicians also have a moral responsibility to be honest about their reasons for accepting or refusing a role in euthanasia. Euthanasia is not the answer to the physician's inadequacy, frustration, or emotional exhaustion as a healer. Refusing to accept one's own finitude or that of one's patients is not justification for ineffective, burdensome, or futile treatment.

All members of the health-care team should play a part in comprehensive palliative care. Still, the physician remains the focal point of the effort. Harm results from dividing the tasks of terminal care, unless there is someone to coordinate that care, interpret it, and to make changes when needed. Again, physicians unwilling to assume this focal role should not undertake the care of fatally ill patients. They must be honest and morally responsible enough to yield the primary role to physicians best fitted by temperament and training to care for the incurably ill patient in a humane and competent way.

The advocates of legalized euthanasia are right when they insist that the physician is crucial to any effective social policy permitting patients to be killed on request. Doctors do have the necessary knowledge. They do control the prescription of the necessary lethal agents. They do know when the patient's diagnosis and prognosis portend a painful and inevitable death. These very facts impose an enormous moral responsibility on the profession to resist becoming moral accomplices or society's designated killers.

If euthanasia is legalized, the medical profession will bear a large burden of the blame if it does not educate the public to the dangers and if it fails to refuse to participate. The profession must also work to alleviate the societal conditions that foster euthanasia--the attitude of hopelessness and futility before death and dying, the financial pressures that all too forcibly convince the patient that he is a burden, and the illusion that life must be perfect and that any chance illness is an affront to human dignity. The profession as a whole must make it morally mandatory to make competent use of all measures that relieve pain and suffering.

There is much that physicians, individually and as a profession, can--and must--do short of killing patients to eliminate the problem of suffering. Legalization of euthanasia poses a far deeper moral challenge than the profession may appreciate. It challenges us to define what it really means to be a physician.

All morally responsible, compassionate, and merciful physicians share the same goal when confronted with a suffering, dying, terminally ill human being. They all strive to assist the suffering person to achieve a gentle and good death. They all share the "objective to do good," to use the phrase from Trollope's novel that I have used as an epigraph. What we do not share is the definition of "the good to be done." A good death does not, I have argued, include killing the patient, nor can one be a good physician and do so.

ACKNOWLEDGMENTS

I am indebted to Pat McCarrick and Mary Coutts for invaluable bibliographic assistance.

NOTES

1   D.C. Thomasma and G.C. Graber, *Euthanasia: Toward an Ethical Social Policy* (New York: Continuum, 1991), 1-11.
2   C. Van der Meer, "Euthanasia: A Definition and Ethical Conditions," *Journal of Palliative Care* 4, nos.1-2 (1988):103-6.
3   J. Rachels, *The End of Life* (New York: Oxford, 1986), 106-28.
4   M.A.M. de Wachter, "Active Euthanasia in the Netherlands" [special communication], *Journal of the American Medical Association* 23 (1989): 3316-19.
5   E.D. Pellegrino and D.C. Thomasma, *Helping and Healing: Religious Com-*

mitment and Health Care (New York: Continuum, in press).

6   J. Rachels, "Killing and Starving to Death," *Philosophy* 54 (April 1979):159-71.

7   *Hippocrates*, vol. 2, trans. W.H.S. Jones, Loeb Classical Library Series (Cambridge, MA: Harvard, 1981):193-203.

8   D.E. Callahan, "Euthanasia Question Complicated by Need to Ration," *Commonweal* 115 (July 1988):397-404.

9   N. Coyle, "The Last Four Weeks of Life," *American Journal of Nursing* 90 (December 1990):75-78.

10   M. de Unamuno, "The Tragic Sense of Life," in *Men and Notions*, trans. A. Kerrigan, Bollingen Series 85, no.4 (Princeton, NJ: Princeton University Press, 1972), 224.

11   Agency for Health Care Policy and Research, *Clinical Practical Guideline: Acute Pain Management: Operative or Medical Procedures and Trauma* (Washington, DC: US Department of Health and Human Services, 1992).

12   J. Lynn, "The Health Care Professional's Role When Active Euthanasia Is Sought," *Journal of Palliative Care* 4, nos.1-2 (1988):100-2.

13   D. Humphrey, *Final Exit* (Secaucus, NJ: Hemlock Society, 1991).

14   E.D. Pellegrino, "The Healing Relationship: The Architectonics of Clinical Medicine," in *The Clinical Encounter: The Moral Fabric of the Patient-Physician Relationship*, Philosophy and Medicine Series 4, ed. Earl Shelp (Dordrecht, the Netherlands: D. Reidel Publishing, 1983), 153-72.

15   L. Kass, "Neither for Love Nor Money: Why Doctors Must Not Kill," *Public Interest* 94 (Winter 1989):25-46.

16   E.D. Pellegrino, "Trust and Distrust in Professional Ethics," in *Ethics, Trust, and the Professions: Philosophical and Cultural Aspects*, ed. E.D. Pellegrino, R.M. Veatch, and J.P. Langan (Washington, DC: Georgetown University Press, 1991), 68-89.

17   E.D. Pellegrino, "Rationing Health Care: The Ethics of Medical Gatekeeping," *Journal of Contemporary Health Law and Policy* 2 (Spring 1986):23-45.

18   R. Fenigson, "A Case Against Dutch Euthanasia," *Hastings Center Report* 19, no.1 (1989):522-30; R. Fenigson, "Euthanasia in the Netherlands," *Issues in Law and Medicine* 6, no.3 (1990):229-45.

19   H. Ten Have, "Euthanasia in the Netherlands: The Legal Context and the Cases," *HEC Forum* 1, no.1 (1989):41-45.

20   I. Van der Sluis, "The Practice of Euthanasia in the Netherlands," *Issues in Law and Medicine* 4, no.4 (1989):455-65; B. Bostrom, "Euthanasia in the Netherlands, A Model for the United States?" *Issues in Law and Medicine* 4, no.4 (1989):467-86; C.F. Gomez, *Regulating Death: Euthanasia and the Case of the Netherlands* (New York: Free Press/Macmillan, 1991).

21   Van der Meer, "Euthanasia."

22   P. Carrick, *Medical Ethics in Antiquity* (Boston: Dordrecht, 1985), 127-50.

23   E.D. Pellegrino, "The Medical Profession as a Moral Community," *Bulletin of the New York Academy of Medicine* 66A, no.3 (1990):221-32.

24 *Euthanasia: Report Council on Ethical and Judicial Affairs of the American Medical Association* (Chicago: AMA, 1989); *Euthanasia: Report Working Part to Review the British Medical Association Guidance in Euthanasia* (London: BMA, May 1988), 69.

25 H. Tristram Engelhardt, Jr., "Fashioning an Ethic for Life and Death in a Post-Modern Society," *Hastings Center Report* 19, no.1 (special supplement: *Mercy, Murder and Morality: Perspectives in Euthanasia*, 1989):13-15.

26 R. Fenigson, "A Case Against Dutch Euthanasia."

27 A. Trollope, *The Fixed Period*, ed. R.H. Super (Ann Arbor: University of Michigan Press, 1990).

28 P.J. Van Der Maas, J.J.M. van Delden, L. Pijnenborg, and C.W.N. Looman, "Euthanasia and Other Medical Decisions Concerning the End of Life," *Lancet* 338 (14 September 1991):669-74.

29 J. Lachs, "Active Euthanasia: Theoretical Aspects," *The Journal of Clinical Ethics* 1, no.2 (1990):113-15; J.H. Van Der Berg, *Medical Power and Medical Ethics* (New York: Norton, 1978).

30 K.L. Lyle, "A Gentle Way to Die," *Newsweek,* 2 March 1992, 14.

31 C.A. Brandt, P.J. Cone, A.L. Fontana, *et al.*, "Model Aid in Dying Act," *Iowa Law Review* 75, no.1 (1989):125-215.

32 J. Rachels, *The End of Life*, 187.

33 S.H. Wanzer, D.D. Federman, St. Edelstein, *et al.*, "The Physician's Responsibility Toward Hopelessly Ill Patients, A Second Look," *New England Journal of Medicine* 320 (1989):884-89; C.K. Cassel and D.E. Meier, "Morals and Moralism in the Debate Over Euthanasia and Assisted Suicide," *New England Journal of Medicine* 323 (1990):750-52.

34 T.E. Quill, "Death and Dignity: A Case of Individualized Decision-Making," *New England Journal of Medicine* 324 (1991):691-94.

35 These are etymologically dubious euphemisms for socially designated functionaries who would administer lethal drugs if doctors refuse to cooperate.

3

The Quality of Mercy: An Examination of The Proposition "Doctors Must Not Kill"

Fredrick R. Abrams

This essay explores the proposition "doctors must not kill." In their 1988 article, Drs. Gaylin, Kass, Pellegrino, and Siegler present compelling arguments against physician aid in dying.[1] In examining this proposition, this essay argues that enough exceptions may be found to make that untenable as an absolute prohibition. For those who acknowledge that such exceptions exist, the problem has been how to prevent abuse, once deliberate aid in dying is permitted.

IS THERE A UNIVERSAL MEDICAL ETHICS?

"Doctors must not kill." To enter into a discussion of this imperative, one must first examine the notion that there is a monolithic medical ethics to which physicians universally subscribe. There are a great many ethical precepts to which most physicians agree, but there is no set of universal rules that a lay person may find that will predict any physician's behavior in any given circumstance. The only proposition that is likely to reach universal agreement is, "I will practice medicine to benefit my patients." But the interpretation of "benefit" will vary widely. In dealing with each other, our legal regulatory mechanisms are secular, founded on a fundamental view regarding freedom.[2] Of course, that does not exclude permissions and prohibitions that are found in both religious and secular systems, some so strong that they are made into law.

Yet, most of our behavior is not governed by law. How we relate to different members of family, to business associates, to teammates, to lovers, to authorities, is guided by ethics. Roles play an important part in interpersonal relationships. A lifeguard has a different obligation to a drowning person than does a passerby. A fireman is expected to behave differently from a neighbor when a hazardous rescue is contemplated. Less settled is the role of a physician, for physicians have been seeking and changing their professional roles and obligations since ancient times.

The Hippocratic Oath, often cited as if it could settle these difficult issues, deserves recognition for being an early public revelation of principles by a professional group. But persons who cite its authority usually select only the parts they prefer. Today, codes of medical behavior serve only as guidelines developed by professional societies such as the American Medical Association, the American Society of Internal Medicine, the American College of Obstetricians and Gynecologists, and the American Academy of Pediatrics. Basic ethical behavior of the physician is not learned as part of the curriculum in medical school. Most physicians have learned ethical precepts the same way nonphysicians do--from religious and philosophical instruction, formal and informal, as they grow and mature as human beings. It is important to reiterate that there is no universal medical ethics binding all physicians.

THE SEPARATIST THESIS

As various professions promulgated codes of ethics, a debate emerged, characterized succinctly by Gewirth as the *Separatist Thesis.* According to this thesis:

> Professionals by virtue of their expertise and their consequent roles, have rights and duties that are unique to themselves and that may hence be not only different from, but even contrary to, the rights and duties that are found in other segments of morality. . . . by virtue of this separateness, the professionals' rights may justifiably infringe certain of the moral right of his clients or of other persons.[3]

A dichotomy is noted between those physicians of Separatist leaning and others who believe that "medical" ethics is contextual, founded on the relations between doctor and patient. The tendency of the Separatist physician is to value professional goals in the abstract, such as preserving life or healing. Dealing with the patient is contingent upon how these doctors place themselves in the world, what they believe their role to be. To be sure, the patient is an important part of that world, but the doctor's decisions are made from the *doctor's perception* of what promotes the patient's good. Treatment is based on the Golden Rule, "Do unto others as you would have them do unto you."

Alternatively, the non-Separatist physician places greater emphasis on the relationship itself, between doctor and patient, seeing the patient as a person with unique, perhaps idiosyncratic, needs. Medical skills are applied to those needs as the *informed patient* perceives them. If there is conflict between the beneficent intent of the physician (in pursuit of his or her professional interpretation of what will promote the patient's health) and the patient's wishes, the

respect for the competent patient's autonomy dominates. The patient sometimes holds health subordinate to the other values. Professionals, therefore, *are
not privileged to violate their patients' rights, even in the pursuit of beneficent ends.*
Their Golden Rule would be rephrased, "Do unto others as they would wish you
to do unto them."

In an untidy moral universe, there is virtue in breeding discussion and
debate, negotiation and compromise. Although a majority of the population,
including physicians, identify themselves as belonging to a religious group, in a
pluralistic society such as ours, there is no *single* authority for religious or moral
truth. Until there is, patients must seek physicians who can agree with diverse but
ethically defensible positions compatible with their own.

Physicians work in a utilitarian world largely devoted to outcomes, with the
objective to produce the best medical outcome for the patient in keeping with
agreed-upon health objectives. It is a dynamic relationship, and changing goals
and interventions occur as the course of illness unfolds. Sometimes cure is not
possible, and the caring aspects of the relationship become the focus. Whatever
the course, physicians are impelled by the principle of beneficence, which
imposes the duty to apply their medical skill on behalf of the patient. The
principle of beneficence in medical practice is precisely parallel to what philosophers and theologians call *agape* in contextual ethical decision making. *Agape* in
Greek means love or concern for persons. Whereas utilitarian ethics has been
characterized by the rubric "the greatest good for the greatest number," the
individual physician needs to act for the greater good for his or her individual
patient, to whom fidelity is owed and for whom the physician must advocate.

It is argued that doctors must be devoted to life and health. This is a useful
but abstract notion. It must be specifically applied by a doctor to the life and
health of each patient. That patient has no interest in life and health as
abstractions. Rather, he or she is devoted to very concrete desires regarding life
and health, and correctly expects the physician to apply medical skills to achieve
these goals. That patient has no interest in the survival of random tissues or
organs, but has a great interest in the integrated function of the unified mind and
body that is his or her persona.

If there are limitations of mind or body (or both), only that patient may
determine whether that very specific (not speculative) quality of life is sufficient
to serve his or her ends. A physician ought to respect the patient's values and the
decisions they engender, whether it involves accepting or refusing medical
interventions.

WHAT MIGHT A PATIENT ASK OF A DOCTOR?

What might a patient ask of a physician if the patient determines that a time
has come when death is preferred to life? He or she may ask one of three things.
(1) He or she might ask simply to be left alone; to have medical interventions
withheld or withdrawn permitting the disease process to run its natural course,

leading to death sooner than might occur if interventions prolonged the process. (2) He or she might ask to be *supplied* with a lethal dose of medication that would enable the patient to end her life quickly and painlessly. (3) He or she could ask to have the doctor *administer* a lethal dose of medication resulting in the patient's death, directly and quickly.

REFUSAL OF CARE

How may a physician respond to the patient's wish for the physician to withhold or withdraw life-sustaining treatment, to assist in suicide, or to directly administer a lethal medication? Such requests ought not be taken at face value when initially made.[4] A patient may believe this dramatic request is the only way to capture the attention needed to deal with other problems. To use his skills on behalf of an informed, competent patient, the physician must interact with great care and in depth with the patient in order to determine the patient's needs. The physician must inform the patient of available remedies--their harms, risks, and benefits--and the consequences of nonintervention, and he or she must be satisfied that the patient has the capacity to make such decisions.

A patient may make an unwise decision in terms of optimal medical treatment, but once all measures have been taken to ensure that the patient has the capacity to choose, a physician may not impose his or her ideas of what will best benefit that patient. The patient may hold some values above health and life. Decisions may be made that seem eccentric or tragic, but if they are those of a competent patient, they should be honored. There are those who feel that the politics of selfishness and the pressure of economics will lead to a societal retreat from the defense of the great value of life. The Massachusetts court in the Saikewicz case responded to that concern specifically, saying:

> The constitutional right to privacy . . . is an expression of the sanctity of individual free choices and self determination as fundamental constituents of life. The value of life as so perceived is lessened not by a decision to refuse treatment, but by the failure to allow competent human beings the right to choice.[5]

ASSISTED SUICIDE

Regarding suicide, there is a presumption that it is irrational. Like any presumption, it can be overcome by contrary evidence. Many religious systems find suicide unacceptable on the basis that a person's life is held in trust, given by God and to be taken only by God. This is a decision based on faith, and for those who have that faith, it may serve them well. But many persons, religious and otherwise, agree that there are circumstances of unbearable suffering that justify suicide, and that this ought to be a choice remaining with the patients for whom suffering plays no redemptive role in their cosmology. If they had ready access to lethal medications, such patients would not need to call upon physicians for prescriptions. But, in the United States, these drugs are not readily available by any legitimate means.

Physicians are licensed by society to dispense medications, providing a check and balance against ill-considered, impulsive acts. There are philosophers and physicians who say the profession would be ill advised to collaborate even "once removed" in a patient's self-administered death. But there are philosophers and physicians who accept the enormous burden of evaluating the plight of each individual fellow human being. *They are aware that refusing to participate is a decision also.* And, if there *were* a method by which desperate patients might approach their doctors for aid-in-dying, it seems equally plausible that as many lives might be saved as lost. Those patients who misunderstood the diagnosis or prognosis, those who were temporarily depressed, those who were not currently in pain but who feared or anticipated pain, and those who simply needed to know someone supported them in their difficulty might be persuaded to forbear. However, once satisfied that temporary depression, misinformation, or misunderstanding play no role in a competent patient's decision, some doctors permit their compassion to overcome their reservations. Ceasing to act as an agent of a strictly paternalistic profession, they allow access to medications and enable their patients to bypass the obstacles standing in the way of self-determination.[6]

How does this square with the ancient oath of Hippocrates? Few of those persons who believe that quoting the oath settles arguments about euthanasia would countenance physicians who have sworn to all of the pagan gods and goddesses of ancient Greece. Nor would they expect physicians to maintain and support their teachers and the children of their teachers. Many of those doctors who voiced the oath (encountered for the first time at graduation) left immediately for a residency in urology fully aware they would soon "cut for the stone" in violation of their pledge. The evidence is convincing that these admonitions against surgery, abortion, and euthanasia were the precepts of the Pythagorean cult.[7] Historical notice of the oath was first made centuries after the death of Hippocrates. Christian teachings found this compatible with their theology and made authoritative use of it by appending Hippocrates' name--although it was far from Greek and Roman contemporaneous practice. In fact, the ancient physician's direct participation in euthanasia (literally, "a good death") by poisoning or phlebotomy was undertaken (along with the interdicted surgery and abortion) at the discretion of the physician upon the request of the patient.[8]

Early in the Christian era, references first appeared in the Greek and Roman teachings permitting drugs to relieve pain but not to cause death. This entered Catholic teachings as the Principle of Double Effect, whereby an evil outcome may be foreseen but not intended. Medication given to relieve pain may hasten death, but it is given with only the intention of relieving pain. An overzealous district attorney could cite the rather vague laws that speak of the crime of "aiding" or "encouraging" suicide to bring charges, despite the fact that this is a widely practiced and accepted medical intervention.

Sometimes having access to lethal medications enables patients to feel enough control over their fates that they never use them. They are strengthened simply by knowing that they, personally, can set the limit to their suffering and they need not depend on the unpredictable behavior of medical attendants who may at the end know very little about them. Assisting suicide remains illegal in most jurisdictions[9] but many physicians have encountered patients[10] for whom there is ethical justification for relinquishing control over the means of release, thereby enabling patients to control their own demise in the way they believe is most appropriate. Can the patient be mistaken? If so, that is the price of liberty.

How else can we respond to the stress of our aging population who do not fear death as much as dementia? They have seen it in family and friends. They fear that they will be physically and mentally incapable of enduring their lives when its quality is terribly diminished. What can we say to a genteel and fastidious person who fears fecal and urinary incontinence, his or her unrestrained and inappropriate aggressiveness, the need for imprisonment by restraints or isolation, and loss of social inhibitions in language and sexual behavior? Is this something more than simple aesthetic disapproval? Research continues, but experience tells us that there will be no sudden discovery, no magic bullet that will banish this problem by some technological quick fix.

Dworkin maintains that autonomy consists of authenticity and independence.[11] To be sure, a physician must use his or her knowledge of disease and how it impairs judgment and affects emotions in order to determine whether the desire for death is authentic, a true reflection of that person's essence. Jackson and Youngner have written about clinical and psychological problems that complicate the concept of patient autonomy.[12] "Is the function of medicine to preserve biological life or to preserve the person as he defines himself?" Eric Cassell asks this question and then answers it: "I believe that the function of medicine is to preserve autonomy and that preservation of life is subservient to the primary goal."[13]

ACTIVE EUTHANASIA

Regarding an active and deliberate intervention to bring about the patient's death, wise and respected commentators strongly oppose a physician's deliberate action to accomplish this.[14] They offer good arguments. First, a physician must be dedicated to preserving life. In response, ought one be dedicated merely to life, to vitalism, without regard to the patient's suffering or expressed wishes? Second, a physician who kills, even mercifully, may lose the trust of patients and of his other colleagues. In response, a patient would probably trust a doctor even more who is dedicated to helping the patient, responding to competent requests, and relieving agony and suffering, rather than one who is devoted to an exceptionless principle. These doctors, whose agonizing deliberation brought them to the conclusion that their patient's request for a quick and painless death was warranted, were not committed to an idea but rather to a patient. Having failed to heal or to cure, they do not fail their patient. Knowing no more can be done against a disease, they do what they can in their patient's interest, *as only the patient can truly decide.* Third, society cannot be trusted to refrain from wanton killing once the barrier to killing is broken. This is a very cogent caveat, yet the very essence of moral decision making is the search for stopping places on the slippery slope. In euthanasia by refusal of life-sustaining treatment, and in euthanasia by suicide, only the patient need act. But in administering a lethal dose, a person other than the patient is given license to act; thereby, the risk of abuse is greater because it may be imposed on a patient who is unable to resist. That is why the initiative must always come from the patient. No one else may decide what kind of a life is worth living and what is not, unless the patient has delegated this authority.

It may be that there is no way safely to endorse a law permitting the practice of euthanasia. Rachels has addressed the slippery-slope arguments by dividing them into logical and psychological.[15]

Logically, it is argued, once the practice of killing is accepted, there can be no reason to stop, so we dare not cross the barrier. Since there is clearly a difference between random, unsolicited killing and the considered request of a competent adult with whatever other preconditions may be desired, this argument is not sustained. There is a clear stopping place on the slippery slope. It is buttressed by the fact that society has accepted and delineated other clear conditions for accepted killing.

The psychological argument is different. It is based on conjecture. It argues that when certain practices are accepted, people will go on to less acceptable ones. They are not logically committed to do so, but it is speculated that this is what they will do. We must guess if this is, in fact, going to happen. Rachels points out that, with this fear in mind, persons wish to "leave well enough alone." But he goes on to say that the present policy is not simply a benign and harmless policy being compared to a dangerous new alternative. There is evil and suffering now. How can we change that suffering without inviting abuse? If a method were available to individualize each case, rather than give blanket permission, then fear of conspiracies and abuses might be allayed.

Rachels suggests that mercy killing, like self-defense, should be an acceptable defense against a charge of murder or manslaughter. The elements of proof consist of (a) the patient, while competent, requested aid in dying; (b) the patient was suffering from a painful, terminal illness. When such a defense is offered, the burden of proof is on the defense. Since the crime has been admitted, it is a reversal of the usual burden of proof. But this would not mean that everyone would have to go to court, although everyone would be liable to an investigation. Surely anyone contemplating mercy killing would have his witnesses, proofs, and evidences carefully lined up, and he would be unlikely to hazard the procedure without strong evidence that the conditions were fulfilled. In clear cases, most district attorneys would not bring charges. The need to write complex legislation would not be necessary. Another safeguard would be to make the failure to report each case to authorities a separate crime.

Rachels's approach is remarkably similar to the Dutch case law, regarding physician aid in dying, which involves the following:

1. There must be physical or mental suffering, which the sufferer finds unbearable.
2. The suffering and the desire to die must be lasting.
3. The decision to die must be the voluntary decision of an informed patient.
4. The person must have a correct and clear understanding of his or her condition and of other possibilities.
5. The person must be capable of weighing these options and must have done so.
6. There is no other reasonable solution to improve the situation.
7. The time and manner of death will not cause avoidable misery to others.
8. A medical doctor must be involved in the decision and prescribe the correct drugs.

The latter requirement is found particularly objectionable by Gaylin *et al.*, who in their article cited above said, "We must say to the broader community that if it insists on tolerating or legalizing active euthanasia, it will have to find non-physicians to do its killing."[16] To this I would say, surely we do not want a cadre of professional killers unconcerned with anything but the technique and the efficiency of the job. The Dutch realize that each death must be agonized over. A person must love dearly someone whom he would mercifully kill.[17] Can our society be trusted to adhere strictly to the rigid guidelines of self-determination so that we may know that no person other than the competent patient may ever determine when it is appropriate to shorten life? It is almost inevitable that political and economic pressures will work to establish aid in dying. Indeed, it would be less worrisome if there were universal access to medical care to deemphasize economic factors. Perhaps the motivation will not always be in the interest of self-determination, but our obligation is to ensure that it serves that end, regardless of motive. It would be wise to establish guidelines now, to bring this practice out of the shadows from whatever degree it is currently done without public approval, and subject it to compassionate regulations by society. The Dutch guidelines as a legal defense against the charge of homicide or manslaughter would be appropriate.

NOTES

1   W. Gaylin, L. Kass, E. Pellegrino, and M. Siegler, "Doctors Must Not Kill," *Journal of the American Medical Association* 259 (1988):2139.
2   H.T. Engelhardt, Jr., *The Foundations of Bioethics* (New York: Oxford Uni-

versity Press, 1986).

3   A. Gewirth, "Professional Ethics: The Separatist Thesis," *Ethics* 96 (1986):282-300.

4   D. Jackson and S. Youngner, "Patient Autonomy and Death with Dignity," *New England Journal of Medicine* 301, no.8 (1979):404-8.

5   *Superintendent of Belchertown State School vs. Saikewicz*, MA 370 NE2d, 417 (1977).

6   T.E. Quill, "Death and Dignity: A Case of Individualized Decision Making," *New England Journal of Medicine* 324, no.10 (7 March 1991).

7   L. Edelstein, "The Hippocratic Oath: Translation and Interpretation," *Bulletin of the History of Medicine* (Supplement No. 1, 1943):1-64.

8   D.W. Amundsen, "The Physician's Obligation to Prolong Life: A Medical Duty Without Classical Roots," *Hastings Center Report* 8, no.4 (August 1978):23-30.

9   H.T. Englehardt, Jr., and M. Malloy, "Suicide and Assisted Suicide: A Critique of Legal Sanctions," *Southwestern Law Journal* 36 (1982):1003-37.

10   F. Abrams, and E. Gee, "Withholding and Withdrawing Life Sustaining Treatment: A Survey of Opinions and Experiences of Colorado Physicians," (Denver: Center for Health Ethics and Policy, University of Colorado, 1988).

11   G. Dworkin, "Autonomy and Behavior Control," *Hastings Center Report* (February 1976):23-28

12   Jackson and Youngner, "Patient Autonomy and Death with Dignity."

13   E. Cassell, "The Function of Medicine," *Hastings Center Report* (December 1977):16-19.

14   Gaylin, Kass, Pellegrino, and Siegler, "Doctors Must Not Kill."

15   J. Rachels, "The Letters of Life and Death," in *Matteers of Life and Death: New Introductory Essays in Moral Philosophy,* ed. T. Reagan (Philadelphia: Temple University Press, 1980); 28-66; J. Rachels, *The End of Life: Euthanasia and Morality* (New York: Oxford University Press, 1986).

16   Gaylin, Kass, Pellegrino, and Siegler, "Doctors Must Not Kill."

17   D. Humphrey, ed., *Assisted Suicide: The Compassionate Crime* (Los Angeles: Hemlock Society, 1982).

Part II

Euthanasia in the Netherlands

4

Euthanasia in the Netherlands: Brief Historical Review and Present Situation

Else Borst-Eilers

In this contribution I will deal with euthanasia in the Netherlands mainly from the medical viewpoint. The legal aspects will be described elsewhere in this volume.

DEFINITIONS

To understand the Dutch discussion on euthanasia, it is important to know the definitions used.

In the Netherlands, *euthanasia* is defined as the deliberate termination of the life of a person on his request by another person. Essential in this definition is the request. Without such a request, the termination of a life would be murder. This also holds true if the termination of a patient's life is carried out by a doctor. Incompetent patients are therefore not eligible for euthanasia, unless prior to their becoming incompetent they have drawn up a written living will in which they request the termination of their life in the occurrence of explicitly named circumstances.

In view of this definition of euthanasia, the term *voluntary euthanasia* is not used by Dutch physicians, as this would constitute a pleonasm.

There is also formal agreement in the Netherlands that the following medical practices do *not* fall within the definition of euthanasia:

1. Stopping all forms of treatment that have become medically pointless is considered normal medical practice, not euthanasia. This also holds true in those cases where stopping the treatment means that death will possibly-- or probably--come a few days sooner. To determine whether a treatment

has become medically pointless is not always as easy as it sounds. In the case of incurable cancer, for example, stopping or not restarting chemotherapy can be a difficult decision. In a given patient, there may still be a small chance of some temporary improvement. This has to be weighed against the often serious side effects and the risk of complications that could even hasten death instead of postponing it. As long as the patient is still competent, such a decision should be taken by patient and doctor together. But, once again, when they decide to stop, this is not considered euthanasia.

2. Stopping a treatment or not starting a treatment on the patient's explicit request is not considered euthanasia. If the patient has been well informed and refuses (further) treatment, the doctor should respect the patient's wishes. Again, this is not euthanasia but normal medical practice.

3. Treating pain with increasing doses of morphine that are necessary to kill pain, but might at the same time shorten the patient's life, is not considered euthanasia. Here again, if the patient is competent the doctor should obtain the patient's consent for the policy.

HISTORY

It is difficult to decide where the history of euthanasia in the Netherlands starts. Doctors have probably always helped dying patients to end their lives more quickly when suffering became unbearable, but this occurred incidentally and was not discussed in the open. Many older Dutch doctors can recall a few of such cases from their own practice, and no doubt it happened--and still happens --in other countries as well. In 1957, the highly publicized acquittal of Dr. Bodkin Adams, a British general practitioner accused of murder when he was easing the deaths of rich old ladies, implicitly acknowledged the acceptability of administering "fatal doses" of drugs to the dying.

The Royal Dutch Medical Association (RDMA) published its first leaflet on medical ethics in 1936, and since then it has been regularly revised. Euthanasia was mentioned for the first time in the 1959 edition. In the introduction, this leaflet dwells at great length on the doctor's duties at a deathbed, repudiating euthanasia as well as assisted suicide in strong terms, and emphasizing the fact that it is the doctor's duty to preserve life and to do this as long as possible. Attention is paid to the patient's autonomy, but one does not attach much importance to it. In some situations, the doctor is admonished to protect a rash patient from himself. Even if a deathbed entails much pain and suffering, the doctor ought to do all that is possible to preserve life, for it is not up to the doctor, according to the booklet,[1] to wonder whether or not suffering is meaningful.

The Dutch debate over euthanasia was sparked by a 1973 court case in which a general practitioner was prosecuted for ending her mother's life. The mother had suffered a cerebral hemorrhage, was partly paralyzed, had trouble speaking, was deaf, and had repeatedly expressed the wish to die. The daughter, Dr. P, admitted that she had ended her mother's life and that she still believed she had done the right thing. At the time of the trial, eighteen other doctors had signed an open letter to the Dutch minister of justice, stating that they had committed the same "offense" at least once. Dr. P was found guilty. The judge gave her a suspended sentence of one week imprisonment and put her on probation for a year.

During the ensuing years, many statements and articles were published in the Netherlands by political parties, lay societies, by individual doctors, lawyers, and ethicists. The churches also took part in the discussion. In fact, the Dutch Reformed Church had already in 1972 published a "pastoral manual" entitled "Euthanasia. Meaning and Boundaries of Medical Treatment."

The Dutch Society for Voluntary Euthanasia was formed in 1973, nearly forty years after the British Voluntary Euthanasia Society, which was founded as early as 1935 by George Bernard Shaw, H.G. Wells, and others. The Dutch Society has pleaded repeatedly for legalization of euthanasia in the Netherlands. Furthermore, it gives information to patients and family members and helps patients to follow the correct procedure when they want to make a request for euthanasia. The society, on request, distributes model forms for a living will, by which a competent person can state in writing his wish to die by euthanasia should he become incurably ill and mentally incompetent.

In 1979, the Dutch Minister of Health asked the Dutch Health Council to write a report on the opinions within the medical profession and on the practice of euthanasia. The report was published in 1982.[2] First of all, it dealt with the matter of definitions. The Health Council advised not to use the term euthanasia for medical procedures that are generally accepted as normal medical practice, such as stopping a life-prolonging treatment that has become medically point- less. The Health Council recommended to use the term euthanasia only for "actions that are intended to shorten or end the life of another person on that person's request." The report also stated that in the view of many Dutch doctors, active euthanasia by a doctor should be allowed when a patient is incurably ill and when there is intolerable physical or mental suffering that cannot be alleviated by other means. In view of the secret atmosphere around euthanasia at that time, the Health Council could not give reliable information on the number of euthanasia cases per year in the Netherlands or the number of doctors involved. The Health Council's report was an important source of background information for the State Commission on Euthanasia, which was set up in 1982 to make recommendations to the government on future policy. The final report of the State Commission certainly is the most far-reaching report on euthanasia to emanate from an official government committee.[3] Defining euthanasia as the intentional termination of life by another party at the request of the person concerned, the State Commission, by a majority of thirteen to two, advocated a change of the penal code, which would allow doctors to practice euthanasia under conditions similar to those that were developed by the several courts in the Netherlands. The report included a model bill that was designed to implement the proposed reform.

Returning to the medical profession, there is little doubt that the attitudes of Dutch doctors regarding euthanasia were decisive in shaping the course of events leading up to the present situation.

In 1984, the RDMA issued a statement on euthanasia drawn up by its executive committee.[4] It first stressed the fact that in a pluralistic society there will always be differing opinions on matters such as abortion and euthanasia. It then went on to say that if a doctor wanted to grant his patient's wish to have his life ended, it would be proper for the doctor to perform euthanasia, provided the patient's condition fulfilled certain criteria, and provided the doctor followed certain guidelines (see below). If a doctor were to reject euthanasia on principle, the RDMA held that it may nevertheless be expected that he give the patient concerned an opportunity to contact another doctor at the earliest possible stage.

A striking point in the 1984 statement is that the distinction between euthanasia and assisted suicide is abolished. The executive committee felt that from a moral point of view it makes no difference whether the lethal medicine is administered directly by the doctor or is handed by the doctor to the patient (in the case of a drug taken orally). What matters is that the doctor is intensely involved in administering a drug with the explicit intention of bringing about the death of the patient. The guidelines for a "permissible" euthanasia as formulated by the RDMA closely mirror the criteria as laid down by the district courts, the appeal courts, and the Dutch Supreme Court in their several decisions. They amount to the following:

1. The request for euthanasia must come from the patient and must be entirely free and voluntary.
2. The patient's request must be well considered, durable, and persistent.
3. The patient must be experiencing intolerable (not necessarily physical) suffering, with no prospect of improvement.
4. Euthanasia must be a last resort. Other alternatives to alleviate the patient's situation must have been considered and found wanting.
5. Euthanasia must be performed by a physician.
6. The physician must consult with an independent physician colleague who has experience in this field.

Several Dutch hospitals and nursing homes have drawn up formal policies and protocols for terminal care, including euthanasia. Those institutions that allow euthanasia for their patients usually follow the RDMA guidelines, which have thus played an important role in inducing a uniform policy among Dutch doctors who practice euthanasia.

Of the 30,000 doctors in the Netherlands, nearly 25,000 are members of the RDMA. At the end of the 1960s, when the legislation of abortion was a hot issue in the Netherlands, a so-called Pro-Life movement came into being within the Dutch medical profession. These doctors are united in the Dutch Doctors

Association (DDA). The DDA is, on principle, against euthanasia as defined by the State Commission and the RDMA. The DDA has about 1,000 members. Although the RDMA and the DDA hold different views on euthanasia, they respect each other's opinions and they have remained on speaking terms. There are also issues on which their viewpoints are the same: in 1989 they published a booklet[5] together on terminal care, in which they express the hope that an optimal terminal care may minimize the demand for euthanasia.

The opinion of the Dutch population on euthanasia has been monitored by several opinion polls over the years. The percentage of people being in favor of a liberal euthanasia policy has grown steadily over the years: 40 percent in 1966, 53 percent in 1975, 67 percent in 1985, and 81 percent in 1988. Even among the voters for the Christian Democrats Party, 66 percent would want to see euthanasia formally accepted.[6]

In spite of the fact that the majority of the population is in favor of a permissive attitude towards euthanasia, as defined by the State Commission and carried out by a doctor, medical euthanasia has not yet been legalized in the Netherlands. The reason is a political one: the Christian Democrats Party is still opposed to such legalization and has held a strong position in every government coalition up until now.

THE INCIDENCE OF EUTHANASIA: HOW OFTEN DOES IT OCCUR AND WHERE?

When a doctor performs euthanasia in accordance with the guidelines laid down by the RDMA and reports this to the public prosecutor, he will not be prosecuted. (See the chapter by Professor Gevers in this volume for more details) But officially, euthanasia is still a criminal offense and, technically speaking, the doctor is a "suspect" until the moment when the public prosecutor has decided not to prosecute. Moreover, until November 1990, every reported case of euthanasia resulted in a police investigation, involving not only the physician but frequently also the family of the deceased. This procedural harassing is probably the main reason why most doctors did not report euthanasia, but signed the death certificate stating that death was the result of natural causes. In November 1990, the minister of justice introduced a new procedure. The doctor who has performed euthanasia informs the municipal medical examiner, who views the body and reports to the public prosecutor. If the public prosecutor is satisfied that all the guidelines on euthanasia have been followed, he dismisses the case and no further police investigation takes place. Since the introduction of this new procedure, the number of reported cases of euthanasia has doubled (in 1990 the number was 454). Nevertheless, reporting is still certainly far from complete.

The true incidence of euthanasia in the Netherlands has for many years been a matter of guesswork. Estimates varies widely, from 3,000 to 20,000 cases a year. The first reliable figures came from three small studies on the incidence of euthanasia in general practice.[7] The conclusion from these data was that all Dutch general practitioners together probably perform euthanasia between 2,000 and 3,000 times a year. In 1991, a more extensive study on the incidence of euthanasia in general practice was published by Van der Wal.[8] The author, state inspector of health in the province Noord, Holland, held an anonymous survey among 1,000 general practitioners (chosen at random), asking them about their experience with euthanasia in the years 1986 to 1989. The response rate to his survey was 67 percent. From his data he concludes that the total number of cases of euthanasia carried out by general practitioners in the Netherlands is 2,000 per year.

As a state inspector of health, Van der Wal has access to all the records of the formally reported cases of euthanasia in his province. By comparing several characteristics of the reported and the not-reported cases, he has tried to gain more insight into the question of why some cases are reported and others are not. Reporting showed a high correlation with having consulted a medical colleague and with having documented the whole procedure of decision making in writing.

The general practitioners were also asked several questions about their euthanasia patients, such as sex, age, diagnosis, main reason for requesting euthanasia, and probable life expectancy at the time of euthanasia. Nearly 85 percent of the patients who died by euthanasia suffered from a malignancy. In the remaining 15 percent, the diagnoses AIDS, multiple sclerosis, and amyotrophic lateral sclerosis occurred relatively often. Total weakness and exhaustion, complete physical dependence, and loss of dignity were the three most frequent reasons for requesting euthanasia. Severe pain was a relevant factor in only 25 percent of the cases. The estimated life expectancy (of course, a subjective judgment by the general practitioner) was less than two weeks in two-thirds of the patients; natural death still seemed more than three months away in only ten percent of the patients.

Van der Wal is following up his survey among general practitioners by a similar survey among nursing-home doctors. From his pilot data, the incidence of euthanasia in Dutch nursing homes seems to be far below 100 cases per year.[9]

The most extensive study on the incidence of euthanasia, assisted suicide, and other possible medical life-shortening interventions was commissioned by the present Dutch government. This government, when taking office in 1989, was confronted with the still unsolved question of whether to legalize medical euthanasia. The government decided to postpone a decision until reliable information was available about the incidence of euthanasia in hospitals, nursing homes, and family practice. To provide such information, a commission was set up in January 1990, chaired by Professor Jan Remmelink, Attorney General at the Dutch Supreme Court. The commission asked Professor Paul van der Maas, of the Erasmus University of Rotterdam, to carry out an extensive study that would address not only the question of euthanasia and assisted suicide but the total range of medical decisions that may hasten a patient's death--such as nontreatment decisions and the decision to alleviate severe pain by administering possibly lethal does of morphine. The study was also meant to yield information on the characteristics of patients and doctors involved in euthanasia and related procedures, and to investigate under which conditions doctors would be willing to report all cases of active termination of a patient's life.

For political reasons--the government wants to take a definite decision on legislation before the next elections in 1993--the time allotted for the study was only a year and a half.

In order to gain insight into the backgrounds of medical decisions concerning the end of life (MDEL), detailed interviews with practicing physicians are indispensable. On the other hand, reliable conclusions about the number of MDEL can only be obtained by a very large sample of individual deaths. Van der Maas *et al.* decided, therefore, to set up three separate studies:

1. A postal survey among doctors, based on a stratified sample of 7,000 deaths. All Dutch doctors received a letter explaining the study and how anonymity would be guaranteed. The response rate was 76 percent, yielding 5,197 usable questionnaires.
2. In-depth personal interviews with a stratified random sample of doctors. The response in this study was 91 percent, yielding 405 interviews (152 general practitioners, 50 nursing home physicians and 203 specialists working in hospitals).
3. A prospective study. All interviewees from the second study were asked to participate by completing, for every patient in their case who died within six months of the interview, a questionnaire identical to that used in the first study. The rate of response in this study was 80 percent.

The results of the combined studies by Van der Maas *et al.* has been published in a 220-page report.[10] An English version is in press. An English summary of the main results was published in *Lancet*.[11] The Remmelink commission wrote a 70-page comment on the study.[12] The study not only yielded reliable information on the true incidence of euthanasia and other MDEL in the Netherlands, but also provided valuable insights into medical decision making concerning the end of life and insights into the attitude of Dutch doctors to euthanasia and related procedures. Within the context of this paper, only the main results and conclusions can be mentioned. See Table 1 for a summary of the estimated incidence of the different types of MDEL in the Netherlands

The total number of deaths per year in the Netherlands is about 129,000. The true incidence of euthanasia and assisted suicide is, therefore, 2,300 and 400 respectively. The majority of these 2,700 deaths takes place at home (nearly 2,000). The incidence of euthanasia in hospitals is probably about 700; in nursing homes euthanasia is a very rare event (far less than 100 cases per year). These figures correspond to the answers given by physicians in the interviews. Of the general practitioners, 62 percent had ever practiced euthanasia or assisted in suicide; for the specialists and nursing home physicians these figures were 44 percent and 12 percent respectively.

Table 1
Estimated Incidence of the Different Types of
Medical Decision at the End of Life (MDEL) in the Netherlands

Type of MDEL	Percentage of All Deaths
Euthanasia (according to the official definition)	1.8
Assisted suicide	0.3
Life-termination without a recent explicit and persistent request	0.8
Alleviation of pain and symptoms with possible life shortening effect	17.5
Non-treatment decisions	7.5
Total MDEL	37.9

As in all previous studies, cancer appeared to be the most frequent diagnosis in euthanasia patients (83 percent of all cases). The two main reasons for asking for euthanasia were defacing and loss of dignity, with severe pain coming in third. This, too, is in accordance with other studies.

The number of requests for euthanasia is about twice the number performed. The study clearly revealed that Dutch doctors are reluctant to carry out euthanasia and try hard to find other alternatives to alleviate the patient's suffering. If such alternatives cannot be found, 88 percent are willing to end the patient's life. Another 8 percent are not willing to do so, but would refer a patient to a colleague who does not object on principle. Only 4 percent of Dutch doctors would never perform euthanasia or refer the patient to a colleague with a more liberal view.

Because Van der Maas *et al*. had set up their study to cover *all* types of MDEL, they also obtained information on active termination of life without an explicit and persistent request from the patient. They found that this occurred in about 0.8 percent of all deaths, which means about 1,000 times a year. Further analysis of these cases yielded the following information. Nearly all patients were no longer capable of making decisions at the time of their deaths. In more than half of the cases, however, euthanasia had been discussed earlier between doctor and patient, or the patient had expressed a wish for euthanasia if his suffering would become unbearable. In the remaining cases, the decision to end the patient's suffering by ending his life was taken without knowledge of the prior wishes of the patient. Nearly always, however, the doctor discussed the decision beforehand with medical colleagues, the nursing staff, and/or the family of the patient. In the total study, only two cases were found where the patient was still mentally clear and competent, yet the doctor had taken the decision on his own. Both cases had occurred several years ago and both doctors stated that, in the euthanasia climate of today, they would have discussed the situation openly with the patient.

In judging the ethical aspects of the 1,000 cases discussed above, one should bear in mind that more than 70 percent of the patients were expected to die within a week, and more than 20 percent within one to four weeks. In more than 60 percent, the "lethal drug" was morphine, a much higher figure than in the true euthanasia cases (26 percent). This suggests that in many cases, the doctor's primary goal was to kill pain, although he fully realized that it could hasten the patient's death. Despite formal agreement on the distinction between euthanasia and active termination of life, on the one hand, and possibly life-shortening treatments on the other hand, it is a fact that many doctors, especially those working in a hospital setting with its high-technology medicine, still have difficulty in making this distinction.

The Remmelink Commission, after studying the data very carefully, concluded that the great majority of the cases of active termination of life without explicit and persistent request ought to be defined as "medical help in dying" and to be regarded as acceptable medical practice. Nevertheless, they recommended that such cases be fully reported in the future, in order to be reviewed by the public prosecutor.

A last interesting finding from Van der Maas's is that 80 percent of the interviewees would be willing to report euthanasia to the authorities, provided certain conditions are fulfilled (such as no police interrogation, no confiscation of the body, and no prosecution). The other 20 percent regard euthanasia as a private matter that ought to remain between doctor and patient.

Van der Maas et al. conclude from their study that MDEL occur frequently in modern medical practice and will occur even more frequently in the future, because of the shift toward older populations, more cancer patients, and more life-prolonging technologies. Adequate care for ill patients nearing the end of life requires a combination of medical skills and human qualities. Medical students and young doctors in training should receive more explicit teaching about medical decision making and fatally ill patients. They should also obtain full knowledge of all appropriate technical and legal procedures, and they should be encouraged to report their decisions openly and to make them available for review. (The legal and political implications of the study by Van der Maas et al. are dealt with in a later chapter in this volume by Professor Gevers.)

ACTIVE TERMINATION OF LIFE IN INCOMPETENT PATIENTS

The euthanasia debate in the Netherlands has entirely concentrated on euthanasia according to the definition given earlier in this article, the right to self-determination being the main argument for a liberal euthanasia policy. As a result, termination of the life of patients who suffer intensely from an incurable disease but who are unable to make a request for euthanasia has, to a large extent, remained outside the picture. No case law has been developed, nor has the medical profession laid down clear guidelines for such cases.

This situation has changed recently. In the last couple of years it has become increasingly clear that doctors are badly in need of some guidance in their conduct toward mentally incompetent patients, such as severely handicapped newborns and patients in a state of irreversible coma. On the first of these issues, both the Dutch Pediatric Society and the RDMA have recently published a discussion report. The RDMA is also going to issue in the near future a report on irreversible coma.

On the actual life-shortening practice of Dutch doctors in cases of mental incompetence, very little is known. The general attitude is one of extreme caution; the overall policy is not to interfere in situations where the patient himself is not seriously suffering and where the burden of suffering is mainly carried by the family or the nursing staff. In the following paragraphs, I will deal briefly with the three categories mentioned above.

Severely Handicapped Newborns

In 1987, the Dutch Pediatric Society carried out a survey among eight centers for neonatology.[13] From this survey, it appeared that seven of these centers had developed guidelines on how to reach a decision on stopping life-prolonging treatment or not starting it in the first place. In one center there was no formally stated policy on such cases: doctors acted as they thought best for each individual baby.

In all eight centers, the decision to stop life-prolonging measures was not made solely on the baby's vital prognosis: the quality of life to be expected was also taken into consideration. In other words, the struggle to keep the baby alive was sometimes given up because the medical team and the parents had come to the conclusion that the life they were trying to save would bring with it so much suffering that it would not really be worth living.

Thus, stopping life-prolonging measures seems to be a generally accepted practice among Dutch neonatologists. Much more difficult for them is the question of active termination of a baby's life in those cases where life-prolonging measures have been stopped but where death does not follow. In five centers, it was openly admitted that the policy in such (exceptional) cases was to terminate the baby's life by the administration of a lethal drug. In the other three centers, this was only considered acceptable if the baby had spontaneously gone into the "dying phase."

Even more delicate is the issue of actively terminating the life of a severely handicapped newborn in the first place, because its defects are so severe that a speedy death seems the most merciful solution. The policy in three of the eight centers permitted such an action in exceptional cases. It is hardly necessary to add that such a step is only taken after a very carefully conducted process of decision making, in which several other people participate besides the parents and the doctor. However, it is generally agreed that only the doctor carries the ultimate responsibility for whatever action is taken, and that he can be called upon to defend his decision afterwards.

A fundamental point is, of course: Which criteria do the neonatology centers apply in reaching the decision that the baby's life will be one of unbearable suffering? It is not surprising that there is no absolute agreement on this. We are dealing here with a weighing process, in which different people may give different weight to the several defects and disabilities present in a given case. However, from the policies followed in the several centers, it appears that there is agreement that, generally speaking, the following criteria are deemed important in determining the quality of life to be expected: the ability to communicate with others, the ability to cope for oneself, the degree to which the child will remain dependent on medical care, the degree of suffering to be expected, and the expected lifespan.

Irreversible Coma

There are no systematic data available on the life-shortening practice of Dutch doctors in cases of irreversible coma. It is public knowledge that there are several patients lying in an irreversible coma in nursing homes, hospitals, and occasionally even at their own homes. In cases where the patient is dependent on artificial respiration, several doctors follow the policy of stopping the ventilator when it has become clear that the patient will never wake up again. The most difficult cases are those where the patient breathes spontaneously and is only dependent on artificial feeding in order to stay alive. It is generally known that in some of these cases, the medical team, the nursing team, and the relatives have together decided to stop the administration of food and fluids in order to let the patient die. Some nursing homes, however, do not allow such a policy, on religious grounds. Dutch courts have ruled inconsistently on whether artificial feeding in these cases is (futile) medical treatment or falls within the definition of normal nonmedical care.

Intercurrent fatal infections, such as pneumonia, are often not treated in coma patients. Such a policy is also a matter of agreement between the doctor and the patient's nearest relatives.

Severe Dementia

Severely demented people are generally well cared for in the Netherlands, in the so-called psychogeriatic nursing homes. Everyone in the Netherlands is fully insured for this type of care (by means of the General Special Health Costs

Act), without any limitation as to the duration of care. Because of poor planning, however, there is now a waiting list for this type of care. The present minister of health has promised a larger budget to solve this problem as soon as possible.

When a demented patient has, while still of sound mind, written and undersigned a request for euthanasia in case he should become severely demented, this is considered a valid request, especially when the request has been written or re-signed not longer than five years ago. In such cases, euthanasia has been performed. The number of cases per year, however, is probably small: the data by Van der Maas indicate an incidence of about twenty cases per year. The present prime minister has caused some upheaval in his own party (the Christian Democrats) by publicly admitting that he has written such a request for himself.

It seems to be rather common practice not to treat undercurrent fatal diseases in completely demented persons but to confine medical and nursing care to the alleviation of symptoms that cause suffering to the patient. "Pneumonia is the old man's friend" is still regarded true wisdom for demented people.

SOME POINTS FOR DISCUSSION

The facts about euthanasia in the Netherlands are no doubt of some interest because they give us an indication on how many people in modern Western society might want to die by euthanasia, when given a free choice. That number seems to be in the order of 2 percent, but may be even higher in a completely "permissive" society, which even the Netherlands are not (yet). The demand for euthanasia is, of course, also to a large degree determined by the morbidity pattern in a given population, a factor that changes over time.

More interesting than the actual facts about euthanasia are the moral aspects. There is little disagreement on the statement that euthanasia can be a blessing to individual patients, but there is wide disagreement on the question of whether it does harm to society. Several people, also in the Netherlands, are convinced that legalization of euthanasia *will* harm society, because it violates such fundamental norms and values as the taboo on killing a fellow human being and the traditional social role of the medical profession as a "healing" profession. If a liberal euthanasia policy would be a threat to society, then the next question would be how the rights of the individual ought to be balanced against the values of society. These are two central issues that deserve discussion. In the following paragraphs I will deal with them very briefly.

Does Legalization of Euthanasia Harm Society?

Opponents fear that a liberal euthanasia policy will: (1) lead to a loss of respect for human life in general, and (2) inevitably lead to the *involuntary* termination of patients' lives. Regarding the first point, I want to stress that there is no evidence that the Dutch population values human life less than other

Western societies. On the contrary: the death penalty has been abolished long ago, individual citizens are not allowed to possess a firearm without a special permit, and the abortion rate is the lowest in Europe (one abortion to ten live births), although the request for an abortion is usually granted in practice. In my opinion, there is not a scrap of evidence that the open practice of euthanasia leads to a lesser respect for human life.

The second fear is less easy to reject or confirm. Opponents have stated that there are several ways by which a policy of euthanasia could lead to the involuntary ending of patients' lives by doctors. They fear that, once the taboo of never actively killing a patient has been broken, the following phenomena will gradually occur: (1) "encouraged euthanasia," whereby chronically ill or dying patients may be pressured to choose euthanasia to spare their families further emotional stress; (2) "surrogate euthanasia," where, once voluntary euthanasia becomes permissible, society might go on to permit killing incompetent patients on the basis of substituted judgement; and (3) "secret euthanasia," meaning that vulnerable patients will be killed without their consent.[14] Singer and Siegler suppose that especially in a society like the United States, where many citizens live in a very vulnerable position and where many millions of people do not have access even to basic health care, the legalization of euthanasia "would create another powerful tool with which to discriminate against groups ... whose rights are already in jeopardy."

The fear that legalization of euthanasia gradually leads to a policy of involuntary termination of patients' lives has also been expressed during the political debate in the Netherlands. It is probably one of the reasons why the present government has financed the previously mentioned large confidential survey among Dutch doctors with the purpose of getting better insight into how doctors make decisions that influence the moment of death. The medical profession has been cooperating in this study. They too are anxious to lift the veil of ignorance and to establish, by actual fact-finding, if there is any ground for the accusation that some Dutch doctors are indeed on the slippery slope from euthanasia to involuntary termination of life, because *they* think that is the best solution for the patient. Some people might argue that the small number of severely defective newborns whose lives have been actively terminated--when they did not die spontaneously from their disorders and they seemed to suffer very much--are already proof that things have gone too far. In view of the very careful procedure of decision making in these cases, involving the medical team, the nurses, the parents, and a pastor or psychosocial worker, I do not agree with that conclusion.

In view of some of the arguments from North American opponents to euthanasia, it may be important to note that in the Netherlands there are no financial incentives to terminate a patient's life. Everybody has full health-care insurance, and nobody has to pay out-of-pocket money for institutional care in hospitals or nursing homes. Dutch doctors are never shareholders of the hospital or nursing home in which they practice.

Does Euthanasia Harm the Image of the Medical Profession as a "Healing" Profession?

In my opinion, those who ask this question miss the whole point of euthanasia. There are situations in which the best way to heal the patient is to help him die peacefully. The doctor who, in such a situation, grants the patient's request acts as the healer "par excellence."

NOTES

1   Th.G.J.J. van Berkestein, *et al.*, *Medische Ethiek en Gedragsleer* (*Medical Ethics and Code of Behavior*) (Amsterdam, the Netherlands: Royal Dutch Medical Association, 1959).
2   Gezondheidsraad (Health Council), *Advies inzake euthanasie* ('s-Gravenhage, the Netherlands: Staatsuitgeverij, 1982).
3   "Final Report of the Netherlands State Commission on Euthanasia: An English Summary," *Bioethics* 2 (1987):156-62.
4   KMMG (Royal Dutch medical Association), "Standpunt inzake euthanasie," *Medisch Contact* 39 (1984):990-98.
5   H.L. van Aller, W.L.H. Smelt, J.A.J. Stevens, and J.G. Verhoeven, *Stervensbegeleiding: Praktische Adviezen voor Hulperleners* (*Care for the Dying: Practical Advice for Health-Care Professionals*) (Utrecht, the Netherlands: Bunge, 1990).
6   "Nederlandse Vereniging voor Vrijwillige Euthanasie" (brochure, 1989).
7   A.P. Oliemans and H.G.J. Nijhuis, "Euthanasie in de huisartspraktijk," *Medisch Contact* 41 (1986):691; A.I.M. Bartelds, *et al.*, *Studies from the Continuous Morbidity Registration Sentinel Stations* (Netherlands Institute of Primary Health Care, *1989*), *259-83; Jaarverslag 1987 van het Amsterdamse peilstatiionsproject* (Amsterdam, the Netherlands: 1988).
8   G. Van der Wal, "Euthanasie en help bij zelfdoding door heisartsen," *Medisch Contact* 46 (1991):171-76, 211-15, 237-41.
9   G. Van der Wal, personal commmunication.
10   P.J. van der Maas, J.J.M. van Delden, and L. Pijenborg, *Medical Decisions Concerning the End of Life* (in Dutch) (The Hague, the Netherlands: Staatsuitgeverij, 1991).
11   P.J. van der Maas, J.J.M. van Delden, L. Pijenborg, and C.W.N. Looman, "Euthanasia and Other Medical Decisions concerning the End of Life," *Lancet* 338 (1991):669-74.
12   van der Maas, van Delden, Pijenborg, and Looman, *Medical Decisions*.
13   Dutch Pediatric Society, *Ned Vereniging voor Kindergeneeskund. Doen of Laten?* 1989.
14   P. A. Singer and M. Siegler, "Euthanasia: A Critique," *New England Journal of Medicine* 322 (1990):1881-83.

5

What the Law Allows: Legal Aspects of Active Euthanasia on Request in the Netherlands

J.K.M. Gevers

INTRODUCTION

Developments concerning active voluntary euthanasia in the Netherlands continue to receive considerable attention in other nations, including the US. If there is any country that seems to embrace the often-claimed principle that everybody has a right to die in dignity or even to choose to die, that country would seem to be the Netherlands.

However, under Dutch law the "right to die" is only recognized to a limited extent. Protection of life remains a major concern of the law. This goes without saying where incompetent persons are concerned--for instance, severely ill, comatose patients. If there is no advance directive in which such a patient has expressed his will, life-sustaining treatment must be provided, unless the responsible physician is convinced that these interventions are pointless from a medical point of view. In the few court decisions that deal with incompetent patients, the courts have been very reluctant to accept quality-of-life arguments as a basis for withholding treatment or to allow for substituted judgement by relatives or next of kin. Actively terminating the life of such patients is not allowed.

As to competent patients, there is a consensus that the patient has a right to refuse any therapy or treatment, even if this results in death, provided that the patient is sufficiently informed about the consequences of his or her decision. Furthermore, an attempt to take one's own life is not a criminal offense. But it is against the law for a relative or intimate friend of the patient to assist in suicide.

What about doctors? In principle, physicians also must refrain from assistance in suicide and from terminating a person's life at that person's request.

And if the patient's situation is one of unacceptable suffering without any prospect of improvement--a situation in which, according to the courts, a doctor may be acquitted if he carries out euthanasia on request or assists in suicide--there is no right of the patient to demand euthanasia from his doctor. The latter, although he has entered into a medical contract with the patient to help him (including alleviating his suffering), can never be obliged to terminate the patient's life. Euthanasia is not an enforceable right and it is not likely to (and should not) develop into such a right.

THE LAW AND ITS APPLICATION

The current penal code states in Article 293 that anyone who takes another person's life, even at his explicit and serious request, will be punished by imprisonment of, at the most, twelve years. A comparable provision, with a more limited punishment, exists with regard to assisting in suicide (Article 294).

How have doctors who have been prosecuted for these crimes defended themselves? Some of their lawyers simply argued that Article 293 was not written for the termination of the life of a severely suffering patient. The Supreme Court rejected this argument; rightly so, because otherwise anybody would be free to terminate the life of a seriously ill patient on the patient's request. Another argument, which avoids this undesirable consequence, is that hastening the death of a patient who is in a desperate situation can be part of medical practice and that--like other medical acts--this act should be governed by the rules set by the medical profession, not by societal rules such as the provisions in the penal code. As we will see, this appeal to a medical exception was also dismissed by the courts: like abortion, euthanasia cannot be considered normal medical practice and the state has a legitimate interest to regulate such acts. Thirdly, it was argued that voluntary euthanasia, although in conflict with the wording of Article 293, is basically not against the substance or the spirit of the law, because a large part of society would consider it justified as an ultimate remedy in a situation of unbearable suffering. The Supreme Court rejected this argument also, if only because according to its view, euthanasia was not generally accepted.

The one plea for acquittal that was not dismissed is the invocation of a situation of emergency in which the defendant carefully balanced his conflicting duties and made a decision that could objectively be justified, taking into account the special circumstances. The first instance in which the Supreme Court accepted this argument was in a case from Alkmaar. In this case, the defendant, a doctor, had given a series of injections resulting in the death of his patient, a ninety-five-year-old woman who was seriously ill with no chance of improvement. The weekend before her death, she suffered substantial deterioration, was unable to eat or drink, and lost consciousness. She had pleaded with the doctor several times to put an end to her agony. After regaining consciousness, she declared that she did not want to go through such an experience ever again and, with great emphasis, urged her physician to perform euthanasia. The defendant had discussed the matter several times with his assistant physician and the patient's son, both of whom had approved of such measures. Finally, the defendant decided to act according to the patient's wishes as, in his opinion, every single day of life would be nothing but a heavy burden to the patient, whose pain was unbearable.

The defense invoked a conflict of duties. The Court of Appeals of Amsterdam rejected this argument and convicted the doctor. According to the Supreme Court in its decision of 1984, the Court of Appeals had not given sufficient reasons for its decision; in particular, it should have investigated whether, according to responsible medical opinion measured according to the prevailing standards of medical ethics, an emergency had existed. In this case the court of appeals should, for instance, have taken into account:

- Whether, and to what extent according to professional medical judgement, an increasing disfigurement of the patient's personality and/or further deterioration of her already unbearable suffering were to be expected;
- Whether it could be expected that soon she would no longer be able to die with dignity under circumstances worthy of a human being;
- Whether there were still opportunities to alleviate her suffering.

The Supreme Court referred the case to the Court of the Hague, which acquitted the doctor.

The Supreme Court's decision has been welcomed by many since it allowed some room for euthanasia. Still, the reasoning leading to its conclusion has been criticized for different reasons. Some have argued that the court was right in referring to medical ethics, but that it was not consistent enough in its reasoning. In this view, if medical ethics are to be decisive, it is the medical profession who has to develop norms. Medical acts, including active euthanasia upon request, should primarily be judged by the profession itself, in particular, by the disciplinary courts. As long as a doctor acts according to accepted professional standards, he should never be held liable under criminal law, according to this view.

Others have criticized the Supreme Court's decision because of its reference to medical ethics. According to these critics, first, there is strong disagreement within the medical profession itself on the ethical acceptability of euthanasia. Secondly, the question whether euthanasia should be allowed, and if so in what circumstances and under what safeguards, would exceed the competence of the medical profession.

Two years later, in 1986, the Supreme Court had the opportunity to answer its critics. It had to review the decision of a lower court that had suggested that if a physician acts carefully, according to professional standards, termination of a patient's life at the latter's request does not come under Article 293 of the Penal Code. In this second decision, the Supreme Court explicitly rejected this "medical exception," but it reaffirmed the approach it had adopted in its first decision.

Since the Supreme Court made its landmark decision, ten to fifteen other euthanasia cases have been decided. In most of them, the invocation of a situation of emergency by the defendant resulted in acquittal. In some cases, the physician concerned was convicted, either because he had failed to establish the will of the patient beyond doubt, or because he had been negligent in consulting another independent physician. In several cases, the physician was not convicted for euthanasia, but he received a penalty for writing a false death certificate, disguising the fact that the patient had not died a natural death.

FURTHER LIMITS TO VOLUNTARY EUTHANASIA

The developing pattern of court decisions leaves room for euthanasia or assisted suicide, provided such help is given by a physician after another physician has been consulted; the patient's request is persistent; his situation is desperate; his suffering is unbearable; and there are no other solutions to his situation. This summary of what the courts allow leaves many questions unanswered, in particular as to whether there are any further limits to voluntary euthanasia. I will briefly discuss four of these questions:

1. Must the patient must be terminally ill?
2. Is it sufficient that only the patient experiences his situation as unbearable?
3. Can mental suffering can be a basis for euthanasia?
4. May a minor may request euthanasia?

In general, the courts do not require that the patient be terminally ill and that his death be imminent. In one of the first cases, which was decided in 1973, the court in question argued that patients with incurable diseases, which entail very serious physical and/or mental suffering, may live for many years in that situation and that therefore it would not be just to limit the possibility of help in dying to situations where death would inevitably ensue. For instance, in 1985, the Court of the Hague acquitted an anesthesiologist who had performed euthanasia upon the request of a very ill patient suffering from multiple sclerosis.

What the courts do require, however, is not only that the patient is in a desperate situation with no prospect of improvement, but also that there are no other, reasonable solutions to improve his condition. Whether such a situation exists depends, first of all, on the patient's own assessment. In 1986, for example, in the aforementioned Alkmaar case, the Court of Appeals of the Hague decided that the physician could take into account that the patient herself felt that she would no longer be able to die with dignity. The court also acknowledged that a possible alternative may no longer be available when the patient refuses it. But, in the final analysis, the existence of unbearable conditions is not merely determined by the patient's subjective experience. The physician, also, must satisfy himself that there are no practical alternatives, and that the situation of the patient can be considered as untenable.

The rulings of the courts do not exclude the possibility of euthanasia or assisted suicide in cases of unbearable psychological suffering. The court of Rotterdam, for instance, stated in 1981 that assistance in suicide could remain unpunished in case of physical *or* mental suffering experienced as unbearable by the person in question. In the literature, however, the general opinion would seem to be that requests for help in dying, made on the basis of mental suffering only, should be approached with great caution. This holds in particular for patients suffering from a mental disorder, in which case it will be difficult to establish whether the request of the patient is based on free will and has been made after careful consideration. This last point was the central issue in a decision of the Central Disciplinary Court of the Netherlands (1990), in which the court reviewed a complaint against a psychiatrist who helped a patient end his life: the patient was about sixty years old, seriously and chronically depressed, and suffering from severe lung emphysema. According to the complaint lodged by the National Health Inspectorate, the patient's wish to die was not an independent expression of his will, but rather part of his illness. The psychiatrist was personally convinced that the patient was able to make a free decision to die and this view was supported by two colleagues in the same hospital. However, as to the question whether this decision was influenced by the patient's mental illness, there was no definite and unambiguous answer. Therefore, according to the Court, the physician should not have cooperated in the patient's suicide.

Finally, enabling patients to request euthanasia inevitably raises the question as to what extent "mature minors" may make such a request. If we acknowledge that all persons have a right to self-determination, and that minors must be enabled to exercise that right to the extent that they have the mental and psychological capacities to do so, it is difficult to accept that a physician could disregard their views simply because they are not yet eighteen years old (the age of majority in the Netherlands). One case in which a pediatric oncologist assisted in the suicide of a sixteen-year-old minor by providing him drugs to end his life has caused considerable public debate. According to a draft bill on euthanasia submitted to parliament by the Dutch government at the end of 1987, the parents or legal representatives must always be involved and can always veto a decision of a doctor to provide help in dying. According to the advice of the National Health Council, however, a minor of sixteen years should have the option to object to parental involvement. There are no court decisions on this particular issue.

PROSECUTION

Since active euthanasia and assisted suicide are not regarded as causes of natural death, the physician cannot write a death certificate. This means that the medical examiner (a physician operating at municipal level who is authorized to investigate all cases of unnatural death) will be involved. He will then report to the public prosecutor, that is, the district attorney. It is at the discretion of the prosecutor, whether the case in question will be brought before the court. From 1982 onward, reported cases were discussed at a national level in the meetings of the attorneys general. They decided whether the physician would be prosecuted; the criteria for this decision were derived from the court rulings. Although the number of cases reported to the authorities has been rising (in 1989, 336 cases were reported; in 1990, 450 cases), in the large majority of cases (estimates are about 95 percent) the public prosecution was not informed because physicians disguised the facts.

Although there was general agreement that what physicians do in the domain of euthanasia and assisted suicide should be open to public scrutiny, and that the relevant procedures should be designed in such a way as to permit retrospective assessment of the way in which a decision to terminate life was taken and carried out, there was criticism of the existing procedure. On the one hand, the procedure was considered unreasonable and unfair to doctors who, after having made the difficult decision to help the patient in dying, felt they were treated like criminals and were exposed to the possibility of an often not very discreet police investigation. On the other hand, many (including members of the public prosecution itself) considered the procedure to be ineffective, because considerable time was spent on those cases which were most likely to meet the accepted criteria. In order to make the procedure less deterrent and more effective, several proposals were made, mostly to increase the role of the medical examiner and to reduce the role of the police. In some districts, attorneys and local associations of doctors reached an agreement on the notification and review of cases of euthanasia, but for several years the Ministry of Justice has refused to officially approve these local conventions. In 1990, the Ministry of Justice agreed to a procedure in which the medical examiner, after having received a complete account from the physician, reports to the district attorney. The latter may then order a police investigation or issue a certificate of no objection to burial or cremation. If the police are involved, they will act as discreetly as possible. It is expected that this procedure will increase the willingness of doctors to cooperate in the notification and review of cases of active euthanasia or assisted suicide.

CHANGING THE LAW?

For many years, there have been calls for legislation. The courts have opened the door to voluntary euthanasia, but they have not succeeded in developing completely uniform and unambiguous standards concerning proper medical procedure and careful decision making. Their decisions remain determined by the particular facts of each case. Patients and doctors are left with a considerable degree of uncertainty. Moreover, the courts cannot surpass the existing criminal law; they can only be lenient in applying that law. Statutory regulation would not only have the advantage of providing more legal certainty, but also of making existing medical practice more subject to societal control. Legislation could even be an indispensable instrument to establish such control.

Over the past ten years, several proposals and draft bills have been submitted to parliament, among them the proposal of the State Commission on Euthanasia, which reported in 1985. I will not discuss these proposals. For various reasons, no law legalizing euthanasia and assisted suicide has been adopted so far in the Netherlands, because the Christian Democrats oppose any legalization of the current practice, and their role is crucial in any government coalition. In 1991, the committee of inquiry set up in 1990 to investigate the practice of euthanasia published its report (see previous chapter by Else Borst-Eilers). One of the findings is that in 0.8 percent of all deaths, lethal drugs were administered with the explicit intention to shorten the patient's life without the patient's persistent request. The study suggests that in these cases, death was imminent and the patient was suffering heavily; in more than half of the cases the decision had been discussed with the patient when he or she was still competent or the patient had in a previous phase of his or her illness expressed a wish for euthanasia if suffering became unbearable. These cases (or at least part of them) do not meet the strict criteria for euthanasia. The existing pattern of court decisions does not allow shortening a patient's life without his or her explicit and persistent request, although one can never completely exclude the possibility that the courts would accept an appeal to a conflict of duties in an exceptional situation. In pursuance of the publication of the report, the Dutch government has sent a letter to Parliament proposing new legislation. According to the proposal, the penal code will not be changed: termination of the life of a severely suffering patient will remain a crime, even if the patient has requested euthanasia explicitly and persistently. On the other hand, the notification procedure for cases of euthanasia that was agreed upon in 1990 (see above) will be laid down in regulations under the Burial Act and thereby acquire legal status. That procedure will also apply to situations where death is imminent (because the patient has entered a process of irreversible loss of vital functions) and a doctor shortens his life without his previous request. According to the government, it is desirable to extend the notification procedure to the latter category of cases so that they will be reported and can be submitted to the judgment of the courts.

It remains to be seen whether the Dutch parliament will agree with the proposal. In my view, it is not satisfactory. From a legal point of view it is not consistent to modify existing legislation (Burial Act) so as to provide room for euthanasia (at least implicitly), while on the other hand the absolute prohibition of euthanasia in the penal code remains intact. Furthermore, although apparently it is not the government's intention to do so, the extension of the notification procedure to cases in which there is no request of the patient suggests that these cases can be dealt with on the same basis as cases of euthanasia in the strict sense (that is, when there is a request of the patient). However, the distinction between the two categories remains essential, and the question as to whether, in a situation of unbearable suffering, shortening life without a request could ever be justified, requires a separate, fundamental discussion.

BIBLIOGRAPHY

de Wachter, M.A.M. "Active Euthanasia in the Netherlands." *Journal of the American Medical Association* 262 (1989):3316-19.

Gevers, J.K.M. "Legal Developments Concerning Active Euthanasia on Request in the Netherlands." *Bioethics* 1 (1987):156-62.

Leenen, H.J.J. "Dying with Dignity: Developments in the Field of Euthanasia in the Netherlands." *Medical Law* 8 (1989):517-26.

6

A Physician's Responsibility to Help a Patient Die

Pieter V. Admiraal

She was a forty-seven year old, happily married mother of four children who ranged in age between thirteen and nineteen years. In December 1988, she first noticed a painful swelling in her lower abdomen. She went to her family doctor. She had worked for his family for many years, had helped take care of his children, and looked upon him as a trustworthy advisor and friend. He referred her to the gynecologist in our hospital. Surgery was performed in January, which revealed a malignant tumor of the ovary, so large that it could not be removed entirely. Chemotherapy was begun at the end of January and by June her condition had definitely improved. For the following nine months, she had hardly any complaints and was able to do her housework by herself. In March 1990, the tumor was found to have recurred. She was again treated with, chemotherapy, but in vain. In the beginning of July she was suffering from so much pain that her family doctor had to prescribe narcotics. Her condition deteriorated quickly and she was readmitted to our hospital. I was consulted because her abdominal pain had become intolerable. On my first visit, I told her that it was almost certain that I would be able to control her pain completely. I achieved this within two days by continuous infusion of morphine subcutaneously. This was of great relief to the patient. Like most patients with cancer, she was frightened that the pain in the terminal stage of her illness would be unbearable and that nothing could be done to relieve it. I visited the patient at least once a day. On one occasion, she asked me about the possibility of euthanasia. Her husband was upset by her request. He could not accept that she was terminally ill, even though he realized that we could not do anything more to cure her. I confirmed that euthanasia could be discussed at our hospital when it was requested by the patient, but explained that the final decision regarding euthanasia must be made by a team of two physicians, a nurse, and a pastor. The following day she discussed her request with a Roman Catholic pastor.

Her condition deteriorated quickly. She developed persistent vomiting which required that I place a tube through her nose into her stomach. At the patient's request we made the decision not to feed her intravenously. She received only small amounts of saline by infusion to prevent thirst. She lost weight quickly and became extremely weak. She did not even have enough strength to move around in bed. It was extremely difficult for the nurses to prevent bed sores. In the meantime, her tumor continued to increase in size. It obstructed the veins in her legs, causing her legs to swell. From the date of admission, she was nursed in a room of her own so that members of her family could spend the whole day with her. During the night her husband and one of her children slept in the same room. She was often visited by her family doctor and his wife. The patient remained completely alert until the last moment. She bore her physical deterioration bravely and provided support for her grieving family. She had a strong religious belief and was certain that she would go to heaven. She received the last sacraments of the Roman Catholic Church four days before she died.

And then came, not unexpectedly, the day that she begged us to end her suffering. "God could not want this," she said. Her husband was now able to accept her request because he realized that he was being selfish in his wish not to let her go. There was a family meeting where the oldest son, in spite of everything, still doubted the fact that his mother would never get better. The patient talked to him privately, after which he went along with her request. The nurses who cared for the patient on a daily basis were able to respect her wish to die. The gynecologist, the pastor, and I also agreed that we were prepared to respect the patient's wish. We always hesitate and consider a request for euthanasia to be a cry for help, perhaps as a result of shortcomings in our palliative care. In this case, however, we came to the conclusion that there were no further options to alleviate her suffering. The family doctor and his wife came to say farewell. The patient and I met with the family and arranged for euthanasia to be performed the following day. The patient signed a declaration requesting euthanasia. The following day, the patient again confirmed how much she longed for eternal reunion with her parents. The patient's husband, her two sisters, her pastor, and two of her children were in the room when I administered the lethal drugs. She fell asleep with a smile on her face and died after 8 minutes on August 6, 1990. Her family was especially grateful that we had spared her further suffering. The gynecologist and I signed a checklist which we sent to the prosecutor along with the patient's declaration. The attorney General decided not to prosecute us.

This case history illustrates how we at the Reinier de Graaf Gasthuis in Delft performed euthanasia and have been doing so for more than fifteen years. I will now go into more detail about the following items:

1. The right of self-determination,
2. The request for euthanasia,
3. The role of the family,
4. The role of palliative care,
5. The technique of euthanasia.

THE RIGHT OF SELF-DETERMINATION

I started my medical studies more than foorty years ago. At that time the patient's right of self-determination were not an issue. Patients surrendered their rights completely to the doctor and trusted his skill and judgment without being informed about either the diagnosis or the prognosis of the disease. In those early days, there was frequently little that medical science could do to cure the patient. Patients died at home under the care of their family, pastor, and general practitioner. Today, the situation is very different. From the beginning, patients are fully informed about the diagnosis and prognosis of their diseases, about the therapeutic possibilities and the their consequences, and about the likelihood of overcoming the disease. As a result, patients are frequently forced to decide which course of action should be taken. Every patient in the Netherlands has the right to the most advanced treatment available. They also have the right to refuse treatment without running the risk of being discharged from the hospital. Patients also have the indisputable right to judge when suffering is unbearable and the right to request euthanasia.

THE REQUEST FOR EUTHANASIA

Cancer patients in the terminal phase will request euthanasia if they consider their suffering to be unbearable, choosing to die rather than to live under those circumstances. What factors cause suffering to become unbearable? We must distinguish between physical and psychological causes even though the two are closely related.

Loss of strength makes a patient incapable of any exertion and totally dependent on nursing care. Persistent nausea, vomiting, and hiccuping can also drive a patient to request euthanasia. Pain, however, is often considered to be the most important cause of suffering, although nowadays, pain can be controlled in most cases. In a small number of instances, we may be compelled to administer morphine in such high doses that the patient's mentation is affected. Some doctors and nurses think that the use of high doses of morphine is a form of euthanasia. This is not correct. Morphine, in fact, prolongs life in patients with severe pain. The presumption is correct, however, that patients who are in agonizing pain may ask for euthanasia as a last resort. On the other hand, it is incorrect to presume that a patient with proper pain control will never request euthanasia. Pain is very seldom a reason for euthanasia in our hospital. Most often the reason for euthanasia is psychological suffering.

Practically every patient is plagued by anxiety during the course of a terminal illness. From the moment they hear the diagnosis and learn that death is inevitable, many patients develop fear of pain and grievous suffering. The good physician will assure his patients that medicine has powerful tools to treat suffering and that they will not be alone. Unfortunately, many physicians provide poor information or withdraw from the patient entirely. Much more difficult to combat is the anxiety about spiritual and physical decay. Patients also fear that they will become totally dependent on others. The fear of loneliness and isolation is also terrible. Many patients spend long sleepless nights alone with their thoughts and fears.

Anxiety about dying itself can have various causes. Dying is the loss of the world in which one has lived, worked, and loved. There is also anxiety about the moment of dying. Patients fear what comes after death. This can vary from a vague anxiety about the unknown to a literal "deathly" fear of punishment which may be eternal. The suffering of a human being is strictly individual and is largely hidden from our objective observation. Consequently, it is difficult for one person to judge the suffering of another.

THE ROLE OF THE FAMILY

The family also suffers during a terminal illness. They ask themselves how much longer it will last. It is easy to understand a request for euthanasia from the family. However, their request should never be fulfilled. It is only the patient who can ask for euthanasia. Of equal importance is that the family cannot prevent euthanasia if the patient is insistent.

THE ROLE OF PALLIATIVE CARE

One often reads that patients never request euthanasia if they are receiving good palliative care. It has even been suggested, in the Anglo-American anti-euthanasia literature, that a request for euthanasia proves that inadequate palliative care had been provided. Let's face the facts. For more than eighteen years doctors, nurses, and pastors have provided good palliative care in our hospital. We have coordinated our efforts and used modern techniques to try to alleviate the suffering of our patients. After all this experience we have only one certainty: we cannot relieve all suffering. We have learned to accept that some of our patients have totally detached themselves from the world and long only for a good death. They regard any hesitation as an unjustified denial of their suffering. But hesitate we must! A request for euthanasia alone is not enough. We always try to improve our care in order to avoid the need for euthanasia.

The decision to carry out euthanasia is made by a team of doctors, nurses, and pastors who must try to realize in their own minds why the patient prefers to die rather than to live under these circumstances. The doctor in the team must remain aware that he bears the final responsibility for the decision. The decision to carry out euthanasia in our hospital is based upon our understanding that euthanasia is a part of palliative care. We all realize that good palliative care is essential. Without good palliative care, there is no euthanasia! But we also realize that good palliative care must offer at least the possibility of euthanasia. About 8 percent of terminally ill patients in our hospital request euthanasia.

THE TECHNIQUE OF EUTHANASIA

Euthanasia in our hospital is carried out either by giving the patient an overdose of barbiturate by intravenous infusion or by a single injection of a barbiturate and a curare-like drug. The barbiturate causes a coma which leads to death within several hours. The curare-like drug causes respiratory paralysis which leads to death within a few minutes. In 1980, I published "Justifiable Euthanasia" with guidelines about how to perform euthanasia. This brochure was written in Dutch and sent to all doctors and pharmacists in our country by the Voluntary Euthanasia Society. In 1986, I was a member of a working party of the Royal Association for the Advancement of Pharmacy, and we published guidelines for doctors and pharmacists that are recommended by the Royal Dutch Medical Association.

EPILOGUE

Euthanasia is a word burdened with a bad history. Because of the crimes committed by Hitler and the Nazi doctors, the word euthanasia is often associated with the senseless murder of innocent people. Many opponents of euthanasia belong to the generation which lived through World War II. This may explain why some people fear that euthanasia will be applied to mentally ill patients and people with disabilities. They fear that tolerance of euthanasia at the request of the dying patient may ultimately lead to "involuntary" euthanasia." I can understand this fear but am of the opinion that we must define our aims today in order to prevent any possibility of such distortion in the future. Acceptance of voluntary euthanasia should go hand in hand with protection against any possible misuse. Some opponents reject any possibility of euthanasia on religious grounds. To them, life is a gift of God which only He can take away. Nobody has the right to stop the life of another person. This sanctity of life principle is not open for debate. We must all respect each other's religious views
.   I have a strong feeling that not euthanasia, but death itself, is the taboo. This should not be surprising in a world where, technically speaking, everything is possible: a world without limits where life-prolonging procedures blur the boundary between life and death. Death seems to exist only to be conquered, to be driven out and forgotten as soon as possible. Euthanasia confronts us with death in its most concrete form. Many of us, however, would rather not be confronted. It is my honest opinion that every doctor has the right and the duty to carry out euthanasia at the request of a dying patient. This should only be done

after a prolonged and thorough deliberation convinces him that he is acting in the patient's best interest. Similarly, every doctor has the right to refuse to carry out euthanasia.

7

Active Euthanasia:
Is Mercy Killing the Killing of Mercy?

D.J. Bakker

INTRODUCTION

In recent decades, medicine has made dramatic progress in the ability to prolong life. While the possibilities of treatment with advanced life-support measures often provide great benefit to individual patients by restoring or prolonging not only their lives but also the "quality" of their lives, there is also the capability to prolong patient's lives beyond the point at which they desire such a continuation. Sometimes the patient does not want continued life support, although we doctors, still think they will benefit from it.

For some patients, literally speaking, the end of their lives can be lost. Medicine, with all its modern abilities, can go too far and sometimes doctors do not know how to stop where they should; instead, they start where they should not and go on "curing," when "terminal care" is required.

Some of the most controversial moral issues in present-day medical ethics involve decision making at the beginning and at the end of life; for example, in severely handicapped newborns and terminally ill patients.

We in medicine seem to lose track when one of the most important and decisive parts of a patient's life, the end, is near. Because of the problems we can have with this terminal phase of our patient's life, we sometimes take refuge in measures that seem to be more a solution for the embarrassment of the doctor than for the benefit of the patient.

Moreover, over the past two or more decades, bioethics has been secularized. Once dominated by medical and religious tradition, it is in our days shaped more and more by secularized philosophical and legal concepts.

The lack of consensus on many fundamental questions, the absence of authority in present-day ethics, and the strong development of the idea of individual autonomy as a heritage of the Enlightment, has caused a pluralism in reasoning up to a point where every individual has his or her own set of principles and values. Discussion about these principles and values is sometimes considered unjustified and unethical.

There is no general agreement on what I consider to be the fundamental rule in the doctor-patient relationship: *Patient and doctor act in mutual agreement on responsibilities, under the authoritative guidance of the doctor, using a common moral standard.*

In our day there can hardly be "mutual agreement," when the autonomous patient is the only decision maker; when "authoritative guidance" is considered to be old-fashioned paternalism; where "moral" is unscientific, and when a "common moral standard" is impossible, due to a fundamental lack of consensus and the above-mentioned pluralism.

God is no longer acknowledged as the Giver, Sustainer, and, ultimately, the Receiver of life. We are no longer able to see that life with awe and wonder, and we no longer believe in a death that is of the body only and non-final. As K. Jaspers formulated it: "The loss of transcendent reality has increased the earthly will-for-happiness to the absolute," and, in characterizing the nature of present-day medicine as mainly technological: "all difficulties should be eliminated through technical measures on the basis of science."[1] From a mystery for everyone, death has become a problem for experts. We have transformed death into an act of human deliberation and technological manipulation.

In this chapter, we will discuss the eventual admissibility and eventual desirability of legalization of active euthanasia, against the background of the situation in the Netherlands. The importance of the answer to this question, is of course, not restricted to the Netherlands.

ACTIVE EUTHANASIA

Euthanasia is defined in the official medical and juridical literature as "The deliberate action to terminate life, or active killing, of a patient, at his or her request by a physician." Discussed nowadays is whether killing should also be made possible in "cases without a request," when "others" or "society" judge this to be in "the best interest" of a certain individual.[2] This involves incompetent people like severely handicapped newborns or comatose patients in persistent vegetative states, and demented old people. Although this is, of course, not or not yet the official standpoint, one has to be very careful in a country where this is not only openly discussed in official bodies like the Royal Dutch Medical Association (KNMG) and others, but where, in fact, acceptance of "voluntary" active euthanasia is growing.[3]

According to two polls in 1985 and 1986, 70 percent and 76 percent of the Dutch people (respectively) said they accepted active euthanasia. So there seems to be not only growing acceptance to deny life-saving treatment to certain individuals under certain circumstances, but even active killing is considered as an acceptable possibility when asked for by a patient. This can be interpreted as a public choice in favor of voluntariness in these matters, freedom of choice, and the right to die in a way one chooses. More threatening, however, is that a majority of the same public also says they accept "involuntary" active euthanasia. This can be interpreted as a choice for involuntariness, no freedom of choice, and the denial of the right to live under certain circumstances to certain human beings.[4]

Active euthanasia is still forbidden in the Penal Code, but we find a growing difference between the law and the feelings of the general public. This acceptance of not only voluntary, but also involuntary euthanasia under certain circumstances (after some years of discussion under a Penal Code in force that forbids even voluntary euthanasia) is threatening and indicates the existence of a "slippery slope" in moral reasoning. This is very clearly demonstrated by a recent survey in the Netherlands showing that 2,300 cases of active euthanasia were performed per year. However, in 400 cases assisted suicide was performed, and the lives of another 1,000 patients were ended actively without their request. In addition, pain and other symptomatic medication was given to 22,500 terminally ill patients, and doctors declared in 20 percent to 30 percent of cases (4,500 to 6,750 patients), that euthanasia was one of the goals of this medication.[5]

HISTORY

Euthanasia is not a new problem, nor is it or specific to this time. It dates back to Greek and Roman classical culture and even before.[6] Problems of terrible suffering and difficult dying have existed since the first human being. Solutions to these problems have been found through all ages. No doubt that hastening of death or even active killing was performed from time to time, but then it concerned exceptional situations. The word "euthanasia" in the antique world meant a quick and easy death without suffering. We know from the Roman emperor August that he prayed to his gods for this "euthanasia" every time he heard of a friend's quick and easy death, during sleep, without preceding illness and apparently without suffering.

In Christianity, the word *euthanasia* was used to indicate the death of a believer, who could die quietly because he or she trusted his or her soul in the hands of God and believed in a non-final death and eternal life in Heaven afterwards. In Europe during the nineteenth century, euthanasia acquired the meaning of active killing. In this sense it has been generally forbidden by law until this very day, also in the Netherlands. The majority of the medical community, which was very much influenced by the Hippocratic Oath and Judeo-Christianity, rejected euthanasia. This has influenced medicine enormously for many centuries despite historical, cultural, and religious differences. Also notwithstanding the fact that the Hippocratic Oath was originally entirely or in part a Pythagorean manifesto, thus representing only a small minority of physicians in the fourth century BC, and even that is not sure.

Although called "euthanasia" too, the termination of lives and killing of certain unwanted groups in society by the Nazis during World War II is an entirely different thing; it is not unwise, however, to remember from time to time what doctors can do, when officially allowed, by a satanic government.

WHAT IS NOT EUTHANASIA?

We defined euthanasia as "active killing of a patient, on his or her request, by a physician." However, for a better understanding, we must also discuss briefly what is *not* euthanasia. Although the definition is clear, persistent misunderstandings still exist. We will drop the term "passive" in conjunction with euthanasia because euthanasia is, by definition, "active."

1. *Refusal of medical treatment by a patient who, as a result of this refusal, dies.* No competent patient can or may be treated against his or her will. Treatment without consent is impossible and must be called ill-treatment.
2. *Not initiating or terminating medical treatment when this treatment is medically useless and futile, with the acceptance that the patient will die.* Inclusion of a certain amount of subjective reasoning about "quality-of-life aspects" in these decisions cannot always be avoided. In my opinion, it is even wrong to avoid this because the responsibility of the doctor includes the whole patient and not a part.

    A case that recently happened in the Netherlands is more difficult to interpret in this respect. A baby was born with Down's syndrome and duodenal atresia [a lack of a normal passageway in the small intestine]; an easily correctable operable problem. The surgeon, in consultation with the parents, decided, however, not to operate because the child was mentally handicapped and the supposed quality of life afterwards was judged to be insufficient. So the decisive argument in this case was "the supposed quality of life" and not, what should have been in my view, the "medical urgency" of the operation. Down's syndrome is no reason to kill or even let die under normal circumstances. The necessary operation should have been performed.
3. *Symptomatic treatment, for instance, pain treatment with the unintended side effect of shortening the patient's life.* Pain treatment is meant to alleviate suffering and is, as such, the physician's duty. Shortening the remaining lifespan can be an unintended side effect of effective pain killing. This is not

euthanasia, and the rationale behind this is that acts must be defined and judged according to their aims, more than to their side effects.

An important consideration in symptomatic treatment and pain killing is that the intention is to care and not to kill. This type of double-edged intention and bivalent action, also called "double-effect euthanasia" is difficult to assess morally.

Quite another practice is to gradually increase, intentionally, the dose of (for example) morphine until the patient dies. This is done not infrequently, as I have seen personally. In my opinion, this must be called euthanasia or active killing.

EUTHANASIA IN THE NETHERLANDS: PRACTICE, ARGUMENTS

Active euthanasia is distinct from helping to ease dying, unintentionally shortening life, requesting non-treatment, or omitting medically useless treatment. Euthanasia is a criminal offense, but, as said earlier, doctors practicing it are not prosecuted if they follow strict guidelines. There must be an explicit and repeated request by the patient that leaves no reason for doubt concerning his desire to die: the mental or physical suffering of the patient must be severe with no prospect of relief; the patient's decision must be well-informed, free, and enduring; all options for other care must have been exhausted or refused by the patient; doctors must consult another physician (and other people like nurses or pastors, if he wishes so); and finally, the doctor must keep a precise record of the course of events.[7]

In my opinion it is of the utmost difficulty, if it is at all possible, to establish the presence of these conditions beyond any doubt. They can be influenced so dramatically by sources outside the patient, doctor, family, nurses, and so on, that it is in my view virtually impossible to fulfill these. In this way these conditions, meant to protect, can become extremely dangerous for patients, as we will discuss later.

A frequently used argument *in favor* of euthanasia is human self-determination, the principle of autonomy. Where society generally accepts this principle, it is felt as illogical not to maintain it in matters of life and death. Most physicians who are in favor of euthanasia want to have the unprosecuted opportunity to perform it, when it is thought to be the only possible solution by doctor and patient. Legalization is supposed to solve this problem.

ARGUMENTS AGAINST LEGALIZATION OF EUTHANASIA

My personal opposition to euthanasia is a religious one: the belief in a personal God who created life and to Whom life belongs and to whom it will return in the end. My respect for human life is not based on the humanistic respect for life itself, but is based on respect for the Creator of life.

This principle of opposing euthanasia must be clear. At the same time, however, we know that there is hardly any problem in medical ethics that can be answered with a simple yes or no, that has a black or white solution. There are always shades of grey, and the simple choice between right or wrong is seldom offered. There are exceptional situations in which one has to compromise. However, legalization of euthanasia marks, in my opinion, the beginning of a society with increasing arbitrariness in matters of life and death. I think that this step has already been taken in the Netherlands by legalizing abortion. With this, an important border has been irreversibly crossed!

The idea that there are lives that are not worth living is obviously accepted. These lives are judged by others, as in abortion, or by the *competent* patient or person herself as in euthanasia at this moment. We have also accepted the idea that the doctor must not only have the possibility, but also the duty, to end the life of another person under certain circumstances.

The discussions on how to act in cases of *incompetence*, with severely handicapped newborns, psychiatric patients, patients in persistent vegetative states, mentally handicapped patients, and so on, not only clearly mention the possibility, but also the duty, to terminate life-sustaining treatment and even to perform involuntary euthanasia under certain circumstances. Our judgement of the quality of their lives plays an important role in these decisions.[8] If legalization of abortion is maintained, it will be very difficult not to legalize euthanasia at some moment in the near future. "Requests for euthanasia by competent patients severely and irremediably suffering as a result of incurable disease may be justified. It is a separate question whether they should be honored. Physicians have an obligation to try to provide treatment and care that will result in a peaceful, dignified, and humane death with minimal suffering. However, statutory legalization of the intentional killing of patients by physicians is against the public interest."[9]

Some of my arguments *against legalization of active euthanasia* are as follows:

1.   When a patient asks for euthanasia, we assume that he is asking to be killed. This patient, however, often does not want to die but *he or she does not want to live any more*, which is a completely different situation. We do not know what it is to be dead. The "I am dead" situation is not included in our or in any others' experience, so why long for something we do not know and even fear under normal circumstances?

The reasons for not wishing to live any more can be many: pain and the fear for future pain, solitude, fear for death without dignity, oppression or the fear of it, and many others. Not recognizing, in the request for euthanasia, the request for help and then exploring this question together with the patient is a grave mistake.

The request for euthanasia can be a manifestation of a failure of companionship or of treatment. The patient does not want to live any more with *this* suffering, with *this* treatment, with *this* escort, with *these* people, or in *this* solitude. We, as individuals and as a society, must be ashamed that investigations show that many requests for euthanasia are based on extreme solitude of patients. It is better that we try to be "better neighbors" than to perform active killing in these circumstances.

The whole environment, the whole setting, can force a patient to the request for euthanasia. A patient might think: "These cool, clean medical technologists must admit they have failed. They like to have a cool, clean technical solution to their problem. Who am I to disappoint them, to oppress them. I have no other choice than to ask for euthanasia." Or: "In this hospital or in this old people's home, I cannot live. I have no other home or I cannot go home. I will ask for euthanasia because I see no other solution." Or the patient might reason, "Why bother my family, their lives, and their careers with my terminal illness. I am ashamed to still be alive and to ask so much from them. In asking for euthanasia I will relieve the living of the almost dead." This is exactly the point where we can obey the most important commandment of the Law: "Thou shalt love thy neighbor as thyself." In my own, and many others' experience, good care and attention by all involved can make the request for euthanasia disappear.

Can every problem be solved in this way? No, of course not. Exceptions to the rule may exist but *legalizing exceptions means promoting exceptions to rules and degrading rules to exceptions. Legalizing euthanasia for exceptional situations makes normal caring become exceptional and exceptional caring normal.*

We must put much more effort and money into investigating possibilities for complete relief of symptoms in the terminally ill. We must put more effort and money into home care.

Above all, we must change spiritually and admit that when "cure" ends, "care" starts, and that there is very much we can do for our terminally ill patients in accompanying them to a quiet death with dignity. This is a very difficult task that requires our whole personality, love, and compassion. This could provide an effective alternative strategy to euthanasia.[10]

2.   When the death of a patient is meant to take away the suffering, then this patient is fully identified with his or her suffering. The *person* who is still present in this suffering is denied completely. I think that this is fundamentally wrong. *Medicine has to fight suffering because of the person, and not the person because of his suffering.*

There are extreme situations, but again exceptional, in which a patient is almost completely identifiable with his suffering. This, however, does not justify a general rule for exceptional cases.

3.   In the secular world of today, people see themselves and experience life in a way that is more and more influenced by a scientific rationality with a purely mechanistical world view. This has led to a functionalistic and hedonistic view of man. A person's value depends on the function he or she fills and to the extent he is useful to society. Health as the ability to function and to enjoy life becomes of the utmost importance. The ultimate consequence of this reasoning is that when the disability to function, illnesses, handicaps, or old age cannot be eliminated and one is not able to enjoy life any more, this life no longer makes sense and can be finished. The quality of life in this situation has sunk below the level of acceptability. This also goes for people who are mentally retarded or physically handicapped.

The danger in this reasoning is that it not only applies to competent people, who are able to ask for or reject euthanasia, but also to incompetent people who are unable to do so. Euthanasia for people in this latter category is considered to be in their own interest if we follow the above-mentioned philosophy. The difference between voluntary and involuntary euthanasia thus fades away. That the euthanasia discussion in the Netherlands focuses more and more on these categories of patients, for example, severely handicapped newborns, patients in persistent vegetative states, and even patients with serious untreatable psychiatric disorders, is an ominous sign, and must warn us that the boundaries between different categories of patients is perhaps less clear and solid than we think.[11] The problem with the "assumed quality-of-life" argument is that it is very relative. A person without legs is completely useless in an army, but his wisdom can make him one of the most valuable people in a religious community. Who can judge the "value" of a severely handicapped daughter to her parents who have taken care of her for many years, causing a completely different life for them than they ever expected? Who can probe or understand the cheerfulness one often experiences in this care? Who can judge the "value" of the life of that specific child? Is this life worthless because it is not in agreement with our standards? Who can and will determine the quality of a patient's life? A group of experts, doctors, lawyers, social workers? Is it possible to establish general rules for this? Will there be a court of arbitration to make final decisions on who shall live and who shall die?

One can reproach me that this is all too much of Orwell's *1984*, threatening predictions like some ominous horror science fiction without any proof. My answer is that one of the tenets of medical ethics until this day has been: follow the facts at a certain distance; for the most part, wait until afterward to make a judgment; at its best, disapprove of an already established practice. Most techniques in medicine were developed without an ethical preview, and it has proven to be almost impossible to change this. Therefore it is time, especially with these very difficult questions, to be prepared and to discuss what can be expected before the facts will catch us again by surprise. *Ethical preview is preferred above ethical review.*

Absolutising a scientific mechanistic concept of man that denies or neglects the importance of spiritual, historical, and social dimensions will lead to the conviction that there is human life that is better off not lived. Acceptance of euthanasia, voluntary and involuntary, will almost automatically follow.

4.   One of the most difficult aspects of our profession is to care for patients when cure becomes useless, to accompany fellow human beings to their death. It is the doctor's responsibility and duty to help his patients die when the time comes. These experiences influence and color, of course, our whole professional attitude and behavior. Acceptance of euthanasia removes a great part of the terminal phase of patients and of the terminal care by doctors and even makes this care unnecessary. The doctor-patient relationship will be negatively changed. Who will take the difficult road when another, "easier" solution is possible? I do not refer in the first place to doctors who live now and have experienced and taken part in the extensive discussion on euthanasia all these years, but to future generations who will grow up with the idea that euthanasia is considered "good medical practice" and even obligatory under certain circumstances.

The Dutch Penal Code dates from 1886. If we legalize euthanasia now, maybe doctors in 2100 will still have the new Penal Code. Performing euthanasia will have been legal for many years then. Who will remember our discussions?

The stimulus for good terminal care will be removed. One hesitation in compassion with a terminal patient can result in a question for euthanasia. A certain resistance by the doctor against further care can cause an involuntary request for euthanasia from the patient.

In this way, the possibility for legal "mercy killing" will certainly "kill the real mercy" we ought to have for terminally ill patients.

When medical treatment has become useless, futile, or even contraindicated, difficult terminal care can be bypassed by following the law: "There is an inherent conflict of interest between the beneficent healing and comforting role in which life and wholeness is sought, and one in which death is caused intentionally."[12] Human beings, doctors included, are not always as good as we would hope for or expect. History shows us this, and it would be very foolish to forget this or to conclude that historical facts of killing, torture, or completely wrong experimentation with human beings were only incidents or, if you like, accidents. Our world in 1991 has hardly changed.

5.   Present-day medicine is scientifically and technically advanced. The statement that such an advanced technological medical science cannot do without euthanasia is perhaps a justified, but also frightening conclusion. It

is remarkable that euthanasia is then chosen as the wrong solution for a wrong development in medicine. A medical science that is in need of euthanasia has to be changed as soon as possible to a medicine that cares beyond cure.

6.   The last point I would like to discuss, although there are more, is whether a request for euthanasia can ever be "voluntary" and completely free of coercion. Supporters of euthanasia demand a completely "free" request from a patient with "a very severe mental or physical suffering with no prospect of relief." The assumed possibility of a voluntary request is based upon the concept of an individual, who by his reasoning can decide about his norms or values and can independently make decisions for his own life. No individual is ever completely free from his surroundings and his fellow human beings, not even when he is healthy and apparently capable of taking care for himself. There is always some kind of dependency on something or somebody. This apparent "freedom of choice" diminishes when a person becomes more dependent on others or on his surroundings. It is very unlikely that a very ill person can really make an independent and free request to be killed. The very fact of deep dependency, of being in a terminal state, influenced by medication that is often given in these situations, makes a "normal" functioning of the brain very difficult, if at all possible.

Dependency excludes, by definition, voluntariness and complete freedom of choice.

A very ill or terminally ill patient is completely dependent on others who, through their attitude, gesture, tone of voice, and so on and so on, can suggest that the patient, even unconsciously, should ask for euthanasia. My conclusion is that a voluntary and completely free choice for euthanasia in the type of patients we are discussing and whose condition would justify euthanasia, is almost always impossible by definition. What remains when euthanasia is requested and performed must be called involuntary.

How about a living will written in advance? There is an important difference in discussions between healthy people who try to anticipate what they think they want to be done or not to be done when they are sick; and those people who are really ill, even terminally ill. It is good to reflect on death and dying when one is still young and healthy, but the real problems are far away. In caring for terminal patients, I am often ashamed and moved by their cheerfulness, their wish to live, and when the end is near, their acquiescence and their ability to comfort me, often more than I think I can do for them. Fortunately, we have very powerful tools in medicine to care for our terminally ill patients when cure has become impossible. This enables us to accompany them to a death with dignity and minimal or no suffering. Open discussion on every aspect of disease and death, including euthanasia, must be possible between patient and doctor. Only in this way can we practice the "art of healing."

ACKNOWLEDGMENT

The author gratefully acknowledges the use of an unpublished article on euthanasia in the Netherlands by H. Jochemsen, PhD, Director of the Prof. dr. G.A. Lindeboom-institute of Christian Medical Ethics, Ede, the Netherlands.

NOTES

1   K. Jaspers, "The Physician in the Technological Age," *Theoretical Medicine* 10 (1989):251-267.

2   Central Committee of the Royal Dutch Medical Association, *Report on Terminating the Lives of Incompetent People: Part I: Severely Handicapped Newborns* (in Dutch) (Utrecht, the Netherlands: KNMG, 1988); Central Committee of the Royal Dutch Medical Association, *Report on Terminating the Lives of Incompetent People: Part II: Patients in a Prolonged Coma* (in Dutch) (Utrecht, the Netherlands: KNMG, 1991).

3   H. Rigter, "Euthanasia in the Netherlands: Distinguishing Facts from Fiction," *Hastings Center Report* (January/February 1989, special supplement):31-32.

4   R. Fenigsen, "A Case against Dutch Euthanasia," *Hastings Center Report* (January/February 1989, special supplement):22-30.

5   P.J. van der Maas, J.J.M. van Delden, and L. Pijnenborg, *Medical Decisions with Regard to Euthanasia* (in Dutch) ('s Gravenhage, the Netherlands: SDU Publishing, 1991); Remmelink Committee, *Offical Report of the Commission Inquiry into Medical Practice with Regard to Euthanasia* (in Dutch) ('s Gravenhage, the Netherlands, 1991); P.J. van der Mass, J.J. van Delden, L. Pijnenberg, and C.W.N. Looman, "Euthanasia and other Medical Decisions Concerning the End of Life," *Lancet* 332 (1991):669-71.

6   P. Carrick, "The Problem of Euthanasia," in *Medical Ethics in Antiquity*, ed. P. Carrick (Dordrecht, the Netherlands: D. Reidel Publishing, 1985), 127-50.

7   Rigter, "Euthanasia in the Netherlands"; J.K.M. Gevers, "Legal Developments Concerning Active Euthanasia on Request in the Netherlands," *Bioethics* 1 (1987):156-62.

8   Central Committee of the Royal Dutch Medical Association, *Report on Terminating the Lives of Incompetent People, Parts I and II.*

9   *The Appleton Consensus: Suggested International Guidelines to Forego Medical Treatment. Report of an International Working Conference, May 15-19, 1988* (Appleton, WI: Lawrence University Program in Biomedical Ethics, 1989), 8.

10   C.M. Saunders, "The Philosophy of Terminal Care," in *The Management of Terminal Disease*, ed. C.M. Saunders (London: Edward Arnold, 1978), 194-202.
11   Central Committee on the Royal Dutch Medical Association, *Report on Terminating the Lives of Incompetent People, Parts I and II*.
12   W. Reiche, and A. Dijck, "Euthanasia, A Contemporary Moral Quandary," *Lancet* 2 (1989):1321-23.

8

Should We Copy the Dutch? The Netherlands' Practice of Voluntary Active Euthanasia as a Model for the United States

Margaret Pabst Battin

Can the Netherlands serve as a model for end-of-life practices in the United States, or for that matter in any other country? Holland (as the Netherlands is informally, but incorrectly, known in the United States) is the one nation in which active voluntary euthanasia is legally tolerated and in which the practice is openly performed; thus, it is the only available model of what might be the case if we in the US were to legalize or otherwise adopt the open practice of euthanasia too. But although it is our only model, the question remains: how good a model is it--for us? Can the US adopt this model, or does it somehow fail to fit? Are we like the Dutch or different, in ways that are relevant to the practice of active euthanasia?

WHY SHOULD WE COPY THE DUTCH?

Why might we want to model our end-of-life practices on those of the Dutch, and hence permit voluntary active euthanasia in the US? There are at least three major reasons for doing so. First, one might argue that the right to aid in dying is a basic human right; I believe this is correct, but since such an argument will not be accessible to those opposed to euthanasia on moral grounds, I will not consider it further here. But there are two additional reasons for copying the Dutch practices.

One of them is what we might call an argument from envy: it concerns social harmony. After a substantial amount of public discussion of euthanasia in

Holland in the late 1970s and early 1980s, marked by inflated figures about the number of cases, by exaggerated reports of abuse, and by such events as the secession of the Dutch Physicians League from the Royal Dutch Medical Association on grounds of opposition to euthanasia, the Dutch seem to have finally developed a policy about euthanasia that is rather generally (though by no means universally) accepted.[1] Social uproar over this issue, it is said, is diminishing: wild estimates of frequency are being revised downward, orderly reporting is increasing, and reports of bizarre cases outside the guidelines are diminishing. For the first time, a careful empirical study is being done.[2] While not everyone agrees with the morality of the practice or believes that he or she would make such a choice, there is a growing consensus that voluntary active euthanasia may be practiced provided it meets the very strict guidelines; that the law will not be changed but will retain its currently delicate treatment of euthanasia (according to which euthanasia remains a violation of statutory law, but case law stipulates conditions for non-prosecution); that any abuse will be dealt with severely; that no international commerce in euthanasia will be allowed; and that, it is rumored, the Dutch Physicians League will rejoin the Royal Dutch Medical Association. The only remaining problem, it seems, is the hordes of foreign writers and reporters tracking through the country to scrutinize Dutch practice.

In contrast, the United States is entering an increasingly volatile period of public debate about end-of-life issues, of which the issue of euthanasia is clearly the most contentious. Right-to-life groups, taking euthanasia as their new focus, are squaring off against Hemlock and other groups who advocate the legalization of euthanasia and physician-assisted suicide. Incidents like the publication of the letter "It's Over, Debbie" in the otherwise august *Journal of the American Medical Association*[3] and Dr. Jack Kevorkian's "suicide machine" have rocked not only the medical world but have also astonished the public. Perhaps widespread public debate over euthanasia, diverse as it will certainly be, cannot be avoided; but it might also be argued that straightforward adoption of a policy as much like Holland's as possible, including its rigorous guidelines, careful hospital protocols, and balanced legal status for euthanasia, would be the best way to short-circuit this dispute or at least to reduce its acrimony. If we envy Holland's restoration of comparative social harmony over this issue, so this argument goes, we ought to copy Holland's practice.

Not only might we be concerned about social harmony, but there is a second, still more compelling reason for emulating the Dutch as well. Active euthanasia is legally tolerated in Holland, but is illegal in the United States. This does not mean, however, that active euthanasia occurs only in Holland; on the contrary, active euthanasia is indeed performed in the United States, but since it must always be "under the table," it is not subject to judicial review, medical supervision, or to any other protection. There are no guidelines for euthanasia in the US: every physician who ends the life of a patient--and there is reason to believe that euthanasia is not infrequent[4]--does so on his or her own and must necessarily do so in a clandestine way. There is no provision for review by a second physician of independent judgment; no protection for voluntariness; no documented request on the part of the patient; no evidence that other ways of relieving the patient's suffering have been tried--in short, no protection for the patient at all. Nor is there any secure means of transmitting medical information or means among physicians that might enable them to practice euthanasia in a reliable, fool-proof way. Like abortion, sustained legal suppression does not put an end to the practice; it only means that it occurs in more precarious, dangerous circumstances than would otherwise be the case.

Why, then, might we want to model ourselves on the Dutch? Even for those who do not accept the claim that assistance in dying is a matter of moral right, consideration of social harmony and of the protection of patients may still be persuasive. Even so, this does not yet answer the central question here: would it be possible for us Americans to simply copy Dutch practices and install them in our own world, or would this produce results that would require us to reject euthanasia even despite the arguments considered above? To answer this question, I think we must look rather carefully at several important differences between ourselves and the Dutch.

HOW THE DUTCH ARE DIFFERENT

While the Netherlands and the United States are alike in being advanced industrial democracies, with similar demographics involving long average life-spans and well-developed medical systems, there are a number of differences that are crucial to notice in considering the issue of active euthanasia.[5]

1. The Nature of the Physician/Patient Relationship

Different cultures exhibit different patterns of contact and involvement between physician and patient, and these patterns are of enormous relevance in an issue like euthanasia. In Holland, primary care is typically provided by the *huisarts*, the general practitioner or family physician, who also refers the patient to specialist physicians for specific problems. While the relationships between specialists and patients in Holland are similar in many ways to those between specialists and patients in the US, the relationship of the Dutch *huisarts* and the patient is distinctive. For instance, a *huisarts'* practice, usually covering about two thousand people, is typically centered in a neighborhood; the *huisarts* lives in this neighborhood, makes house calls frequently, and often maintains an office in his or her own home. Also, the *huisarts* is usually the physician for the other members of the patient's family, as well as for most of the neighbors, and will remain the family's physician throughout his practice.

In Holland, unlike the US, about 50 percent of patients die at home. In practice, this usually involves a scenario in which the *huisarts*, supported by the visiting nurse and other professional personnel, provides frequent, ongoing care for the patient in the patient's home, usually after the patient has left the hospital when aggressive treatment is no longer successful and has come home to die. For a patient in severe distress, the *huisarts* may make house calls as often as once a day, twice a day, or more (after all, he lives in the neighborhood), and is in continuous contact with the family. In contrast, the traditional American institution of the family doctor who makes house calls is rapidly becoming a thing of the past, and while some patients who die at home have access to hospice services and receive housecalls from their long-term physician, many have no long-term physician and receive most of their care from staff at a clinic, emergency room, or housestaff rotating through the services of a hospital. (Indeed, we sometimes speak of the new "doc-in-the-box" style of instant, anonymous medical care.) About 80 percent of Americans die in hospitals or other institutions, often without close contact with a long-term, trusted physician.

These differences in the character of the physician/patient relationship between Holland and the US have considerable bearing on issues in euthanasia. For example, during the housecalls the Dutch *huisarts* is likely to make for the dying patient, he has ample opportunity to observe the general character of intrafamilial relationships. Does the family seem to be a loving one, genuinely concerned about the welfare of the patient? Or is there evidence of friction and familial psychopathology? Is the family providing adequate nursing care? Is there evidence of real economic distress? Is there a row of gin bottles on the kitchen sink? Because the American physician typically sees the patient in a clinic or in an inpatient setting, not in the patient's home, he has much less opportunity to detect familial, economic, and other pressures on the patient that might be relevant in choices of euthanasia, and thus much less opportunity to protect the patient's genuine freedom of choice.

2. The Nature of the Legal Climate

Second, the US has a much more volatile medico-legal climate than Holland; our medical system is increasingly lawyer-infected, one might want to say, much more so than that of any other country in the world. Medical malpractice action remains at a very low rate in Holland (though it is beginning to climb); while, in contrast, fears of malpractice action or criminal prosecution color much of what US physicians do in managing the care of patients--including patients who are dying. In the US, this has tended to operate in the direction of extending treatment for patients even where it is of questionable efficacy or is not clearly desired by the patient.

A second difference in the legal climate is also relevant to the issue of euthanasia. The Dutch and American legal systems are unlike in many fundamental respects, inasmuch as one is a Napoleonic code system and the other is a common-law one. Furthermore, the administrative arrangements under which a circumstance like that of euthanasia falls are also different. In Holland, euthanasia remains designated by statute as a criminal offense; while at the same time, lower and supreme court decisions have specified conditions under which the physician who performs euthanasia cannot be prosecuted. Furthermore, the five regional *prosecutors générales* form a policy-making body that controls local prosecutors, and hence can determine on a national basis whether, despite the existence of a statute prohibiting it, euthanasia meeting the guidelines is ever prosecuted. This delicate balance between technically illegal status on the one hand and, on the other, protection by the courts and prosecutors, ensuring that every case can be reviewed but not suppressing the practice, is not as easily achieved in the US legal system. Hence, it might be said, protections like those under Dutch law would be less easy to develop in the United States.

3. The Role of Health Insurance

The Netherlands, like all other industrialized democracies except the US (and South Africa), has a program of national health insurance. In the US, some 37 to 40 million people (at least two and a half times the entire Dutch population) have no health insurance; at least that number, and perhaps double that number, have some health insurance, but coverage is seriously inadequate.[6] Many of the best health plans still require a substantial copayment, often as high as 20 percent or higher even on major medical procedures. Thus, dying occurs in a very different financial climate in Holland than in the US. In Holland, the patient is not directly responsible for the costs of treatment or supportive or palliative care; consequently, the patient's choices about terminal care and/or euthanasia need not take financial considerations into account. Even for the patient who does have health insurance in the US, many kinds of services are not covered under specific policies; whereas in Holland, a very broad range of services directly relevant to choices about dying are provided: not only physician care, specialist care, surgical care, and all inpatient treatment, but also at-home physician care (that is, care by the *huisarts*), home nursing care, home respite care, care in a nursing home or other long-term facility, dietician care, rehabilitation care, physician therapy, psychological counseling, and so on. The patient in the US needs to attend to the financial aspects of dying in a way that patients in Holland do not. In the US, thus, both the patient's choices and the physician's recommendations are shaped by considerations of the financial impact on the patient. This may in part explain why we are so nervous about the prospect of euthanasia: financial considerations *per se* will almost always operate to favor choice of euthanasia, since euthanasia precludes further medical expenses, over continuing care. After all, euthanasia is the cheapest health-care choice a patient could make. This is the disturbing consequence of the fact that we in the US must make our choices about dying against a background of money; patients in the US are thus subject to a kind of pressure patients in the Netherlands are not.

4. The Role of First and Second-Party Decisions

There is a further difference between Holland and the US which, while difficult to document, is reflected in two rather different sets of legal cases. Both Holland and the US, like the other advanced nations, have been responding to the dilemmas posed by medicine's new capacities to prolong life. But the right-to-die tradition that has been developing in Holland, and that is expressed in the lower and supreme court cases, in effect establishes guidelines under which active euthanasia may be performed and differs from the developing tradition in the US in a central way. The US now has a large body of case law concerning right-to-die issues, beginning with *Quinlan* and continuing through *Saickewicz, Spring, Eichner, Storar, Conroy, Brophy,* and *Jobes* to *Cruzan,* but there is a central difference: these are all cases concerning second-party decisions about someone else's life.[7] In each of them, the patient is already incompetent and someone else must therefore determine whether to continue or discontinue treatment; and while many of these cases do appeal to what the patient would want if she could survey her current circumstances (for example *Quinlan*) or would have wanted had she expressed it (for example *Cruzan*), these are not cases concerned with the full range of choices about death a competent patient may permissibly make. Of course, the classic 1914 case *Schloendorff v. Society of New York Hospital* articulates the patient's right to refuse treatment on any grounds, even if this may result in death; but there are no cases (at least not until *Michigan v. Kevorkian,* almost certainly brewing the future!) directly testing the issue of whether a competent patient may choose suicide (which, except in a handful of US states, is not a violation of the law), whether assisted by a physician or not, or may choose physician-performed euthanasia. The closest are cases like *Bouvia,* in which it is discontinuation of treatment, not direct termination of life, that is at issue. Nevertheless, virtually all the significant US cases concern second-party decisions about withholding or withdrawing treatment from someone else. In contrast, the Dutch cases are about physicians aiding patients who are making first-party choices. While Americans often view the Dutch as risking the slippery slope by practicing euthanasia, fearing that medical killing will be likely to expand, the Dutch view the Americans as having already stepped out on the slippery slope by routinely resorting to decisions one person makes about another person's life. The risk here, many Dutch would say, is that Americans do not really understand or respect *voluntary* choice.

Furthermore, I sense--though I know of no study corroborating this hunch --that the very term "euthanasia" is understood more frequently in the US to mean a procedure chosen and performed by the physician upon the patient, rather than one requested by the patient and carried out by the physician. In the Dutch understanding of the practice and even the use of the term, *euthanasia* means only voluntary euthanasia; and medical killing is involuntary or nonvoluntary on the part of the patient is not called euthanasia at all.[8] In the US, in contrast, the term *euthanasia* is often understood as another among a repertoire of medical procedures, one which a physician might come to recommend for a variety of medical or other reasons, and it is often understood in a "post-Nazi" sense, in which death is imposed for political or other extraneous motives. Thus, in the US, unlike Holland, "euthanasia" is something a second party, including the physician, might decide on for somebody else; this clearly invites the erosion of voluntary choice.

5. Differences in Social Climate

Finally, there are a number of differences between Holland and the US in social factors that have both direct and indirect bearing on the practice of euthanasia, some of them related to points made above. In the US, for instance, there is much greater economic disparity between rich and poor, and with it enormous disparities in health-related phenomena like basic nutrition, access to preventive care, general health-care knowledgeability, and so on. In the US, there is extensive homelessness, while in Holland there is virtually none. The US is much more afflicted by racism than Holland, by gaps between urban and rural conditions, and by impaired communication between health-care providers and non-English-speaking minority groups. Holland is a comparatively small, homogeneous country with a tradition of tolerance; the US, in contrast, is a huge and diverse nation with a recent history of severe polarization and social friction over controversial social topics like abortion. The issue of euthanasia may well follow the same course.

CAN WE BE LIKE THE DUTCH?

Some of these differences--in the physician/patient relationship, in the legal climate, in health insurance and the consequent financial implications of medical choices, in social conditions, and in biases toward first or second-party decision making--are quite substantial. Does this mean that the US cannot follow the Netherlands in accepting the practice of euthanasia? Would it be impossible for us to be like the Dutch, and if so, does this mean that we would be better off not permitting the practice of euthanasia at all?

I must confess that this question makes me rather uneasy. America's much greater economic inequities, its increasing distance between physician and patient, its emphasis on second rather than first-party decision making, and the unavoidable permeation of medical choice by personal financial consideration look like a joint recipe for disaster: precisely the kind of disaster those who warn of the slippery slope predict. While active euthanasia is practiced in Holland virtually without abuse, according to the evidence available, I am not so sanguine about the possibility of its practice without abuse in the United States. In particular, it is especially risky at a moment when health insurance in the US has become even more chaotic, with private insurers increasingly employing cream-skimming, experience-rating, and other risk-avoidance measures to exclude from coverage altogether those people who are most likely to need health care. But, of course, these are precisely the people for whom decisions about euthanasia are most likely to arise, since they are the ones who are most ill, and they will be the people under the most severe financial pressures. The biggest single impediment to abuse-free euthanasia in the US, I believe, is the absence of a national health care program, which might insulate patients against being forced to consider costs in deciding when and how they wish to die.

Such impediments do not, of course, change the moral issue of whether voluntary active euthanasia is ethically permissible or not. My own view is that it is a matter of fundamental right for the person facing an intolerable end to expect help from his or her physician in the matter of dying. This may include both physician-performed euthanasia and physician-assisted suicide and should not be restricted to reliance only on withholding or withdrawing care. But I also have come to think, after seeing the humane and virtually abuse-free way in which the practice of euthanasia is conducted in Holland,[9] that conditions for it are must less favorable in the US. Yet patients should not be denied what is their right. As a kind of realistic compromise, I think patients in the US would find themselves better protected against abuse by preferring physician-assisted suicide to physician-performed euthanasia, since physician-assisted suicide incorporates one final level of patient choice as a further protection against second-party decision making, though I do think it is possible to erect adequate protections.[10] But I also think American patients--in fact, Americans generally --must realize that one unfortunate effect of tolerating what is currently a profoundly inequitable health-care system is that it corrupts the free choices about dying we ought to be able to make.

NOTES

1   The best available accounts of Dutch practice is M.A.M. de Wachter, "Active Euthanasia in the Netherlands," *Journal of the American Medical Association* 262, no.23 (15 December 1989):3316-19; and P.J. van der Maas, J.J. van Delden, L. Pijnenborg, and C.W. Looman, "Euthanasia and Other Medical Decisions Concerning the End of Life," *Lancet* 338 (14 September 1991): 669-674. This is colloquially referred to as the "Remmelink Commission" report, named after its chairperson.

2   A summary of this study in English is provided in the Remmelink Commission report.

3   "It's Over, Debbie" (anonymous letter to the editor), *Journal of the American Medical Association* (8 January 1988).

4   For some time Hemlock, the California, then Oregon-based organization advocating legalization of voluntary active euthanasia and physician-assisted suicide, collected physicians' reports of euthanasia they had performed, but destroyed these records at the threat that they might be subpoenaed.

5   M.P. Battin, "The Way We Do It, the Way They Do It," *Journal of Pain and Symptom Management*, 6, no.5 (July 1991).

6   *Consumer Report* published an extensive, two-part examination and evaluation of commercially available health insurance policies in 1991. This series, addressed to the public in the same format as *Consumer Report's* other product assessments, revealed extensive flaws with many brands of health insurance. See also R.P. Huefner and M.P. Battin, eds., *Changing to National Health Care: The Ethical Issues* (Salt Lake City: University of Utah Press, forthcoming 1992).

7   There are, of course, a handful of first-party cases, for example, *Bartling* and *Bouvia*. For a review of right-to-die cases, see B.R. Furrow, S.H. Johnson, T.S. Jost, and R.L. Schwartz, *Health Law: Cases, Materials and Problems*, American Casebook Series (St. Paul, MN: West Publishing, 1987). Information on right-to-die cases is also available from the Society for the Right to Die/Concern for Dying, 250 West 57th St., New York, NY.

8   M.P. Battin, "7 Caveats Concerning the Discussion of Euthanasia in Holland," *Perspectives in Biology and Medicine* 34, no.1 (Autumn 1990):73-77; and *Newsletter of the American Philosophical Association Committee on Medicine*, 1990.

9   The Remmelink Commission's finding that "life termination by administering lethal drugs without an explicit and persistent request from the patient," which occurs in about 0.8 percent of all deaths in the Netherlands, has been widely interpreted in the United States to mean that about 1,000 patients were killed against their will. The study found, however, that in more than half of these cases the decision had been discussed with the patient or, in a previous phase of the illness, the patient had expressed a wish for euthanasia should suffering become unbearable; in other cases, possibly with a few exceptions, the patients were near to death and clearly suffering grievously, yet verbal contact had become impossible. The study finds no examples of patients to whom euthanasia was administered against their wishes. Nor do other studies find concrete evidence of involuntary euthanasia for which real documentation is provided.

10   M.P. Battin, "Voluntary Euthanasia and the Risks of Abuse: Can We Learn Anything from the Netherlands?" *Law, Medicine and Health Care* 20, no.1 (May 1992).

Part III

Do-Not-Resuscitate Orders

9

Impact of the New York State Do-Not-Resuscitate Law on Clinical Practice in a Cancer Research Institution

The Ethics Group of the Memorial Sloan-Kettering Cancer Center

INTRODUCTION

The history of contemporary health care will be replete with accounts of medical, ethical, and legal controversies, many of which have resulted from the tension between a technology increasingly capable of sustaining life in the critically ill and the intensified societal imperative to insure autonomy and the right to self-determination in the same patients. Nowhere have the horns of this dilemma been more pronounced than in response to the use of cardiopulmonary resuscitation (CPR). It has become essential, in this social climate, for hospitals and health-care facilities to develop guidelines about the use or withholding of CPR to assist physicians and to assure that individual patients or their surrogates participate in that decision-making process. Particular attention has been focused on New York State, where the first law governing the application and withholding of CPR took effect in April 1988.[1]

Reactions of physicians to the new law have been varied and intense. Many laud the thrust of the law, which seeks to protect patients from covert decisions about their care and, thus, encourages more open, early, and honest dialogue between physicians and patients. Others have stridently opposed the restrictive and intrusive aspects of the legal mandate. In a moving account of his own discussions with terminally ill patients, one New York State physician echoed the sentiments of those who feel burdened by the law: "I believe that the relationship between a dying patient and his or her caregiver is as intimate as any human relationship can be and deserves freedom from unreasonable regulatory intrusion and governmental scrutiny."[2]

However, the discussion of how the last minutes of life will be managed with the patient has not been easy for physicians to introduce. In part, this is because of the long-held view that such a discussion would be too painful for a patient, and hence the person should be "protected" from the discussion, as has been the custom in relation to revealing the diagnosis of cancer or a poor prognosis. Such discussions were often held with a relative alone, thereby creating a "conspiracy of silence" around the patient. Physicians were trained that it was their *obligation* to make the decisions as part of their responsibility. This paternalism came under increasing criticism as medicine and other institutions were questioned in the social unrest of the 1960s in the United States. Indeed, several abuses of informed consent in clinical trials were revealed, and the need to equalize "power" between the patient and the doctor became a social imperative.

The availability of cardiopulmonary resuscitation brought new pressure to end-of-life decisions, as it became widely (and sometimes inappropriately) applied. The social climate and greater control over the time of dying through use of resuscitative efforts led to the demand for greater visibility as to how decisions were made. A *New England Journal of Medicine* editorial in 1976 stated it was time that surreptitious decisions about resuscitation come "out of the closet."[3] Guidelines for using or withholding CPR have developed increasingly since the mid-seventies, subjecting the decision making to a more open process. However, no law had been promulgated to regulate the procedure until New York State passed legislation in 1988. The impact on medical practice in the state has been followed with interest.

The impact of the law on our major cancer research hospital in the state has been of particular interest. The hospital is widely known as an institution that develops and applies new treatments for cancers that are often otherwise incurable. Patients come with a strong conviction to "turn the last stone," and physicians choose to work at the institution because of a commitment to seeking improved treatments for cancer. The particular views of these patients and physicians create a unique tension in regard to discussions and decisions around terminal care. The history below outlines how the social changes and the state law have impacted this institution. It provides a perspective on the law that is useful to analyze and document.

EARLY CHANGES IN PRACTICE (1976 TO 1984)

In 1984, Memorial Hospital, a 565-bed cancer hospital, elected to follow the widely used classification developed by the Massachusetts General Hospital in Boston to determine the level of care to be provided to patients. Using a four-level classification from A (in which all life supports were to be applied) to D (in which comfort care alone, without resuscitative intervention, was deemed appropriate), this shorthand system was designed to assure the communication of the information from one shift to another in teaching hospitals. The system was effective, but the classification was not routinely placed in the hospital chart and it was not regularly discussed with the patient. A *New England Journal of Medicine* article of 1976 suggested that the decisions must be made explicit to patients and families, and that they should be justified and documented in the hospital chart.[4]

Memorial Hospital was made the center of the public debate by a tabloid article in 1984, describing the use of a "secret system"[5] in which patients' resuscitation status was revealed on a blackboard. It was similarly cited that a hospital in Queens used "purple dots" on charts for indicating patients on whom resuscitation was to be withheld.[6] These two incidents, along with public concern, encouraged the state to consider legislation governing the procedures. At the same time, Memorial Hospital and many other institutions began to develop their own do-not-resuscitate (DNR) guidelines that outlined the circumstances for withholding CPR, and the fact that a discussion with patients and families would be conducted and written documentation provided.

Do-not-resuscitate guidelines were formally implemented at Memorial in May 1984. They have remained substantially the same, but have been expanded to accommodate to legislation and regulation. In July 1984, an audit was carried out to assess compliance with the procedures outlined in the DNR guidelines. The audit addressed documentation of irreversible disease, prognosis, the consent to DNR in patients with capacity, and the use of therapeutic exception. The writing of the order in the order book and a note in the progress notes justifying it were reviewed, as well as the fact that the order was reviewed at three-day intervals. The audit indicated a high level of compliance in most areas, 75 percent or more. However, problems highlighted were the absence of documentation of the patient or family's consent to DNR, the reason why a patient's consent was not obtained, the reason for the therapeutic exception, and the lack of the renewal of the order each ninety-six hours.[7] The audit recommended educational efforts to familiarize both physicians and staff with the requirements for obtaining, documenting, and renewing a DNR order.

FORMATION OF AN ETHICS COMMITTEE (1985) AND DNR GUIDELINES AUDITS

In 1985, the Ethics Committee was established at the recommendation of an ad hoc committee of the Medical Board with the threefold mandate of educating, advising administration regarding policy issues with ethical ramifications, and offering clinical consultations to staff in cases where conflict or questions arose. A major initial thrust of the educational effort of the committee was the dissemination of information about changes in the law, the implementation of institutional DNR policy, and assisting staff in becoming more comfortable with the DNR discussion.

The majority of the early consultations dealt with the timing and writing of a DNR order (see Table 1). Physicians found the discussions difficult and tended to delay the discussion with the patient until it was held only with a family member. Tension was created with house staff and nurses who wanted to know the "DNR status" earlier than physicians felt it appropriate to bring up the issue with patients. There was concern that some resuscitations were being done due to the absence of a DNR order and that admissions to the Intensive Care Unit and the number of patients on respirators were increased.

Since most problems occurred when patients were treated on the medical oncology floors, a committee was appointed by the chairman to review the impact and procedures to improve the situation. A one-week period in June 1985 was chosen in which the charts of all the admissions to the Department of Medicine (four floors) were reviewed at forty-eight hours and two weeks after admission. Charts were reviewed with two goals: DNR status, as noted in the chart, and determination of those patients who might have been appropriately designated DNR by virtue by physical status, based on a clinician's judgment in reading the history, physical findings, and laboratory values. Of the 110 patients admitted, 107 remained in the hospital two weeks later.

The data collected were age, sex, primary diagnosis, the reason for the admission, stage or extent of disease, prior therapy, and resuscitation status. For those patients with a DNR or a TBR (to-be-resuscitated) order, further investigation was directed at ascertaining whether that status was recorded in both the order book and the progress notes, whether or not the status had been discussed

---

Table 1
Ethics Committee Consultations
January through November 1989

Reason for consult	Number
Clarification for patients of DNR issues	15
Discussion of DNR never initiated or initiated too late	11
Medical futility or inappropriate demands for DNR	10
Questions related to validity of DNR consents	7
Sub total	43
Staff conflicts	7
Intensive Care Unit related issues	5
Psychiatric problems	3
Criticism of staff behavior by patients/families	2
Total	60

71.6 percent related to issues surrounding DNR

---

with the patient or family, and whether there was an accompanying care plan in the progress notes.

Each of the remaining charts of patients with a DNR or a TBR order was then reviewed by one of three physicians, assessing the extent of disease and prior and current treatment. The physician made a judgment as to whether a DNR order *should* have been written.

It was noted that 15 percent of patients surveyed had either a DNR or a TBR order forty-eight hours after admission and 18 percent at two weeks, with the DNR order noted for 11 percent. Of the patients without a documented resuscitation status at the end of the two weeks, clinicians estimated that 47 percent would have been appropriate for a DNR order, based on medical status, and several patients with TBR status would actually have been appropriate for a DNR order.

An identical audit was conducted in 1986, using the same time period. Admissions to the Department of Medicine were 101. Demographic and medical characteristics were similar. At forty-eight hours after admission, 16 percent of the patients had a DNR or a TBR status; at two weeks, it was 19 percent, paralleling the 1985 study, with 15 percent of those patients with a resuscitation status noted to be DNR. Of those patients without a resuscitation status noted, 49 percent were deemed appropriate for a DNR order (see Table 2).

Table 2
MSKCC DNR Reviews
Second Week of June, 1985, 1986, 1988, and 1990

	1985	1986	1988	1990
Patients admitted to medicine	107	101	90	88
	Percent			
DNR status noted (two-week audit)	11	15	15	17
Judged appropriate for DNR order (by independent clinician review)	47	49	49	40

In 1985, Dr. John Mendelson, Chairman of the Department of Medicine, MSKCC, appointed a committee to examine the DNR order implementation. Chaired by Dr. Thomas Hakes, Solid Tumor Service, the committee included Drs. Jimmie Holland, Psychiatry; Jeremy Miransky, Quality Assurance; Lee Schwartzberg, Chief Medical Resident; Stewart Fleischman, Psychiatry; and Susan Wolf, JD, Associate for Law, Hastings Center. The committee was responsible for the DNR surveys in both 1985 and 1986. The compliance study of 1989 was conducted by Dr. Daniel O'Hare, Fellow-in-Ethics, Psychiatry Service. The 1988 audit and the 1990 review were under the direction of Dr. Miransky and the Department of Quality Assurance.

In the fall of 1986, the Ethics Committee began an intensive program of in-service presentations on all units and on all shifts. A series of grand rounds presentations were held at which the DNR guidelines were reviewed, as well as the Ethics Committee consultation function. The discomfort in conducting a highly emotional discussion about death with patients was identified as a significant problem for the physicians. A videotape produced through a grant from the American Cancer Society, "The DNR Dilemma--When the Time Comes," was designed to provide a role model for the presentation of the option for DNR. The film highlighted the frustration that is often generated between nurses, house staff, and physicians when the DNR discussion with a patient is delayed. The video was shown widely to hospital staff to facilitate discussion of the problem. (The video can be ordered through Carle Medical Communications, Champaign-Urbana, Illinois.)

NEW YORK STATE DNR LAW ENACTED (1988)

Effective January 1988, the Joint Commission required institutions to have DNR guidelines in place. In New York, this was quickly followed by state legislation to govern the withholding of cardiopulmonary resuscitation. This legislation was the result of a lengthy deliberation by the New York State Task Force on Life and the Law, appointed by Governor Cuomo. The task force represents both religious and professional groups; and they continue to review and recommend on ethical issues in special areas.

Enacted to facilitate the discussion of resuscitation status and to ensure patients' participation, the legislation has created unexpected problems. First, the law reenforced the presumption that *without* "clear and convincing" evidence to the contrary, consent *for* resuscitation is presumed. While it was not intended to alter reasonable clinical judgment and practice, physicians have felt legally bound and concerned that legal action could be taken against them if they did not resuscitate a patient whose wishes were unknown or unclear, even where medical judgment would question the appropriateness of resuscitation. There has been a strong sense by some physicians that they are disenfranchised and unsupported in utilizing their judgment appropriately, under the new law. The law, as implemented, seemed to demand that physicians conform to legal constraints at the expense of reasonable medical judgment.

Secondly, the legislation defined an extremely narrow concept of when medical futility was an acceptable reason for not resuscitating a patient. Medical futility was defined in the law as follows: "Resuscitation will be unsuccessful in restoring cardiac and respiratory function or the patient will experience repeated arrests in a short period before death occurs."[8] This is a particularly limited definition since it allows no recognition of the fact that the patient may have widely metastatic cancer. In fact, a 1991 study by Vitelli and colleagues found that among 114 patients with cancer who received CPR in a three-year period, only 10.5 percent were ever discharged from the hospital, and among those spending greater than 50 percent of their time in bed at the time of resuscitation, only 2.3 percent had a chance of being discharged alive.[9] Physicians feel constrained by the narrow definition; there is hesitation and fear of legal action to extend the definition of medical futility, even when it is based on sound medical judgment. Moreover, concern was expressed that the difficulty and frustration experienced in invoking medical futility would lead to closeted directives for "slow" or "show" codes, which are illegal and an unwanted outcome of the law.

In light of the legislative initiative, Memorial undertook a third one-week identical survey of patients admitted to the Department of Medicine to ascertain the frequency of DNR orders in the new legal climate in 1988. No statistically significant variations were observed in either the demographics of the patients or in the severity of their illnesses. Despite the enactment of the legislation, there was no greater percentage of patients who, in the two-week period of the audit, had a resuscitation status determination recorded in their charts. At the close of the 1988 two-week survey, only 15 percent of the patient population admitted to the Department of Medicine had a DNR status, despite the fact that nearly 50 percent were judged, by independent clinical review, to have been appropriate for such an order.

Memorial adopted the New York Department of Health's system of six consent forms for documentation of the DNR order in 1988. An investigation of compliance with the use of those forms was initiated by the Ethics Committee in 1989, one year after the DNR legislation took effect in New York. The 1989 study by the Ethics Committee reviewed charts of patients for whom the DNR had been written. Was the order written in the order book? Were accompanying directives in the order book and progress notes? Was the appropriate consent form used and completed? And, did documentation of the discussion appear in the progress notes? Despite some lapses, the findings were impressive. More than 67 percent of the DNR orders written in a two-week period in May were both correctly and completely executed. Of sixty-seven orders written in that two-week period, thirteen months after the law took effect, forty-five were in full compliance; only twenty-two were incomplete, due to minor record-keeping points.

The most recent survey at Memorial of the DNR order was conducted in May 1990. Identical to the previous studies, the charts of eighty-eight patients who were admitted to Medicine were reviewed. Of that number, at the two-week audit, 17 percent were judged to be appropriately DNR. A slight decrease to 40 percent was noted in those without a resuscitation status who were judged by independent clinicians to be appropriately DNR (see Table 2).

The analysis of the 1990 data suggests some improvement and reason for optimism: the discussion of resuscitation is taking place more frequently and in a slightly more timely fashion (a change from 11 percent with a DNR order in

1985 to 17 percent in 1990). This means that those discussions which are initiated earlier are more likely to be able to involve the patient in the discussion.

NEW YORK STATE HEALTH CARE PROXY LAW (1990)

A 1991 review by Misbin *et al.* (personal communication) of deaths at Memorial during a two-month period found that most had a DNR order recorded in their chart at the time of death, though many were still written in the days immediately before death.[10] This likely means that the DNR discussion is still being done later in illness than desirable and that a significant percent of patients who should have a DNR order do not because of a delay in the discussion until near the time of death, a situation that often results in the discussion about DNR being held with a family member only. However, passage of the New York Health Care Proxy Law (1990) and the federal Patient Self-Determination Act (1991) has led to greater public awareness of these issues, along with the visibility in the media. Information about resuscitation options must be available, under the Patients' Bill of Rights, to all patients upon admission to New York State hospitals. The result of this unemotional approach to the information and the legally mandated provision of it is reducing the hesitation of staff and physicians to initiate the issues of appointing a proxy and writing advance directives. Patients are now asked routinely on admission about the status of their advance directives and whether they have selected a surrogate for health-care decision making.

SUMMARY

In summary, adherence to legal mandates has led to increased communication between physicians and patients about treatment decisions at the end of life. This positive benefit, enhanced by strong educational efforts, has been apparent in a cancer hospital where deaths are frequent, yet expectations are high for survival in most patients who come for treatment. Compliance with the law is good, in general, yet the nature of that compliance (for example, the time of conducting the DNR discussion), remains an issue. Aspects of the law should be examined for an unintended negative impact by the narrow definition of medical futility that does not address the patient's overall medical status, such as metastatic cancer with poor prognosis. The sense of disenfranchisement of health professionals has led to low morale and distress with yet another legal constraint in an increasingly regulated professional environment. Education of staff and the opportunity to request participation in thoughtful changes needed in the state law remain the avenues for obtaining a positive result from this first state law regulating resuscitation.

ACKNOWLEDGMENT

This chapter was developed and presented at "Controversies in the Care of the Dying Patient" in Orlando, Florida, by Daniel G. O'Hare, PhD, Ethicist and Fellow-in-Ethics at Memorial Sloan-Kettering Cancer Center, New York. The text was prepared by the members of the Ethics Group of the Memorial Sloan-Kettering Cancer Center: Jimmie Holland, MD; Robert Timberger, MD; James Dougherty, MD; Philip Exelby, MD; Kathleen Foley, MD; Jeffrey Groeger, MD; Marguerite Lederberg, MD; Daniel O'Hare, MD; Valerie Rusch, MD; Mary White, MD; Genevieve Foley, RN; Sherry Schachter, RN; Matthew Loscalzo, MSW; Janice Levy, and Roger Parker.

NOTES

1   Article 29-B, Statute 413A. State of New York Public Health Law, effective 1 April 1988.
2   P.T. Swendler, "Reflections on the New York Do Not Resuscitate Law," *New York State Journal of Medicine* (February 1989):58.
3   C. Fried, "Terminating Life Support: Out of the Closet!" *New England Journal of Medicine* 295 (1976): 390-1.
4   *Ibid.*
5   J. Nicholson, "Secret Grade System for Cancer Patients at Top Hospital," *New York Post*, 24 March 1984.
6   R. Sullivan, "Hospital's Data Faulted in Care of Terminally Ill," *New York Times*, 21 March 1984.
7   *DNR Audit Final Report of the Quality Assurance Committee,* (New York: Memorial Sloan-Kettering Cancer Center, July 1984).
8   New York State DNR Legislation, Article 2961.9.
9   C.E. Vitelli, K. Cooper, A. Rogatko, and M. Brennan, "Cardiopulmonary Resuscitation and the Patient with Cancer," *Journal of Clinical Oncology* 9, no.1 (January 1991): 111-15.
10   R.I. Misbin, D. O'Hare, M.S. Lederberg, and J.C. Holland, "Compliance with New York State's Do-Not-Resuscitate Law at Memorial Sloan-Kettering Cancer Center: A Review of Patient Deaths," *New York State Medical Journal* (in press).

10

Should a Terminally Ill Patient Have the Right to Demand Resuscitation?

Howard Brody, MD

I will argue that the terminally ill patient does not have a right to demand cardiopulmonary resuscitation (CPR), but does have a right to other aspects of treatment that are ultimately much more important and desirable. Those who are upset with the notion that the physician might unilaterally refuse to provide CPR often confuse a duty to provide CPR with a duty to provide other, more meaningful aspects of care. If those critics were fully to grasp the lack of any necessary connection, their disquiet would, I think, be eased considerably.

I will not address, at first, the patient for whom CPR offers some predictable, significant chance of benefit or success. I do not think there is any dispute over the accepted notion that providing CPR in the event of cardiac arrest is standard treatment in acute-care hospitals, and a do-not-resuscitate (DNR) order should be entered only with the discussion and consent of the patient. Therefore, I will restrict discussion initially to the patient for whom, based on the published medical literature and on the reasonable judgment of the attending physician, CPR is very unlikely to restore heartbeat or to improve the chances for even short-term survival.[1] In a later section, I will briefly address some more difficult cases, after the more fundamental points about futile CPR have been established.

I will also avoid discussion of patients in chronic or extended-care facilities, as those settings present some problems that require special analysis. I will also accept as the paradigm case the competent patient who accepts or refuses various therapeutic modalities. In the case of the incompetent patient, the same principles will apply, only the discussion will occur between the physician and the appropriate surrogate or proxy decision maker, usually a family member (or members).

WHY PATIENTS CANNOT DEMAND CPR

The Hastings Center *Guidelines* on life-sustaining treatment and terminal care propose four central values which may be used to inform ethical decisions: patient well-being, patient autonomy, moral integrity of the health professional, and justice.[2] The reason patients ought not to have the right to demand CPR when it is viewed medically as being futile is that such a right would run counter to each of these four values. I will discuss them in turn.

Patient Well-Being

By definition, patient well-being cannot be served by administering a treatment which predictably will not work. What "will not work," of course, is a complicated notion, which requires specifying both the goals to be sought and the acceptable means toward those goals.[3] If the only acceptable goal of medicine is to ward off death, then all medical treatment is ultimately futile. On the other hand, if a legitimate goal of medical treatment is to give the appearance of "doing something" so as to mollify the patient and family, then virtually no medical treatment is futile. Somewhere between these two extremes lies a reasonable account of medical futility.

Suppose, as has been proposed in the literature, that we can predict with reasonable certainty that CPR will either not restore heartbeat at all, or else will prolong existence for merely a few hours with a very low level of functioning, in certain categories of patients. If we explain to these patients that CPR is predictably nonbeneficial for them, and they nevertheless demand it, what are we to make of their demand? It would seem either that they did not understand the facts we have presented; or that they do not believe those facts to be true; or that performing CPR would for them serve some other goal besides the restoration of heartbeat and respiration. If they do not understand or believe the relevant facts, then we have little obligation to honor their demand for CPR. If CPR would serve some other goal then it remains to be seen whether we cannot offer them an another means of achieving that goal that will not require a useless charade of medical therapy; and that will be addressed in the next section.

Patient Autonomy

I have already noted that when a patient demands futile CPR after all the facts have been presented, the ability of that patient to make a truly autonomous choice has necessarily been called into question. However, before blaming the patient, it is important to note that the ability of the patient to render an autonomous choice is altered not only by the patient's capacity to choose, but also by whether the physician has created an environment which encourages thoughtful and effective deliberation of the key issues at hand. To claim that the patient has a right to demand futile treatment is to insist that the physician send an inherently confusing message to the patient: "This treatment will not work, *and* I feel compelled to offer it to you." A patient has the right to assume, other things being equal, that if a physician feels obligated to offer a treatment, there must be some chance that it *will* work. (I am grateful to Loretta Kopelman for pointing out, in personal communication, that the phrase "futile therapy" really ought to be viewed as an oxymoron.) And so which part of the self-contradictory message is the patient to believe? If after being thoroughly confused in this fashion the patient goes on to request or demand futile CPR, we can hardly malign his inherent mental capacities.

Simply put, the purported duty to offer CPR to the patient, even if futile, illustrates that it is a mistake to think that we automatically enhance patient autonomy *whenever* we offer the patient an additional choice.[4] Some choices, like Sophie's choice, are inherently subversive of autonomy.

Integrity of Professionals

If CPR in a certain case really served patient well-being and patient autonomy, then possibly the moral integrity of the health professional would be a second-rank consideration. I have argued, however, that autonomy is not served by offering futile CPR and that if well-being is served, it is by a misleading and circuitous route. Therefore, the integrity of medicine and nursing ought to carry considerable moral weight when addressing this issue.

Just as forcing the unwilling patient to accept the physician's preferred treatment violates patient autonomy, forcing the physician to provide predictably useless treatment violates the physician's own moral integrity. When we observe a professional administering treatment, we have a right to assume that the professional has carefully selected that treatment with the patient's particular circumstances in view, precisely because professional judgment indicates that the treatment's likely benefits are substantial and outweigh the foreseeable harms. When these assumptions are false, and we nevertheless force professionals to go ahead with the treatment, we force them to engage in a public act of fraud. We also force them to perpetuate the sad situation--since the more we force them to offer CPR, the more we convince the world at large that CPR is an *expected* treatment to which every patient has an unquestioned right.

The fraud we force professionals to practice is at a real, not just a theoretical level. In discussing futile CPR with physicians and nurses, I have universally been informed that a "code" that appears futile or unreasonable to the professionals, and is being called simply because of required policy, is seldom if ever conducted in the same way as a "real code." Fewer things are done; the procedure is stopped much earlier; the staff's heart simply isn't in it. It is a charade, a so-called "slow code" or "show code." If we created a so-called "patient right" to demand medication at every visit to a physician, we might predict that placebo prescriptions would increase dramatically, which would hardly foster the moral integrity of the profession. We have done the same thing by creating policies that require futile CPR.

Justice

When medical resources are scarce, there seems no justification for using them on patients who cannot benefit. This is especially true in CPR when (as not infrequently happens) CPR is effective in restoring heartbeat, but ineffective in prolonging the patient's life for more than twelve to eighteen hours. In such cases, the additional twelve to eighteen hours almost always requires intensive life support with mechanical ventilation, pressor agents, and possibly even more invasive means; and the patient remains unconscious throughout. To devote such expensive resources to prolonging unconscious life for less than a day seems grotesquely wasteful.[5]

PATIENTS' MEANINGFUL RIGHTS TO TREATMENT

To say that the patient has no right to demand CPR sounds (in our present state of technology-addicted medical practice) as if we were advocating patient abandonment; and it is no wonder that critics of the futility concept react with horror at the idea of abandonment. The mistaken image of abandonment can best be refuted by reminding ourselves (along with the patients and their families) which modalities of treatment will continue, those to which the patient has an unquestioned right. I should, however, note that we live in a world where some physicians think it is abandonment to refer a patient to a hospice program, or generally to do anything other than to treat every medical problem heroically until the last gasp. We cannot expect the notion of futility to be discussed with full rationality in such a world.

The Right to Compassion

Patients with poor prognoses, or indeed with good prognoses but who will not be helped by some particular technology that is in common use, have a right to demand a sensitive and compassionate explanation of this state of affairs. Critics of this sort of dialogue with patients assume that any refusal to offer CPR will necessarily be cruel and will destroy any hope the patient may have left.[6] We should be reminded that these same arguments, in the 1960s and 1970s, were trotted out consistently to oppose ever telling a patient that she had cancer.[7]

Stating that CPR will not be offered can be fully compassionate if it is coupled with a firm promise of non-abandonment and a listing of those treatments that *will* be beneficial and that will be continued. Ideally, the announcement that CPR is not being offered will come *after* the patient has been offered a "treatment package" that includes the modalities predicted to be helpful. In the cases we are considering, these treatments may be primarily palliative, or they may be curative but focused upon a discrete, readily reversible process (such as antibiotics for pneumonia). The physician will then explain why CPR is not a useful part of the "package." (The fact that medical teams often fail to consider an *overall plan of care*, and instead consider individual technological interventions one at a time for various indications that may arise on a day-to-day basis, may explain why the refusal to offer CPR is so readily equated with abandonment and cruelty.)

Moreover, for a number of patients, possibly the majority, the announcement that CPR will not be done will be perceived as compassionate regardless of what other treatments are or are not offered. Many individuals fear medical heroics more than they fear medical neglect, but for a variety of reasons may have hesitated to make their wishes known to the caregivers.[8]

The Right to Disclosure

A pernicious outgrowth of the debate over medical futility has been the proposal that physicians need not discuss treatment non-use with patients so long as futility, rather than the patient's quality of life, is the basis for the non-use.[9] Many physicians fail to see the distinction between disclosure and consent; hence, when it is suggested that patient *consent* is not required for a DNR order based on futility, the reader may mistakenly conclude that *discussion* with the patient need not occur.

Anecdotal reports have persuaded me that many physicians are profoundly uncomfortable discussing with patients anything that seems remotely related to death or to a hopeless prognosis; therefore, they will grasp at any reed, however thin, as an excuse not to engage in this painful discussion. I think this is rooted both in the view that every death is somehow a personal failure for the physician and also in the modern physician's deep reluctance to reveal to the patient anything that smacks of uncertainty.[10] It is obviously critical that nothing in the futility debate be phrased so as to add fuel to this unfortunate tendency toward silence and avoidance.

Disclosure is essential for two reasons: one related to autonomy, the other to well-being. The autonomous patient (or, in most relevant cases, the family of the patient who now lacks the capacity to choose) has no right to demand futile CPR; but the family may have a right to a second opinion if they feel that the conclusion of "futility" is hasty or unsupported. I have already noted that patient well-being may be served even if the goals sought by the patient, for which CPR is demanded, are different from the medical goal of restoring heartbeat. Because many of the family's goals will be emotional or symbolic, frank discussion with the family will reveal the unmet emotional needs and will point the physician toward alternative means to address the vital issues. This will allow the patient's or family's goals to be addressed directly, rather than through the roundabout route of pretending to offer CPR.

The Right to Good Medical Care

We might have difficulty defining what "good medical care" consists of and yet we agree without hesitation that useless treatment is bad medical care. To say that a patient has a right to bad care is to propose a peculiar addition to any list of "patients' rights." In any case, forcing physicians to provide futile care undermines the rights of patients to expect that physicians will provide good care.

MORE DIFFICULT CASES

The principles argued for so far depend upon an empirical assessment of a vanishingly low likelihood of success of CPR. That is, all parties to the debate agree upon what would be a good or a bad outcome for the patient, and the scientific facts dictate that the probability of that good outcome being achieved by means of CPR is very close to zero.

Can these principles be applied to either of the following two cases?

1.   Helga Wanglie, eighty-seven, was in a persistent vegetative state and dependent upon mechanical ventilation. The medical staff of the hospital declared that continued respirator support, in the absence of any realistic prognosis for recovery of consciousness, was not serving the best interests of the patient and sought a court order allowing them to discontinue the respirator. The patient's husband insisted that she would want to live as long as possible, regardless of mental state, and demanded that the respirator be continued.[11] Should the husband's wishes be followed? And what ought to be done if Mr. Wanglie were also to demand CPR for his wife in the event of cardiac arrest?

2.   Another woman, seventy-two, is suffering from advanced senile dementia of the Alzheimer's type, but is otherwise generally healthy. She is found to be acutely short of breath and, on admission to intensive care, is found to have had a recent heart attack with some ventricular arrhythmias. She responds well to initial pharmacologic treatment for these problems and, if she survives the next few days in the hospital, is likely to recover from her cardiac event and could live for another ten years, but of course, still with severe dementia. Should CPR be provided for her while in the hospital, if demanded by the patient's family?

There is not space here to address the much larger question of when physicians may be justified in deciding unilaterally to withhold a medical intervention that patients or their proxies request or demand.[12] I would suggest, however, that these two cases illustrate some important limits of the arguments presented in the earlier portion of this paper.

In Case One, it is important to ask whether the same logic governs offering CPR and continuing ventilator support. An excellent case can be made that offering CPR for Helga Wanglie would fall under the discussion in previous sections of this paper. Given age, ventilator dependence, and underlying neuro-logical condition, there is a vanishingly small chance that CPR would impact positively on patient survival. There would therefore be no physician obligation to offer or to perform CPR. (In the actual case the family, persuaded by these reasons, reluctantly agreed to a DNR order.)

The ventilator, however, has obviously been effective in promoting one goal of the family (and, they argued, of Helga Wanglie herself)--prolonged biological survival even with no chance to recover consciousness. The same logic that is used to refuse to perform CPR, therefore, cannot justify a unilateral decision to withdraw the ventilator.

For the ventilator in Case One, and for CPR in Case Two, we therefore cannot argue that the life-prolonging intervention has a low likelihood of producing an effect that would be considered beneficial *from the patient's or the proxy's perspective*. At issue, instead, is whether the perspective of the patient or proxy should be morally controlling. At least three reasons might be suggested, on review of these two cases, to override the patient's or proxy's request for treatment:

A. The quality of life of the patient in question is far too low to justify aggressive, life-sustaining intervention.
B. The patient is claiming medical resources that, according to sound prin-ciples of distributive justice, ought instead to be allocated to other patients (such as patients with a much greater chance of recovery to full function). The patient thus has no *right* to those relatively scarce resources.
C. The patient is demanding a form of intervention that would violate well-established and widely accepted norms of professional integrity among phy-sicians. The patient has no *right* to demand that physicians violate their own moral beliefs and commitments in order to offer treatment to them.

Assertion *A* would be rejected by most commentators today as far too open to "slippery slope" abuses, that is, whenever outsiders claim the right to judge another person's quality of life based on their own standards and to make life-or-death decisions based on those judgments. I would wish to argue that assertions *B* and *C* can be morally defensible in at least some cases. *B* might apply to the respirator care and intensive-care hospitalization of Helga Wanglie. However, it would then seem that some representative organ of society, and not merely the hospital's medical staff, should be the ones to decide that it is not worthwhile to spend scarce medical resources to prolong the lives of persistently vegetative patients as a class. It is harder to imagine the principled argument by which *B* could be applied to Case Two, unless *B* were simply a disguised version of *A*. *C* seems to apply equally poorly to both of these cases, even though something like *C* seemed to be implicit in the arguments raised by the hospital staff physicians in the *Wanglie* case. If on-going life-sustaining treatment for either patient were to offer no hope of functional recovery, but were instead to inflict severe pain, then one could argue more forcefully that the so-called "treatment" was tantamount to torture and that no physician of integrity would be a party to administering it. But again, appeals to *C* would require fleshing out the notion of the fundamental conditions of moral integrity for physicians in a way that would be agreed upon by almost all thoughtful practitioners, as well as by the informed general public. For all these reasons, assertions that the proxies in Cases One and Two have no *right* to demand continued ventilator support in Case One and CPR in Case Two are problematic in a way that the assertions in earlier sections of the paper are not. And it is quite misleading to suggest that the ventilator in Case One and CPR in Case Two would be "futile."

CONCLUSION

A good deal more needs to be said about how physicians determine futility[13] and what counts as appropriate peer and public review of futility judgments--in part because we need to be sure that already-discriminated-against minority groups are not the only ones for whom treatment is judged to be "futile."[14] These matters can provide many opportunities for thoughtful debate. But I doubt that there could be much meaningful debate over the basic concept presented above. As none of the important values in medical ethics can be served by requiring futile treatment, any proposal that patients have a right to demand such treatment must be based on a misunderstanding.

ACKNOWLEDGMENT

Robert Misbin offered helpful comments on an earlier draft and suggested Case Two.

NOTES

1   L.J. Blackhall, "Must We Always Use CPR?" *New England Journal of Medicine* 317 (1987):1281-85; A.H. Moss, "Informing the Patient About Cardio-pulmonary Resuscitation: When the Risks Outweigh the Benefits," *Journal of Gerneral Internal Medicine* 4 (1989):349-55.
2   *Guidelines on the Termination of Life Sustaining Treatment and the Care of the Dying: A Report of the Hasting's Center* (Braincliff Manor, NY: Hastings Center, 1987).
3   S.J. Youngner, "Who Defines Futility?" *Journal of the American Medical Association* 260 (1988):2094-95.
4   T. Tomlinson and H. Brody, "Futility and the Ethics of Resuscitation,"

Journal of the American Medical Association 264 (1990):1276-80.

5   L.J. Schneiderman, N.S. Jecker, and A.R. Jonsen, "Medical Futility: Its Meaning and Ethical Implications," *Annals of Internal Medicine* 112 (1990):949-54.

6   D.J. Murphy, "Do-Not-Resuscitate Orders: Time for Reappraisal in Longterm-Care Institutions," *Journal of the American Medical Association* 260 (1988):2098-2101; J.C. Hackler and F.C. Hiller, "Family Consent to Orders Not to Resuscitate: Reconsidering Hospital Policy," *Journal of the American Medical Association* 264 (1990):1281-83.

7   H. Brody, "Hope," *Journal of the American Medical Association* 246 (1981):1411-12.

8   B. Lo, G.A. McLeod, and B. Saika, "Patient Attitudes to Discusssing Lifesustaining Treatment," *Archives of Internal Medicine* 146 (1986):1613-15.

9   Murphy, "Do Not Resuscitate Orders," 2098-101; Hackler and Hiller, "Family Consent," 1281-83.

10   J. Katz, *The Silent World of Doctor and Patient* (New York: Free Press, 1984).

11   R.E. Cranford, "Helga Wanglie's Ventilator," *Hastings Center Report* 21, no.4 (1991):23-24; S.H. Miles, "Informed Demand for Non-Beneficial Medical Treatment" *New England Journal of Medicine* 325 (1991):512-15.

12   D. Callahan, "Medical Futility, Medical Necessity: the Problem-Without-a-Name," *Hastings Center Report* 21, no.4 (1991):30-35.

13   Youngner, "Who Defines Futility?" 2094-95; J.D. Lantos, P.A. Singer, R.M. Walker *et al.*, "The Illusion of Futility in Clinical Practice," *American Journal of Medicine* 87 (1989):81-84; Callahan, "Medical Futility," 30-35.

14   R.M. Wachter, J.M. Luce, N. Hearst, and B. Lo, "Decisions About Resuscitation: Inequities Among Patients with Different Diseases but Similar Prognoses," *Annals of Internal Medicine* 111 (1989):525-32.

11

Preserving the Professional Ethics: Physicians Are Not Obligated to Attempt Cardiopulmonary Resuscitation

Nannette B. Hoffman

INTRODUCTION

When physicians are confronted by patients or family members requesting cardiopulmonary resuscitation (CPR) when in the physician's judgment, CPR would be ineffective, a dilemma often results. Even after physician counseling, patients and family members sometimes insist that "everything be done." If CPR is performed under these circumstances, it may only be a half-hearted attempt to satisfy the patient's or family's emotional needs at the time. This "half-hearted" CPR attempt is called by those in the medical profession the "slow code" or "show code." It is performed for any or all of the following reasons: to diminish the family-physician conflict about CPR, to comply with legislative or institutional policies, to reduce potential legal liability, or to ostensibly preserve patient autonomy.[1]

How should physicians approach the situation of patients or family members demanding CPR when it is medically inappropriate? Although not everyone would agree, when CPR has no medical benefit, it should not be attempted just to placate the patient or family. Whether physicians should always discuss with their patients the rationale for not offering CPR is also controversial, as some question why an ineffective procedure needs to be discussed at all.[2]

WHY DO PATIENTS AND FAMILY MEMBERS INSIST "EVERYTHING BE DONE"?

First, what is the rationale for patients' and family members' insistence upon CPR's performance after being informed that it would be unsuccessful for a particular illness? Faced with such an illness, they may either deny its existence or have false hopes about the likelihood of recovery. They also may experience emotional distress from coping with the prospect of death.[3] Furthermore, even if CPR is offered with the physician's expectation of refusal, the patient and family may perceive there is a remote possibility for benefit, since the procedure has been offered.[4] After all, why would the doctor offer CPR if it was of no use? Another reason for insistence upon CPR's performance is the presence of guilty feelings of relatives who have had either no recent contact or some prior conflict with the patient. In this instance, the relatives' guilty feelings would be assuaged with CPR's performance such that they would experience emotional comfort knowing that "everything" was done, regardless of CPR's appropriateness for the patient. Finally, some family members' financial interests may be served by prolonging the patient's life even if such an action is not in the patient's best interest. This latter scenario is probably rare, but should be considered. Should physicians perform "futile" CPR just to "promote some special value of the patient or family" and meet their psychological needs? Some would advocate that CPR in this circumstance is acceptable. Nevertheless, physicians are not obligated to perform CPR if it is useless.[5]

ETHICAL AND LEGAL PRINCIPLE

It is both ethically and legally sound for physicians to withhold useless therapies. Likewise, it is ethically and legally supported for patients to refuse consent for procedures. The latter is embodied in the ethical concept of patient autonomy that has been legally recognized since 1914, when Justice Cardozo rendered the legal opinion: "Every human being of adult years and sound mind has the right to determine what shall be done with his own body." This opinion is called the common-law right of self-determination. The other legal tenet recognizing autonomy is the constitutional right of privacy that has been upheld by the US Supreme Court to protect individuals from government intrusion in personal medical decisions.[6] Hence, it is well established and practiced that once duly informed, competent patients have the right to refuse treatment.

In addition, physicians have a professional ethics to foster the medical profession's integrity. Physicians are not obligated to render useless care, and when they do acquiesce to a patient's request for unnecessary or harmful treatment to respect patient autonomy, physicians' autonomies are reciprocally undermined.[7] If conflict occurs between the respective autonomies of physicians and patients, it is recommended to transfer the patient's care to a physician willing to honor the patient's wishes. Unfortunately, in practice this is sometimes impossible to accomplish, particularly when patients request treatments that are clearly contraindicated. In this situation physicians can be reassured that the courts have upheld physician's professionalism and autonomy with respect to the withholding and withdrawing of life-sustaining therapies when the likelihood for recovery was remote, and that the decision to withhold or withdraw such therapies was based on sound medical judgement.[8]

In conclusion, the ethical principle of autonomy has legal basis such that competent patients have the right to refuse treatment and physicians must respect this right. Nonetheless, physicians have the ethical duty to promote professional integrity by not rendering useless care. When these two ethical standards oppose one another, medical decision making must be guided by scientific and rational professional practice.

NOT RENDERING USELESS CARE: WHEN IS CPR FUTILE?

Disagreement about how to proceed when CPR lacks medical benefit and the patient demands it, results from the supposition that physicians can accurately predict which patients would not benefit from CPR. Clinical determinations of CPR futility are difficult due to inconclusive evidence about CPR efficacy for certain patients, and conflict about the therapeutic goals for the patient among physicians, patient, and family members.[9] Moreover, a "1-percent likelihood" of a successful CPR outcome represents futility to some and, conversely, benefit to others. Because some suggest that designating CPR futility for a particular patient is a value judgement, manifesting paternalism, they believe CPR should be performed on all consenting patients. A problem arises with accepting this premise. In medicine, the decision that a treatment is ineffective is always a matter of probability (however low), and not certainty.[10] Physicians, by virtue of their profession, constantly make value judgments about treatment efficacy for their patients. Likewise, CPR is also a treatment about which physicians must make value judgments regarding its efficacy. Because the result of CPR denial is death, some contend that CPR is unlike other treatments, and thus should be considered differently. This argument really has no rationale. However, when withholding CPR, physicians should be certain this decision has been given thorough consideration and is based upon proper medical practice. Although not everyone would agree, physicians should make a "reasonable" determination about offering CPR when CPR's efficacy is low. The physician, not the patient, must sort out the possibilities, weigh risks and benefits, and recommend a therapeutic plan. This responsibility should not be shifted to the patient in the guise of respect for patient autonomy. Not all would concur: the use of CPR should be justified by a realistic expectation of prolonged benefit, and therefore the treatment plan could exclude CPR in some cases.[11] By necessity this is a value judgement; it is neither pragmatic nor logical for physicians to perform CPR on all patients who request it just because the alternative is death.

Is there information physicians can use to decide when CPR is futile? Indeed, the literature does show CPR's relative ineffectiveness for certain patients when using survival to hospital discharge as the endpoint. Some advocate this endpoint is invalid for all patients, since some patients might wish to live longer in the hospital. Nevertheless, this endpoint is useful in most instances.

Survival to hospital discharge following unwitnessed cardiac arrest averages 1 percent.[12] Sepsis is a uniform predictor of virtually no survival to discharge with an overall survival rate of 1 percent, and 0 percent in many series.[13] Similarly, malignancy, particularly when widespread, is a predictor of a poor outcome from CPR. In many reports, no patient with documented metastatic cancer survived CPR to discharge, and the overall survival rate for all cancer patients was 4 percent.[14] Survival rates for patients with renal failure generally ranged from 0 to 6 percent, with an overall survival rate of 4 percent.[15] Progressive systemic acidosis secondary to respiratory or circulatory failure also predicts abysmal survival.[16] Other conditions associated with a poor outcome, that is, usually less than a 10 percent successful survival to discharge include: significant congestive heart failure, cerebrovascular accidents, and severe physical impairment.[17] (See Table 1.) The overall success rate of CPR in most studies is less than 20 percent in hospital patients and less than 10 percent in nursing home patients. The elderly fare less well than their younger counterparts with respect to CPR outcome, which appears related to concomitant illness and disability.[18] In particular, the "old-old" have the lowest survival rates. One report showed 0 percent survival to discharge in all patients ninety years of age or older. On the other hand, relatively healthy elderly individuals suffering witnessed cardiac arrests with an initial rhythm of ventricular fibrillation have at least approximately a 20-percent chance of survival to hospital discharge following CPR.[19] In the above studies, rhythms other than ventricular fibrillation or tachycardia were associated with very poor CPR survival outcomes regardless of age. Although age should not be the sole criterion upon which to base a CPR decision, it should be remembered that the very old have poor CPR outcomes.

The above information enables physicians to judge the likelihood of a successful CPR outcome and identify those patients for whom CPR would be useless. For example, CPR would be ineffective in a bed-bound stroke patient with renal failure who develops metastatic cancer or sepsis. Such a patient would not live to discharge, based upon our knowledge of the literature about CPR outcome in these disease states. Hence, not only is CPR medically contraindicated in this instance, it should not be offered as a treatment option. Conversely, a patient with mild heart failure without other serious systemic illness who could have a 10 percent chance of survival from CPR should not necessarily be denied this procedure without consent. In summary, if the presumed goal is survival to hospital discharge, then there are circumstances where CPR is obviously useless and should not be offered as a therapeutic modality. This judgment should be made by the physician, based upon the medical literature and the patient's condition. In cases when CPR's benefit is unclear, the risks and benefits should be discussed with the patient and family so an informed decision about CPR performance is made and, hopefully, mutually agreed upon by all parties.[20] If the patient and family request the physician's recommendation, the physician should offer one to the best of his or her professional ability. Patients and families often need guidance and counsel when making a decision to undergo an invasive procedure whose merits might be questionable.

DO-NOT-RESUSCITATE (DNR) ORDERS AND FUTILE CPR

"The purpose of CPR is the prevention of sudden, unexpected death. CPR is not indicated in certain situations, such as in cases of terminal irreversible illness where death is not unexpected." This quote is from the National Council on Cardiopulmonary Resuscitation and Emergency Cardiac Care. Despite the National Council's recommendation, in the 1970s and 1980s CPR was frequently performed indiscriminately in hospitals on all patients regardless of diagnoses. Only recently has there been a trend for physicians to write do-not-resuscitate (DNR) orders for patients who are terminally ill or refuse resuscitation, and for institutions to implement policies about DNR orders.

The three general indications for writing DNR orders are: no medical benefit, poor quality of life after CPR, and poor quality of life before CPR. The latter two should involve the patient or patient's surrogate directly in the decision-making process. The former theoretically does not involve the patient, and is a medical determination by the physician, such that the physician would not offer CPR in the absence of its benefit.[21] However, one state, New York, has legislated the conditions under which CPR can be withheld. This occurred when a grand jury found a New York hospital permitted the use of DNR orders that were neither recorded in patients' medical records nor discussed with patients. Thus, New York State requires the patient's or surrogate's consent to withhold CPR, otherwise CPR must be performed.[22] Unfortunately, the ethical conflict that arises when CPR is medically contraindicated but the patient or surrogate insists upon its use is unaddressed by this legislation. Actually, this legislation refutes the physician's professional ethics not to render useless care. In the above situation physicians cannot adhere to their professional ethics and legally comply with New York State law. Consequently, physicians may reluctantly perform CPR possibly in the form of a "slow code," not perform CPR at all by halting resuscitation immediately after CPR initiation, or finally, perform "proper" but "futile" CPR. In this setting the health-care team might know that CPR will not be performed adequately, if at all, but the patient, surrogate, or family members never know because they have refused consent for CPR to be withheld. The result is that New York State's law and any other institution's similar policy are inherently ethically fallacious because they do not enable physicians to abide by their own professional ethics not to provide useless care.

Table 1
Conditions with Less than 10-Percent Survival to Hospital
Discharge Following CPR

Diagnosis	Survival to Hospital Discharge No. Surviving/Total No. Resuscitated (%)	References
Sepsis	2/148 (1)	Taffet et al.,[1] Saphir,[2] Bedell et al.,[3] Rozenbaum and Shenkman,[4] Urberg and Ways,[5] Kelley et al.,[6] Stiles et al.[7]
Cancer*	12/272 (4)	Taffet et al.,[8] Hershey and Fisher,[9] Bedell et al.,[10] Rozenbaum and Shenkman,[11] Urberg and Ways,[12] Stiles et al.,[13] Peatfield et al.,[14] Jersaty et al.,[15] Sowden et al.,[16] Arena et al.[17]
Cerebro-Vascular Accident	2/48 (4)	Saphir,[18] Bedell et al.,[19] Kelley et al.,[20] Peatfield et al.[21]
Physically Impaired	10/224 (4)	Murphy et al.,[22] Bedell et al.,[23] Rozenbaum and Shenkman.[24]
Renal Failure	7/158 (4)	Murphy et al.,[25] Saphir,[26] Bedell et al.,[27] Rozenbaum and Shenkman,[28] Kelley et al.,[29] Smith and Anthonisen,[30] Hollingsworth.[31]
Congestive Heart Failure	26/357 (7)	Bedell et al.,[32] Urberg and Ways,[33] Peatfield et al.,[34] Sowden et al.,[35] Hollingsworth,[36] Baringer et al.[37]

*   Includes metastatic and non-metastatic cancers.

1   G.E. Taffet, T.A. Teasdale, and R.J. Luchi, "In-Hospital Cardiopulmonary Resuscitation," *Journal of the American Medical Association* 260 (1988):2069-72.
2   R. Saphir, "External Cardiac Massage: Retrospective Analysis of 123 Cases and Review of the Literature," *Medicine* 47 (1968):73-85.
3   S.E. Bedell, T.L. Delbanco, E.F. Cook, *et al.,* "Survival After Cardiopulmonary Resuscitation in the Hospital," *New England Journal of Medicine* 309 (1983):570-76.
4   E.A. Rozenbaum and L. Shenkman, "Predicting Outcome of In-Hospital Cardiopulmonary

Resuscitation," *Critical Care Medicine* 16 (1988):583-86.
5   M. Urberg and C. Ways, "Survival After Cardiopulmonary Resuscitation for an In-Hospital Cardiac Arrest," *Journal of Family Practice* 25 (1987):41-44.
6   C.A. Kelley, D. Watson, C.M. Hutchinson, *et al.*, "Prognostic Factors in Cardiac Arrest Occuring in a District General Hospital," *British Journal of Clinical Practice* 40 (1986):251-53.
7   Q.R. Stiles, B.L. Tucker, B.W. Mayer, *et al.*, "Cardiopulmonary Arrest: Evaluation of an Active Resuscitation Program," *American Journal of Surgery* 122 (1971):282-87.
8   Taffet, Teasdale, and Luchi, "In-Hospital Cardiopulmonary Resuscitation," 2069-72.
9   C.O. Hershey and L. Fisher, " Why Outcome of Cardiopulmonary Resuscitation in General Wards is Poor," *Lancet* 1 (1982):31-34.
10   Bedell, Delbanco, Cook, *et al.*, "Survival," 570-76.
11   Rozenbaum and Shenkman, "Predicting Outcome," 583-86.
12   Urberg and Ways, "Survival After Cardiopulmonary Resuscitation," 41-44.
13   Stiles, Tucker, Mayer, *et al.*, "Cardiopulmonary Arrest," 282-87.
14   R.C. Peatfield, R.W. Sillett, D. Taylor, *et al.*, "Survival After Cardiac Arrest in Hospital," *Lancet* 1 (1977):1223-25.
15   R.M. Jenesaty, T.J. Godar, and J.P. Liss, "External Cardiac Resuscitation in a Community Hospital: A Three-Year Experience," *Archives of Internal Medicine* 124 (1969):588-92.
16   G.R. Sowden, D.W. Robins, and P.J.E. Baskett, "Factors Associated with Survival and Eventual Cerebral Status Following Cardiac Arrest," *Anaesthesia* 39 (1984):39-43.
17   F.P. Arena, M. Perlin, and A.D. Turnbill, "Initial Experience with 'Code-no-Code' Resuscitation System in Cancer Patients," *Critical Care Medicine* 8 (1980):733-35.
18   Saphir, "External Cardiac Massage," 73-85.
19   Bedell, Delbanco, Cook, *et al.*, "Survival," 570-76.
20   Kelley, Watson, Hutchinson, *et al.*, "Prognostic Factors," 251-53.
21   Peatfield, Sillett, Taylor, *et al.*, "Survival After Cardiac Arrest," 1223-26.
22   D.J. Murphy, A.M. Murray, B.E. Robinson, *et al.*, "Outcomes of Cardiopulmonary Resuscitation in the Elderly," *Annals of Internal Medicine* 111 (1989):199-205.
23   Bedell, Delbanco, Cook, *et al.*, "Survival," 570-76.
24   Rozenbaum and Shenkman, "Predicting Outcome," 570-76.
25   Murphy, Murray, Robinson, *et al.*, "Outcomes of Cardiopulmonary Resuscitation," 199-205.
26   Saphir, "External Cardiac Massage," 73-85.
27   Bedell, Delbanco, Cook, *et al.*, "Survival After Cardiopulmonary Resuscitation," 570-76.
28   Rozenbaum and Shenkman, "Predicting Outcome," 583-86.
29   Kelley, Watson, Hutchinson, *et al.,* "Prognostic Factors," 251-53.
30   H.J. Smith and N.R. Anthonisen, "Results of Cardiac Resuscitation in 254 Patients," *Lancet* 1 (1965):1022-29.
31   J.M. Hollingsworth, "The Results of Cardiopulmonary Resuscitation: A Three-Year University Hospital Experience," *Annals of Internal Medicine* 71 (1969):459-66.
32   Bedell, Delbanco, Cook, *et al.*, "Survival," 570-76.
33   Urberg and Ways, "Survival After Cardiopulmonary Resuscitation," 41-44.
34   Peatfield, Sillett, Taylor, *et al.*, "Survival After Cardiac Arrest," 1223-25.
35   Sowden, Robins, and Baskett, "Factors Associated with Survival," 39-43.
36   Hollingsworth, "The Results of Cardiopulmonary Resuscitation," 459-66.
37   J.R. Baringer, E.W. Salzman, W.A. Jones, *et al.*, "External Cardiac Massage," *New England Journal of Medicine* 265 (1961):62-65.

When ineffective, CPR should not be offered to patients and DNR orders should be written without patients', surrogates', or family members' consent.[23] Nonetheless, some recommend that patients and families be informed when CPR will not be performed to facilitate an open discussion about the patient's illness and its outcome. This point remains controversial in the medical ethical literature.

That is, do patients have the right to be informed that CPR will not be performed, particularly if they are in a denial stage about their illness? If patients are not informed, then is this paternalism? Yet if CPR is useless, why even discuss it with the patient since it is not a treatment option? The logical conclusion is not to offer futile CPR to patients and families, because physicians ordinarily do not offer any other ineffective treatment modality to their patients.[24]

CONCLUSION

Physicians must ultimately decide whether CPR is medically indicated and should not offer it when it will be futile. Although, to some extent, futility is a value judgment, futility can be determined in many circumstances based upon the medical literature. Furthermore, physicians have a professional obligation to make such a value judgment about CPR. Institutions need to adopt uniform policies about the withholding of CPR when CPR is inappropriate. In cases of disagreement about CPR initiation, to suggest that physicians are not ethically obligated to prescribe useless treatments, but should simultaneously ignore their professional ethical principles by not writing a DNR order, is illogical and irrational.[25] This practice should never be sanctioned. When medically indicated, physicians should be permitted to write a DNR order and have it implemented without a patient- or surrogate-signed advance directive on the patient's chart. This would substantially decrease the number of "slow codes" and "show codes." Moreover, physicians would not be coerced due to threat of legal or institutional reprisal to endorse a highly invasive and often ineffective procedure. They would be able to adhere to their professional ethics openly, without constraint.

NOTES

1   L.J. Blackhall, "Must We Always Use CPR?" *New England Journal of Medicine* 317 (1987):1281-84; B. Lo and R.L. Steinbrook, "Deciding Whether to Resuscitate," *Archives of Internal Medicine* 143 (1983):1561-63; K.M. Prager (letter to the editor), *Journal of the American Medical Association* 263 (1990):2297; C.T. Plow, (letter to the editor), *New England Journal of Medicine* 318 (1988):1758.
2   Blackhall, "Must We Always Use CPR?" 1281-84; J.C. Hackler and F.C. Hiller, "Family Consent to Orders Not-to-Resuscitate: Reconsidering Hospital Policy," *Journal of the American Medical Association* 264 (1990):1281-83.
3   Blackhall, "Must We Always Use CPR?" 1281-84.
4   Hackler and Hiller, "Family Consent to Orders Not to Resuscitate," 1281-83.
5   S.J. Youngner, "Futility in Context," *Journal of the American Medical Association* 264 (1990):1295-96.

6   US Congress, Office of Technology Assessment, *Life-Sustaining Technologies and the Elderly,* OTA-BA-306 (Washington, DC: US Government Printing Office, July 1987), 91-102.

7   F.M. Marsh, "Refusal of Treatment," in *Ethical Issues in the Care of the Elderly,* vol. 2, ed. D.W. Jahnigen and R.W. Schrier (1986), 511-20; A.S. Brett and L.B. McCullough, "When Patients Request Specific Interventions: Defining the Limits of the Physician's Obligation," *New England Journal of Medicine* 315 (1986):1347-51.

8   Hackler and Hiller, "Family Consent to Orders Not to Resuscitate," 1281-83; *In re Dinnerstein,* 380 NE 2d 134 (Appt. Ct. MA 1987).

9   S.J. Youngner, "Who Defines Futility?" *Journal of the American Medical Association* 260 (1988):2094.

10   T. Tomlinson and H. Brody, "Futility and the Ethics of Resuscitation," *Journal of the American Medical Association* 264 (1990):1276-80.

11   J.D. Lantos, P.A. Singer, R.M. Walker, *et al.,* "The Illusion of Futility in Clinical Practice,"*American Journal of Medicine* 87 (1989):81-84; J.J. Paris, R.K. Crones, and J.D. Reardon, "Physician's Refusal of Requested Treatment: The Case of Baby L.," *New England Journal of Medicine* 322 (1990):1012-14.

12   G.E. Taffet, T.A. Teasdale, and R.J. Luchi, "In-Hospital Cardiopulmonary Resuscitation," *Journal of the American Medical Association* 260 (1988):2069-72; D.J. Murphy, A.M. Murray, B.E. Robinson, *et al.,* "Outcomes of Cardiopulmonary Resuscitation in the Elderly," *Annals of Internal Medicine* 111 (1989):199-205; R. Saphir, "External Cardiac Massage: Retrospective Analysis of 123 Cases and Review of the Literature," *Medicine* 47 (1968):73-85; C.O. Hershey and L. Fisher, "Why Outcome of Cardiopulmonary Resuscitation in General Wards is Poor," *Lancet* 1 (1982):31-34.

13   Taffet, Teasdale, and Luchi, "In-Hospital Cardiopulmonary Resuscitation," 2069-72; Saphir, "External Cardiac Massage," 73-85; S.E. Bedell, T.L. Delbanco, E.F. Cook, *et al.,* "Survival After Cardiopulmonary Resuscitation in the Hospital," *New England Journal of Medicine* 309 (1983):570-76; E.A. Rozenbaum and L. Shenkman, "Predicting Outcome of In-Hospital Cardiopulmonary Resuscitation," *Critical Care Medicine* 16 (1988):583-86; M. Urberg and C. Ways, "Survival After Cardiopulmonary Resuscitation for an In-Hospital Cardiac Arrest," *Journal of Family Practice* 25 (1987):41-44; C.A. Kelly, D. Watson, C.M. Hutchinson, *et al.,* "Prognostic Factors in Cardiac Arrest Occurring in a District General Hospital,"*British Journal of Clinical Practice* 40 (1986):251-53; Q.R. Stiles, B.L. Tucker, B.W. Meyer, *et al.,* "Cardiopulmonary Arrest: Evaluation of an Active Resuscitation Program," *American Journal of Surgery* 122 (1971):282-87.

14   Taffet, Teasdale, and Luchi, "In-Hospital Cardiopulmonary Resuscitation," 2069-72; Hershey and Fisher, "Why Outcome of Cardiopulmonary Resuscitation," 31-34; Rozenbaum and Shenkman, "Predicting Outcome," 583-86; Urberg and Ways, "Survival After Cardiopulmonary Resuscitation," 41-44;

Stiles, Tucker, Meyer, *et al.,* "Cardiopulmonary Arrest," 282-87; R.C. Peatfield, R.W. Sillett, D. Taylor, *et al.,* "Survival After Cardiac Arrest in Hospital," *Lancet* 1 (1977):1223-25; R.M. Jeresaty, T.J. Godar, and J.P. Liss, "External Cardiac Resuscitation in a Community Hospital: A Three-Year Experience," *Archives of Internal Medicine* 124 (1969):588-92; G.R. Sowden, D.W. Robins, and P.J.E. Baskett, "Factors Associated with Survival and Eventual Cerebral Status Following Cardiac Arrest," *Anaesthesia* 39 (1984):39-43; F.P. Arena, M. Perlin, and A.D. Turnbill, "Initial Experience with a 'Code-No-Code' Resuscitation System in Cancer Patients," *Critical Care Medicine* 8 (1980):733-35.

15   Murphy, Murray, Robinson, *et al.,* "Outcomes of Cardiopulmonary Resuscitation," 199-205; Saphir, "External Cardiac Massage," 73-75; Bedell, Delbanco, Cook, *et al.,* "Survival," 570-76; Rozenbaum and Shenkman, "Predicting Outcome," 583-86; Kelley, Watson, Hutchinson, *et al.,* "Prognostic Factors," 251-53; H.J. Smith and N.R. Anthonisen, "Results of Cardiac Resuscitation in 254 Patients," *Lancet* 1 (1965):1022-29; A.L. George, B.P. Folk, P.L. Crecelius, *et al.,* "Pre-arrest Morbidity and Other Correlates of Survival After In-Hospital Cardiopulmonary Arrest," *American Journal of Medicine* 87 (1989):28-34; J.M. Hollingsworth, "The Results of Cardiopulmonary Resuscitation: A 3-Year University Hospital Experience," *Annals of Internal Medicine* 71 (1969):459-66.

16   S.J. Camarata, M.H. Weil, P.K. Hanashiro, *et al.,* "Cardiac Arrest in the Critically Ill: A Study of Predisposing Causes in 132 Patients," *Circulation* 44 (1971):688-95.

17   Murphy, Murray, Robinson, *et al.,* 199-205; Saphir, "External Cardiac Massage," 73-85; Bedell, Delbanco, Cook, *et al.,* "Survival After Cardiopulmonary Resuscitation," 570-76; Rozenbaum and Shankman, "Predicting Outcomes," 583-86; Urberg and Ways, "Survival After Cardiopulmonary Resuscitation," 41-44; Kelley, Watson, and Hutchinson, *et al.,* "Prognostic Factors in Cardiac Arrest," 251-53; Peatfield, Sillett, Taylor, *et al.,* "Survival After Cardiac Arrest," 1223-25; Sowden, Robins, and Baskett, "Factors Associated with Survival," 39-43; Hollingsworth, "The Results of Cardiopulmonary Resuscitation," 459-66; J.R. Baringer, E.W. Salzman, W.A. Jones, *et al.,* "External Cardiac Massage," *New England Journal of Medicine* 265 (1961):62-65.

18   Taffet, Teasdale, and Luchi, "In-Hospital Cardiopulmonary Resuscitation," 2069-72; Murphy, Murray, Robinson, *et al.,* "Outcomes of Cardiopulmonary Resuscitation in the Elderly," 199-205; Saphir, "External Cardiac Massage," 73-85; Hershey and Fisher, "Why Outcome of Cardiopulmonary Resuscitation in General Wards is Poor," 31-34; Bedell, Delbanco, Cook, *et al.,* "Survival After Cardiopulmonary Resuscitation in the Hospital," 570-76; Rozenbaum and Shenkman, "Predicting Outcome of In-Hospital Cardiopulmonary Resuscitation," 583-86; Urberg and Ways, "Survival After Cardiopulmonary Resuscitation," 41-44; Kelley, Watson, Hutchinson, *et al.,* "Prognostic Factors in Cardiac Arrest," 251-53; Stiles, Tucker, Meyer, "Cardiopulmonary Arrest," 282-287;

Peatfield, Sillett, Taylor, *et al.*, 1223-25; Jeresaty, Godar, and Liss, "External Cardiac Resuscitation," 588-92; Sowden, Robins, and Baskett, "Factors Associated with Survival," 39-43; Arena, Perlin, and Turnbill, "Initial Experience with a 'Code-No-Code' Resuscitation System," 733-735; Smith and Anthonisen, "Results of Cardiac Resuscitation," 1022-29; George, Folk, Crecelius, *et al.*, "Pre-Arrest Morbidity," 28-34; Hollingsworth, "The Results of Cardiopulmonary Resuscitation," 459-66; Camarata, Weil, Hanashiro, *et al.*, "Cardiac Arrest," 688-95; Baringer, Salzman, Jones, *et al.*, "External Cardiac Massage," 62-65; G.A. Klassen, C. Broadhurst, D.I. Peretz, *et al.*, "Cardiac Resuscitation in 126 Medical Patients Using External Cardiac Massage," *Lancet* 1 (1963):1290-92; B.S. Linn and R.W. Yurt, "Cardiac Arrest Among Geriatric Patients," *British Medical Journal* 2 (1970):25-27; J.F. Lemire and A.J. Johnson, "Is Cardiac Resuscitation Worthwhile?" *New England Journal of Medicine* 286 (1972):970-72; R. Burns, M.J. Graney, and L.O. Nichols, "Prediction of In-Hospital Cardiopulmonary Arrest Outcome," *Archives of Internal Medicine* 149 (1989):1318-21; A. Peschin and C. Coakley, "A Five-Year Review of 734 Cardiopulmonary Arrests," *Southern Medical Journal* 63 (1970):506-510; R.S. Gulati, G.L. Hhan, M.A. Horan, "Cardiopulmonary Resuscitation of Old People," *Lancet* 1 (1983):267-69; J. Castagna, M.H. Weil, H. Shubin, "Factors Determining Survival in Patients with Cardiac Arrest," *Chest* 65 (1974):527-29; E.J. Stemmler, "Cardiac Resuscitation: A One-Year Study of Patients Resuscitated Within a University Hospital," *Annals of Internal Medicine* 63 (1965):613-18; S.R. Himmelhoch, A. Dekker, A.B. Cazzaniga, *et al.*, "Closed-Chest Cardiac Resuscitation," *New England Journal of Medicine* 270 (1964):118-22; G.E. Applebaum, J.E. King, and T.E. Finucane, "The Outcome of CPR Initiated in Nursing Homes," *Journal of the American Geriatric Society* 38 (1990):197-200; T.F. Kaiser, E.P. Kayson, and R.G. Campbell, "Survival After Cardiopulmonary Resuscitation in a Long-Term Care Institution," *Journal of the American Geriatric Society* 34 (1986):909; W.T. Longstreth, L.A. Cobb, C.E. Fahrenbrock, *et al.*, "Does Age Affect Outcome of Out-of-Hospital Cardiopulmonary Resuscitation?" *Journal of the American Medical Association* 264 (1990):2109-10; M.G. Saklayen, (letter to the editor), *Annals of Internal Medicine* 111 (1989):854; M. Gorden and E. Hurowitz, "Cardiopulmonary Resuscitation of the Elderly," *Journal of the American Geriatric Society* 32 (1984):930-34.

19   Gulati, Hhan, and Horan, "Cardiopulmonary Resuscitation of Old People," 267-69; Longstreth, Cobb, Fahrenbrock, *et al.*, "Does Age Affect Outcome of Out-of-Hospital Cardiopulmonary Resuscitation?" 2109-10; D.D. Tresch, T.K. Ranjun, R.G. Hoffman, T.P. Aufderheide, and H.L. Brooks, "Comparisons of Outcome of Paramedic-Witnessed Cardiac Arrest in Patients Younger and Older than Seventy Years," *American Journal of Cardiology* 65 (1990):453-57.

20   Tresch, Ranjun, Hoffman, Aufderheide, and Brooks, "Comparisons of Outcome of Paramedic-Witnessed Cardiac Arrest," 453-57.

21   T. Tomlinson and H. Brody, "Ethics and Communication in Do-Not-Resuscitate Orders," *New England Journal of Medicine* 318 (1988):43-46.

22   S.L. Sivak, "Effect of New York State's Do-Not-Resuscitate Legislation on In-Hospital Cardiopulmonary Resuscitation Practice," *American Journal of Medicine* 88 (1990):108-111.

23   Hackler and Hiller, "Family Consent to Orders Not-to-Resuscitate," 1281-83.

24   Blackhall, "Must We Always Use CPR?" 1281-84; Youngner, "Who Defines Futility?" 2094; Tomlinson and Brody, "Futility and the Ethics of Resuscitation," 1276-80; Council on Ethical and Judicial Affairs, American Medical Association, "Guidelines for the Appropriate Use of Do-Not-Resuscitate Orders," *Journal of the American Medical Association* 265 (1991):1868-71; W.G. Bartholome, "Do Not Resuscitate Orders," *Archives of Internal Medicine* 148 (1988):2345-46.

25   Lo and Steinbrook, "Deciding Whether to Resuscitate," 1561-63; M.A. Lee and C.K. Cassel, "The Ethical and Legal Framework for the Decision Not to Resuscitate," *Western Journal of Medicine* 140 (1984):117-22.

12

The Hidden Issue in Futility Judgments: Justifying Turning the Traditional Logic of Beneficence on Its Head

Laurence B. McCullough

INTRODUCTION

The concept of futility and its ethical implications play a major role in Dr. Brody's response to the question, "Should a terminally ill patient have the right to demand resuscitation?" When resuscitation is reliably judged to be a futile intervention, Dr. Brody argues, there is no obligation, on any of the accepted bases of bioethics, on the part of a physician or any other health-care professional to perform resuscitation. Interestingly, this conclusion is not peculiar to resuscitation, for it, in fact, applies to any medical intervention that fails to protect and promote patient well-being, patient autonomy, the integrity of professionals, and justice. Writing a prescription for antibiotics in the management of a viral upper respiratory tract infection, for example, fails to protect and promote these values and so it, too, would be non-obligatory.

With respect to the latter sort of examples, Dr. Brody's argument is non-controversial and I agree with it.[1] When it comes to CPR, however, Dr. Brody's argument is controversial because it invites health-care professionals to turn the traditional logic of beneficence on its head. Doing so must be justified. This ethical dimension of futility-based limits on patients' demands for intervention has not been given the attention that it deserves in the literature on futility[2] including Dr. Brody's important and influential work.[3] We can still reach Dr. Brody's conclusion, I believe, but only by a more tortured route and, therefore, with more hesitation.

FUTILITY: TWO DISTINCTIONS

The first way station along this route involves some clarifications concerning the concept of futility. First, futility must be distinguished from impossibility. Impossibility means that something cannot be achieved; it is ruled out as even a possibility. By contrast, futility involves a calculus of probability: the greatest probability is that "something" will not be achieved. Therefore, reasonable people should expect that "something" not to occur. Prudently, they should not plan for the future as if the futile "something" will occur. Dr. Brody's formulations of futility as involving "very unlikely" (page 117) outcomes or interventions "which predictably will not work" (page 118) reflect his awareness of this distinction.

There is, on any ethical theory in the history of the West at least, no obligation to attempt the impossible. After all, "ought" does imply "can." By transposition, "cannot" implies the case that "not ought," or no obligation. This line of logical precision cannot be employed regarding the ethics of futility. The conclusion: " something with the highest probability of not occurring need not be sought as a matter of obligation," must be supported by argumentation about the lack of worth of that "something" and the high probability of adverse costs in attempting to bring about its existence against long odds. More on such argumentation shortly.

Second, the "something" with lowest probability of occurrence must be specified, as Schneiderman et al., are correct to point out.[4] The "something" may be a functional effect of a fairly narrow sort, that is, maintenance of one or more physiological functions. The "something" may be some larger benefit: the patient's overall good as a function of the presence and degrees of those physiological functions that could be maintained. Intuitively, most would agree that the latter sort of outcome (overall benefit), rather than the former (mere physiological function), should be the touchstone for judgments of futility.[5] Dr. Brody seems to share this view, as near as I can tell.

This second distinction is not finely made, however. It assumes a qualitative difference between narrow physiological function and overall benefit. But this assumption hides an ethically significant difference, namely, the difference between vitalist and anti-vitalist concepts of the proper end or purpose of medicine and health care, in general. The vitalist holds, roughly, that maintenance of biological function in a human being, even and especially in the absence of cognitive function, is inherently good and therefore obligatory.[6] Anti-vitalists object, typically on the grounds that vitalism is a misreading of the Judeo-Christian tradition, to which, in fact, vitalism makes appeal for its intellectual and ethical validity.[7] This sort of objection, however, is not sufficient to defeat vitalism in bioethics. We live in a pluralistic society, where the Judeo-Christian tradition (whatever it might be) competes with other religious traditions, as well as with secular points of view. Let us, therefore, consider vitalism and anti-vitalism more closely, in the context of philosophical considerations that attempt to span the pluralism of our society.

VITALISM AND ANTI-VITALISM

At times Dr. Brody talks in his paper about situations in which "CPR is predictably nonbeneficial." There is an interesting ambiguity, I think, in the term "nonbeneficial" in such usages.

The first sense of "nonbeneficial" is that CPR will most probably not produce a benefit, even in the narrow sense of continued cardiopulmonary function, but will *not,* on balance, be harmful. CPR is "nonbeneficial" in the sense of being pointless, but not harmful. There is no obligation in beneficence-based clinical judgment to attempt the pointless but not harmful. Interestingly, neither is there a prohibition against such an attempt. Like the flipped coin that lands on its side,[8] we are free to undertake the pointless or not. The vitalist may elect aggressive management, without strong objection from the anti-vitalist. The anti-vitalist may elect non-aggressive management, without strong objection from the vitalist. That is, sometimes nonaggressive management is futile *vis-a-vis* narrow physiological function, and so is futile even on vitalist grounds. *A fortiori,* it is futile on anti-vitalist grounds. Hence, this first sense of "nonbeneficial" can be understood to be futile without rejecting vitalism.

There is a second sense of "non-beneficial,"[6] however. This sense concerns those outcomes that are not reliably expected to produce benefit, in the narrow physiological sense, but are reliably expected to risk serious, far-reaching, and irreversible harm: harm that is reliably judged not to be worth the low probability of achieving mere physiological function. This sense of "non-beneficial" concerns pointless and harmful interventions, as distinct from pointless but not harmful interventions.

At this juncture, the argument against vitalism must be undertaken, for the vitalist may still insist that the attempt to restore function be undertaken, while the anti-vitalist will claim that the cost of doing so is too high. The difference here can be stated in the following terms.

First, we hear from the vitalist. Beneficence-based clinical judgment endorses the view that aggressive management of patients is justified because aggressive management reduces both mortality and morbidity. After both mortality and morbidity have been reduced to the greatest extent possible, and if incremental reductions of mortality can only be achieved at the price of some persistent rate of morbidity, so be it. This is because no rate or form of morbidity should be regarded as a worse outcome than mortality, and because the only way to reduce morbidity at this point is to allow mortality to rise. The death of patients, even as a result of non-aggressive management, should never be countenanced as a means to reducing morbidity. That is, there is *no* such beneficence-justified outcome as unnecessary morbidity, because an unnecessary and unjustified increased risk of mortality is unavoidably involved in trying to reduce, and thus prevent, unnecessary morbidity.

Second, we hear from the anti-vitalist. Beneficence-based clinical judgment endorses the view that aggressive management of patients is justified because aggressive management reduces both mortality and morbidity. On this point, vitalism and anti-vitalism agree. Here's the difference: after both mortality and morbidity have been reduced as much as possible, and if incremental reductions of mortality can only be achieved at the price of some persistent rate of qualitatively significant morbidity, this is not a justified outcome. This is because some forms of morbidity should ethically be regarded as worse outcomes than mortality. Therefore, increasing mortality is justified as the only way to reduce such morbidity. The death of patients should be countenanced as a necessary means to reducing such morbidity. That is, there *is* such a beneficence-justified outcome as unnecessary morbidity, even if increased mortality is unavoidably --but now justifiably--involved as the means to reduce (and thus prevent) such morbidity. There is a buttressing consideration. If, as Hoffman points out (page 130), the likelihood of a successful resuscitation in a patient with renal failure is only 4 percent, should all patients be subjected to the morbidity of futile cardiopulmonary resuscitation in order to prevent so few deaths? It is not all clear, this line of argument would claim, that these few patients have the right to secure their survival at the price of causing the vast majority (97 percent) of patients with renal failure to suffer unto death.

Put side by side with the argument of the anti-vitalists--that is, all advocates of the Brody-type for futility judgments--the vitalist position doesn't look so bad. The vitalist need not enter the uncharted, perilous ethical and clinical territory of ethically unjustified "unnecessary morbidity," while the anti-vitalist must. Moreover, the anti-vitalist in the end is really concerned with higher central nervous system function, the necessary condition for overall benefit. As a consequence, the anti-vitalist must show that one physiological function, cognition, say, is in all cases more to be valued than another, for example, normal sinus cardiac rhythm.

There is yet another conceptual thicket. The vitalist represents a reasonable version of the traditional logic of beneficence, that is, accepting incremental risk of morbidity as the price of incremental reduction of mortality. By contrast, the anti-vitalist turns that logic on its head, by accepting incremental risk of mortality as the price of incremental reduction of morbidity. This is, surely, a move that is full of conceptual and ethical thickets. The literature on the ethics of futility has seemed unaware of the existence of this dimension of its implicit anti-vitalism. I hope that I have succeeded in bringing this dimension to light. It is high time, therefore, to plunge into the conceptual and ethical thickets of anti-vitalism, so that we can identify and defend a fully articulated concept of futility.

ENTERING CONCEPTUAL AND ETHICAL THICKETS

Turning the traditional logic of beneficence on its head requires anti-vitalists to clarify and justify the concept of unnecessary morbidity. Consider unnecessary death. It would be defined as any death not impossible to prevent. Could unnecessary morbidity, by analogy, be defined as any disease, injury, handicap, pain, or suffering that is not impossible to prevent? This won't do. Consider the following.

Some forms of morbidity, especially pain and suffering, are necessary and acceptable means to prevent or treat the risk of mortality or even forms of morbidity (disease, injury, handicap) other than pain and suffering. Such pain and suffering usually are thought to be temporary. Hence, the mere preventable occurrence of morbidity cannot make it unnecessary; morbidity must be more than momentary to be considered possibly unnecessary. That is, for morbidity to become unnecessary, it must be non-preventable and chronic in nature.

Some pain and suffering, and some diseases, injuries, and handicaps, are both non-preventable and chronic. But, while non-preventable, they are of low or manageable intensity. They permit patients with them to live in and through them.[9] Such morbidity can be distracting, even at times demanding, but not overwhelming. Such morbidity has a point. So, unnecessary morbidity has to do with its chronicity and pointless impact in the life of a patient.

That impact can be pointless when morbidity with highest probability excludes all other outcomes but itself and death. Morbidity is intense, consuming, and is only with lowest probability, a means to relief of other morbidity or mortality. Such morbidity is becoming pointless. On this the vitalist can agree, obliging the anti-vitalist to show why some forms of pointless morbidity are all and only harmful. This is the case for some morbidity because of the dread that its prospect entails for the patient and physician and the dread that its reality entails for both, the dread of relentless suffering of patient and physician alike.

Such dread is repulsive on the assumption that human beings are essentially actors, constructors of their worlds of relationship and meaning, as Leibniz and many other philosophers correctly teach us. Death, of course, ends action and construction. Only harmful morbidity does so too, but it leaves us alive to experience our relentlessly ceasing to act and to construct. Such morbidity arrests us, and then consumes us, while not helping us. It is the ultimate and ultimately horrifying non-lethal pathology.

Is such morbidity worse than death? Death simply kills one. Only harmful morbidity exhausts one, sucking out one's identity and one's presence to others, while leaving enough presence to oneself to serve as the basis for calamitous, horrendous, relentless loss of escape from morbidity. Hence, one's death is not unnecessary. Indeed, it is the only means to end an only harmfully morbid existence.

The argument must go on, for even if some forms of morbidity are worse than death, beneficence-based judgments that such an outcome should be avoided must countenance the reality that the means to do is increased mortality, including mortality of some patients who might have experienced less than ultimate or even less severe morbidity had they survived. Judgments of futility must accept that some patients will survive a futile intervention with less-than-only-harmful morbidity. For those patients, death *is* unnecessary and worse than the morbidity they would suffer if they survived. That is, the benefit to patients with only harmful morbidities is secured at the price of what the anti-vitalist must agree are unnecessary deaths. Moreover, these unnecessary deaths constitute a harm to patients other than those patients who are benefited by the prevention of unnecessary morbidity.

This is not a matter that can be adequately addressed in terms of respect for autonomy, the second of the values Dr. Brody considers. I can consent to the risks of preventing unnecessary morbidity for myself, but I cannot do so for others, especially those who have never been autonomous.

The basic ethical issue here concerns the fourth value that Dr. Brody considers, justice. Is it fair to place on some, who are unable to consent to it, the risk of unnecessary mortality as the unavoidable price of reducing the risk of unnecessary morbidity for others? This is, I believe, the fundamental ethical issue that we encounter when we turn the traditional logic of beneficence on its head, as Dr. Brody would, correctly, have us do. And we must do so if we are to take futility judgments and their implicit anti-vitalism as seriously as Dr. Brody invites us to take those judgments. Some want to exclude such justice-based considerations from the concept of futility.[10] Dr. Brody is to be saluted because he refuses to do so. As he puts it, forcefully, "To devote such expensive resources to prolonging unconscious life for less than a day seems grotesquely wasteful" (page 120).

Dr. Brody is here too compressed in what he says. It is not just that patients have no right to intervention that is futile, because most likely futile intervention will be only harmful and is least likely to prevent unnecessary death. They also have no right, in justice, to make aggressive management in such cases the norm for all patients where such management is reliably judged to be futile. After all, whether aggressive management should always be the norm is the root issue here. There is no right to such a norm, because to put such a norm into practice (as we now, largely, do) imposes a highly likely risk of causing unnecessary morbidity for most patients as the means to secure the highly unlikely benefit of preventing unnecessary death for a tiny fraction of patients. The quality of the cost to those many other patients is too high in beneficence-based judgment. The cost in human suffering can only be imposed with consent of those at risk, and they are under no obligation to potential survivors to consent.

The cost to those who pay health-care bills (that is, all of us), of course, is enormous in financial terms. But this, by itself, does not make that cost "grotesquely wasteful." Further justification is required for such language. It is found in the virtues. To seek for oneself the highly unlikely outcome of unnecessary death at the highly likely price for many, many others--and perhaps even oneself--of unnecessary morbidity is vanity, indeed vainglory. No one has a positive right to the financial--not to mention human--resources of others to finance vainglory. Hence, consideration of scarce resources cannot be eliminated from the concept of futility.

Finally, the pursuit of vainglory by patients breeds hubris in health-care professionals who lend their services and souls to such folly. The health-care professional who fails to see this becomes a Phaethon who will rend irreparably the integrity of health care, to accent the third value that Dr. Brody considers.

CONCLUSION

Judgments of futility thus involve conceptual and ethical thickets that have been insufficiently explored in the recent literature on futility. If my mapping of those thickets is reliable, we may be able to traverse them with our skins still largely intact. These thickets are rooted in the anti-vitalism that is implicit among advocates, such as Dr. Brody, of futility judgments. I have attempted in this presentation to make that anti-vitalism explicit and to provide an ethical justification for that anti-vitalism. That justification centers on providing a justification for the fundamental ethical commitment underlying futility judgments: turning the traditional logic of beneficence on its head. I hope to have shown that, once we gain some clarity about the concept of unnecessary morbidity, such a justification can be given in terms of the four values to which Dr. Brody appeals, namely beneficence, respect for the patient's autonomy, the integrity of the health care professions, and justice.

If this line of argument holds up to critical scrutiny, what follows for clinical practice? First, when aggressive management is reliably thought to be futile for a group of patients, aggressive management should not be the norm. There should be no ethical presumption in favor of aggressive management as the standard of care when aggressive management is reliably judged to be futile. Second, this should be explained to patients (or to the surrogates of patients not able to make their own decisions) and a recommendation against aggressive management should be made.

Third, the physician should be open to the possibility of significant reasons that the patient may have for wanting aggressive management undertaken. In particular, the patient's reasons for such a request may be based on religious or other serious forms of moral convictions. Such convictions should be respected. Asking the patient to reconsider or respectfully persuading the patient to reconsider, for example, by pointing out that such convictions may not always be well-served by aggressive management, are both consistent with respect for the patient's convictions.

There will be very few cases in which the patient will persist in demanding futile aggressive management. Resistance to such demands is justified only if a convincing account can be given of why the integrity of medical judgment should count more than the integrity of the patient's moral convictions. There is no philosophical argument, of which I am aware, that can settle this issue decisively. Thus, it must be explicitly addressed and decided in the democratic process, that is, by legislatures and courts. In the meantime, fulfilling the patient's request seems obligatory, when that request is based on serious moral convictions.

NOTES

1   A.S. Brett and L.B. McCullough, "When Patients Request Specific Interventions: Defining the Limits of the Physician's Obligation," *New England Journal of Medicine* 315 (1986):1347-51.
2   L.J. Blackhall, "Must We Always Use CPR?" *New England Journal of Medicine* 317 (1987):1281-85; D.J. Murphy, "Do-Not-Resuscitate Orders: Time for Reappraisal in Long-Term Care Operations," *New England Journal of Medicine* 260 (1988):2098-101; J.D. Lantos, S.H. Miles, M.D. Silverstein, and C.B. Stocking, "Survival After Cardiopulmonary Resuscitation in Babies of Very Low Birthweight: Is CPR Futile Therapy?" *New England Journal of Medicine* 318 (1988):91-95; D.J. Youngner, "Who Defines Futility?" *Journal of the American Medical Assiciation* 260 (1988):2094-95; J.C. Hackler and F.C. Hiller, "Family Consent to Orders Not to Resuscitate," *Journal of the American Medical Assiciation* 264 (1990):1281-83; S.J. Youngner, "Futility in Content," *Journal of the American Medical Association* 264 (1990):1295-96; L.J. Schneiderman, N.S. Jecker, and A.R. Jonsen, "Medical Futility: Its Meaning and Ethical Implications," *Annals of Internal Medicine* 112 (1990):949-54.
3   T. Tomlinson and H. Grody, "Ethics and Communication in Do-Not-Resuscitate Orders," *New England Journal of Medicine* 318 (1988):43-46; H. Brody and T. Tomlinson, "In-Hospital Cardiopulmonary Resuscitation," *Journal of the American Medical Association* 261 (1989):1581; T. Tomlinson and H. Brody, "Futility and the Ethics of Resuscitation," *Journal of the American Medical Association* 264 (1990):1276-80.
4   Schneiderman, Jecker, and Jonsen, "Medical Futility."
5   *Ibid.*
6   W.E. May, R. Barry, O. Griese, *et al.,* "Feeding and Hydrating the Permanently Unconsicous and Other Vulnerable Persons," *Issues in Law and Medicine* 3 (1987):203-17.
7   R.A. McCormick, "To Save or Let Die: The Dilemma of Modern Medicine," *Journal of the American Medical Association* 229 (1974):172-76.
8   O.D. Bouwsma, *Philosophical Essays* (Lincoln, NE: University of Nebraska Press, 1965).

9   I.C. Lieb, "The Image of Man in Medicine," *Journal of Medical Philosophy* 1 (1976):162-76.
10   Schneiderman, Jecker, and Jonsen, "Medical Futility."

Part IV

Legal, Ethical, and Religious Issues

13

From "Natural Death" to "Aid-in-Dying": Reflections on the American Judicial Experience

Edward R. Grant and Clarke D. Forsythe

INTRODUCTION

Throughout the primitive world the doctor and the sorcerer tended to be the same person. He with the power to kill had power to cure, including specially the undoing of his own killing activity. With the Greeks, the distinction was made clear. One profession, the followers of Asclepius, were to be dedicated completely to life under all circumstances, regardless of rank, age, or intellect . . . [T]his is a priceless possession which we cannot afford to tarnish, but society is always attempting to make the physician into a killer--to kill the defective child at birth, to leave the sleeping pills beside the bed of the cancer patient. . . . [I]t is the duty of society to protect the physician from such requests.[1]

The idea of mercy killing, as this correspondence of Margaret Mead reminds us, is as old as Hippocrates. Yet, it did not engage serious debate within the modern medical profession until the late nineteenth century. In Great Britain and the United States, the campaign for mercy killing remained an academically remote and politically quixotic enterprise throughout most of this century. The cause was undoubtedly hampered by the memory of what had been done in the name of "euthanasia" during Hitler's Third Reich.[2] Until recent decades, most news accounts of euthanasia did not involve legislative proposals, but isolated instances of mercy killing by physicians, spouses, or the grieved parents of handicapped infants.

In the final quarter of this century, the picture was changed, dramatically, by the 1976 case of Karen Quinlan. Here was an image--a pious Catholic family, devoted to their adopted daughter, who now lay in "twilight" between death and life--that could not be farther from the images which had shrouded the concept of euthanasia for a generation. The effect on public policy was remarkable; the trend is compelling. *In re Quinlan* prompted the passage of so-called living will or "natural death" legislation, the first such statute being the 1976 California Natural Death Act. Today, over forty-five states and the District of Columbia have passed natural death laws. Twenty-five states and the District of Columbia have passed laws permitting the written designation of surrogate decision makers for health-care purposes.[3] At least two other states have passed laws providing for surrogate decision making for incompetent patients when no written instrument is left. In addition, appellate courts in over a dozen states have issued rulings allowing the withdrawal of life-sustaining medical treatment including food and fluids.

The post-*Quinlan* era climaxed in 1990 in the US Supreme Court's first "right to die" case, *Cruzan v. Director, Missouri Department of Health*.[4] There, a narrowly divided court held that the states could require clear and convincing evidence of an incompetent patient's intent before allowing the withdrawal of food and fluids, without violating constitutional rights. Instead of applying the constitutional right of privacy to exclude state regulation along the lines of *Roe v. Wade*, the Court deferred to state regulation in this sensitive area.

Nevertheless, the *Cruzan* decision, of ambiguous import, signalled, or at least coincided with, a fundamental change in the nature of the debate. In the wake of *Cruzan*, the movement for natural death has been superceded by the movement for "aid in dying": direct killing of patients by their physicians. A series of highly publicized mercy killings have placed the issue on the front pages of newspapers and magazines. Derek Humphrey's *Final Exit*, a suicide manual, quickly climbed to the top of the summer 1991 best-seller lists. And in November 1991, the state of Washington became the first state to consider and reject a referendum to legalize physician-assisted suicide. Under Initiative 119,[5] a set of proposed amendments to the Washington Natural Death Act (NDA), competent persons who execute a natural death directive would have been permitted to authorize their physicians to administer a lethal injection. Such "aid-in-dying" could only be given to a conscious patient who requested it in writing. After the defeat of Initiative 119 in Washington, efforts were successful in getting a similar referendum on the California ballot for November 1992.

This chapter will briefly review developments in American jurisprudence in the post-*Quinlan* era and use them to analyze the potential long-range impact of proposals such as Initiative 119. The primary thesis--that, once legalized, active euthanasia cannot be limited to competent, profoundly suffering patients with a terminal illness--proceeds from the fundamental principles established in *Quinlan* and its progeny.[6] The section following this introduction explores the judicial origins of these principles. The final section presents a derivative thesis: that the specific text of Washington Initiative 119 is virtually an invitation to immediate and wide expansion of the euthanasia license.

The American experience from the first "natural death" acts of 1976 to the "aid-in-dying" proposals of 1991 suggest that the practice of active euthanasia, if legalized, will not be limited by conditions of voluntariness or terminal illness. The internal logic of euthanasia, the policy assumptions made by American legislatures, and the legal reasoning employed by American courts, including the adoption of quality-of-life considerations, all support this conclusion. Quite apart from the numerous religious, moral, prudential, and utilitarian arguments that may be engaged in this debate, this conclusion offers substantial grounds for questioning the wisdom of any positive legal warrant for assisted suicide, euthanasia, or mercy killing.

QUINLAN TO *CRUZAN*: JUDICIAL EFFORTS AT LINE DRAWING

Over thirty years ago, Professor Yale Kamisar pointed out that the fundamental trouble with euthanasia legislation is that it seeks "a goal which is *inherently inconsistent*: a procedure for death which *both* (1) provides ample safeguards against abuse and mistake; and (2) is 'quick' and 'easy' in operation."[7] This "Euthanasiast's Dilemma" has become the dilemma of American courts since *Quinlan*. The more reflective of jurists have perhaps learned that, in the realm of euthanasia, "specific plans of enforcement are often much less palatable than the abstract notions they are designed to effectuate." Most, unfortunately, have not grasped this point.

This is borne out in the judicial opinions governing the withdrawal of life-sustaining treatment from incompetent patients. The seminal case, *Quinlan*, declared that incompetent patients enjoy a right to refuse life-sustaining medical treatment, that the right is of constitutional stature, and that such right can be exercised for them, through the vehicle of "substituted judgment," by a family member or guardian. Put simply, the principle of autonomy, increasingly protected in the past thirty years under American constitutional law, was utilized to protect a decision made *not* by the patient, but by others *for* the patient. According to the author of the Missouri Supreme Court's opinion in *Cruzan v. Harmon*, the *Quinlan* doctrine requires "wholesale mutations of the principles of law on which it rests."[8] To compensate, courts have often erected elaborate safeguards or limitations on the withdrawal or withholding of medical treatment which create the impression that such decisions are primarily a legal or juridical affair and not a question of medical judgment. In *Quinlan* and its progeny, we gain insight into how the abstract notions of liberty and autonomy actually play out in a scheme of licit euthanasia.

A Clarification of Terms

For reasons set forth at length elsewhere, "euthanasia" is defined here as "the wilful and deliberate killing of oneself or another out of motives of compassion, the desire to save another from suffering, or to promote the 'dignity' of the suffering person." Euthanasia is to be distinguished, although not always easily so, from decisions to withdraw from terminally ill patients medical treatment that is regarded as futile or unduly burdensome in light of imminent death.[9] In some cases life-sustaining medical procedures are withdrawn from patients who would not otherwise have died. This has sometimes been referred to as passive euthanasia.

Withdrawal of Life-Sustaining Treatment from Competent Patients

Withdrawal of treatment so as to deliberately cause death has been protected in certain cases by the common law right of self-determination or constitutional rights of liberty or privacy. In *Cruzan*, the US Supreme Court assumed, without ruling on the question, that a competent person has a constitutionally protected liberty interest in refusing unwanted medical treatment. The court also did not rule on whether this liberty interest would likewise protect a decision to forego tube feeding, stating "[w]e do not think a State is required to remain neutral in the face of an informed and voluntary decision by a physically-able adult to starve to death." Yet, Justice O'Connor, in a concurring opinion, declared that "the liberty guaranteed by the Due Process Clause must protect, if it protects anything, an individual's deeply personal decision to reject medical treatment, including the artificial delivery of food and water."[10] The four dissenting justices in *Cruzan* clearly agreed with Justice O'Connor on this point. Two of these four dissenters--Justices Brennan and Marshall--have since resigned.

However, state courts have addressed the question more directly and endorsed voluntary passive euthanasia for competent patients. In 1987, a Colorado trial court ruled that a thirty-four-year-old patient, Hector Rodas, left quadriplegic and in a locked-in state after a drug-induced stroke, had a constitutional right to refuse all medical treatment, including a gastrostomy tube, even though this would terminate his life.[11] The testimony at the hearing established clearly that Mr. Rodas' intent was suicidal. The court ruled that since a constitutional right was at stake, the hospital had the burden to prove, by clear and convincing evidence, that Mr. Rodas was incompetent when he expressed this intent. The court found that the hospital did not meet this burden, and ruled that the hospital must withdraw the feeding tube and continue to care for Mr. Rodas until his death. Shortly after this ruling, Mr. Rodas' attorneys, affiliated with the American Civil Liberties Union, filed a petition seeking a declaration that Mr. Rodas be permitted to receive a lethal injection to end his life. However, this petition was almost immediately withdrawn and the opportunity for judicial consideration of active euthanasia was averted.

In a more celebrated case, that of Elizabeth Bouvia, a California court of appeal ruled in 1986 that she had a constitutional right to refuse medical treatment, including nutrition and hydration, even if the effect of that refusal was to commit suicide. The court held that the decision was neither a medical question, nor one for the courts. "It is a moral and philosophical decision that, being a competent adult, is [Ms. Bouvia's] alone."[12] Justice Compton, concurring, went further and wrote:

> Elizabeth apparently has made a conscious and informed choice that she prefers death to continued existence in her helpless and, to her, intolerable condition. I believe that she has an absolute right to effectuate that decision. The state and the medical profession instead of frustrating her desire, should be attempting to relieve her suffering by permitting and in fact assisting her to die with ease and dignity. The fact that she is forced to suffer the ordeal of self-starvation to achieve her objective is in itself inhumane. The right to die is an integral part of our right to control our own destinies so long as the rights of others are not affected. That right should, in my opinion, include the ability to enlist assistance from others, including the medical profession, is making death as painless and quick as possible.[13]

Justice Compton's opinion is at the extreme end of the spectrum of opinions permitting passive euthanasia, but his reasoning is clearly relevant to the future of euthanasia jurisprudence.

Two 1990 opinions from the high courts of Nevada and New York confirm the emerging consensus in favor of a *competent* patient's virtually absolute right to refuse medical treatment, regardless of condition or prognosis. In *Fosmire v. Nicoleau*,[14] the New York Court of Appeals held that a woman who had hemorrhaged after a caesarean section had a common law and statutory right to refuse blood transfusions that her doctors claimed were necessary to save her life. The woman's intent was not suicidal; she objected to the blood transfusions on religious grounds, although the court did not reach the question of religious freedom in addressing her case. In *McKay v. Bergstedt*,[15] the Nevada Supreme Court relied on *Cruzan* to hold that a thirty-one-year-old quadriplegic had a constitutional liberty interest to refuse continued use of a respirator to sustain his life and echoed the opinion in *Bouvia*:

> At some point in the life of a competent adult patient, the present or prospective quality of life may be so dismal that the right of the individual to refuse treatment or elect a discontinuance of artificial life support must prevail over the interest of the state in preserving life. In instances where the prospects for a life of quality are smothered by physical pain and suffering, only the sufferer can determine the value of continuing mortality. . . . The State's interest in the preservation of life relates to meaningful life.[16]

The court demurred, however, at explicitly endorsing suicide: "there is a substantial difference between the attitude of a person desiring non-interference with the natural consequences of his or her condition and the individual who desires to terminate his or her life by some deadly means, either self-inflicted or through the agency of another."

Withdrawal from Incompetent Patients

Incompetent patients, however, have been the focus of the seminal cases concerning the "right to die," most often, patients who have no prognosis for returning to a condition of competence. The two most important of these cases --*Quinlan* and *Cruzan*--act as chronological bookends to the debate and judicial developments of the past fifteen years.

Philosopher Paul Ramsey claimed that the rationale of *Quinlan* (and, he might later have added, its progeny) had "gone a long way toward obliterating the distinction between voluntary and involuntary euthanasia and weakening legal protection of life from involuntary euthanasia."[17] Ramsey did not claim that the removal of the respirator would itself constitute euthanasia. Rather, he focused on the legal reasoning that permitted Karen Quinlan's constitutional right of privacy--indistinguishable here from the concept of personal autonomy--to protect a decision made by another person, her father. Of course, in her disabled state, Karen had no autonomy--no capacity of governing herself --or at the very least, no means of exercising such governance. The New Jersey court ruled that although the *capacity* for autonomy had been lost, the *right* to autonomy had not. Rather, the right must be preserved, by lodging it with the decision-making capacity of a family member or guardian.

Neither *Quinlan*, nor its progeny, yet support the blanket transfer of autonomy rights to surrogates in all cases. *Quinlan* limited its relief, at that time, to a small number of patients: those with no prognosis of recovery to a cognitive, sapient state. Such patients, the New Jersey court held, had a constitutional right to be allowed to die without further medical intervention, a right not trumped by the state interest in preserving life. In evaluating Professor Ramsey's claim, therefore, it is important not to overreach in interpreting *Quinlan*, or to focus solely on its novel declaration of constitutional doctrine. Chief Justice Hughes strove to discern and articulate a consensus that death resulting from the withdrawal of mechanical life-support from a patient such as Miss Quinlan was contrary neither to medical ethics, nor to the law of homicide.

Nor is it fair to suggest that *Quinlan* or its progeny have unleashed an unfettered, nationwide practice of euthanasia-by-omission. Indeed, life-sustaining medical treatment is both widely available and widely utilized in American medicine. Thousands of treatment-withdrawal decisions are made in American hospitals each day. It is virtually impossible to assess in how many cases inevitable death is allowed to occur, and in how many cases death is deliberately willed. Moreover, as the law has recognized since before *Quinlan*, the difficulty of distinguishing between such cases virtually negates the possibility of prosecution for passive euthanasia. Numbers, however, are not all that matter. The relatively small number of cases in which handicapped infants were left untreated and allowed to die, for example, did not mitigate the moral reprehensibility of such decisions, or the public and political outcry against them.

What, then, of the charge that *Quinlan* would open the door to involuntary euthanasia? Do these data, and the opinion's own limitations, refute the claim? To the contrary: for two reasons, the claim seems to be validated by the events of the past decade and the prospects for the next. First, *Quinlan* did not declare a set of moral-legal principles regarding care of the dying, but, rather, followed what it viewed to be the attitudes of society and medical profession on the subject. *Quinlan* postulated that if the patient were "miraculously lucid" for a moment, she "could" consent to the withdrawal of the respirator. The court added that her putative decision, as expressed by her family, "should be accepted by a society, the overwhelming majority of whose members would, we think, in similar circumstances, exercise such a choice in the same way for themselves or for those closest to them."[18] Legalizing active euthanasia would affect this social consensus and the courts' interpretation of it. Should an "overwhelming majority"--or even a simple majority--of society conclude that terminally ill patients may call upon the active cooperation of their physicians in causing their deaths, it would follow, from *Quinlan*, that this right should be available to incompetent patients as well. *Quinlan* was silent on the question of active euthanasia *per se*. But it was attentive to the moral and medical culture that it perceived as supporting decisions to withdraw treatment from patients in a dying state. Should society accept active euthanasia upon the request of a competent dying patient, a court relying upon *Quinlan* could easily rule that it should likewise accept the administration of active euthanasia for similarly situated patients who are incompetent.

Second, *Quinlan's* blurring of the distinction between voluntary and involuntary decision making is of utmost importance as long as euthanasia proponents rely upon alleged "voluntariness" as both the sole warrant for mercy killing and the conclusive safeguard against abuse. Even if we accept the euthanasia lobby's claim that mercy killing must necessarily be limited to cases of voluntary consent--a claim that is open to serious question[19]--we must reckon with what the American courts have done to the concepts of "autonomy" and "voluntariness" in the context of passive euthanasia cases. These terms have been dismantled and re-arranged to protect decisions which, while not positively contradicted by the expressed will of the patient, are in essence the decisions of third parties. One does not have to reject the validity (or even necessity) of such decisions in order to seriously question whether they should receive *legal* protection under the guise of the patient's personal liberty. After *Quinlan*, voluntary consent cannot be considered an immutable concept, and autonomy is not a bedrock upon which a limited license for euthanasia can be firmly anchored. Rather, under the doctrine of substituted judgment, the autonomy of incompetent patients is conditioned upon what is judged appropriate by their friends and families and approved by society and the medical profession.

Even where substituted judgment is rejected in favor of a standard of "clear and convincing evidence" of a patient's intent, as is the case in Missouri under *Cruzan*, truly voluntary consent may not be required. This is illustrated by the denouement of the *Cruzan* case itself, where her parents brought to court new evidence of statements allegedly made twelve years earlier by Nancy when she was employed as a teacher's assistant for handicapped children. During the process of feeding a disabled child, Nancy purportedly said that she would never want to be tube-fed if she were left in a debilitated condition after an accident. The court found this to satisfy the clear and convincing evidence standard, granted authority to remove the tube feeding, and Nancy died two weeks later. Thus, an evidentiary standard more strict than substituted judgment still may permit vague and remote statements to constitute "clear" evidence of an intention to die. Should the acceptable means of death be expanded to include active euthanasia, there is no reason to conclude that such evidence would not likewise be accepted as constituting the requisite voluntary consent.

EUTHANASIA BY ANY OTHER NAME: AID IN DYING

"Dr. Death" and "Debbie": Some Lingering Questions

Similar lessons can be drawn from the remarkable series of assisted suicides linked to Dr. Jack Kevorkian. Dr. Kevorkian--who had previously spent decades advocating that condemned prisoners be given the right to consent to the performance of lethal medical experiments under deep anesthetic in lieu of execution gained notoriety in 1990 for his "suicide machine," first used in the death of Janet Adkins. Mrs. Adkins, a fifty-two-year-old woman in the early stages of Alzheimer's disease, travelled to Michigan after hearing about the "machine," a relatively simple device permitting autonomous intravenous injection of an anesthetic, and then, a fatal dose of potassium chloride. It was widely speculated that since Dr. Kevorkian had not actually operated the intravenous device, other than to place the intravenous line, Michigan authorities would not be able to prosecute him. Although homicide charges were eventually filed, they were dismissed, after a preliminary hearing, on grounds that Michigan had no statutory prohibition on assisted suicide and that Dr. Kevorkian's actions did not constitute homicide. Two months later, however, a circuit court entered a permanent injunction against Dr. Kevorkian's use of the suicide machine or his participation in the suicide of any person. Since that time, however, Dr. Kevorkian has participated in three other killings, the most recent in April 1992.

The death of Janet Adkins was not the first instance of physician participation in active euthanasia or "mercy killing," nor was it the first in which the physician suffered no legal penalty. Doctors have also, wittingly or unwittingly, "assisted" in the death of their patients through prescriptions of medicine later taken by the patient in a lethal overdose. The impact of the Kevorkian-Adkins case upon the euthanasia argument, and euthanasia in practice, is a story whose conclusion is yet unwritten. However, several lessons can already be drawn from the incident which have an undeniable relevance to the legal discussion.

First, Janet Adkins was not a "patient" of Dr. Kevorkian. She first consulted him, two days before her death, for the sole purpose of using his advertised device. This raises the salient question: if active euthanasia is legalized, who will perform it? Specifically, will the patient's attending physician undertake the task? Although such participation is assumed in most euthanasia literature, it should not be taken for granted. The likelihood that the attending physician, after applying his professional skills to cure disease, alleviate pain, and promote health, would willingly accept a direct role in causing the patient's death is an entirely unproven hypothesis with profound implications. As Margaret Mead noted, the impact would be manifested in the physician's own professional self-definition, as well as in the physician-patient relationship. Many, if not most, physicians would balk at this role. They would respond to a patient's or family's plea for euthanasia by addressing the underlying cause, whether it be pain, fear, or depression. Such care would, hopefully, dissuade many patients and families from requesting euthanasia, but not all. If euthanasia were legal, therefore, a small coterie of doctors would likely become the "euthanasia specialists." Presumably, such physicians would not have long-term relationships of caring for patients who request euthanasia from them. Thus, the presumption against killing, as manifested through the fabric of the physician-patient relationship, would not exist. The condition of Mrs. Adkins prior to her death relatively healthy, active, and mentally competent shows how widespread the euthanasia license can become when this presumption against killing is abandoned.

Second, any "informed consent" given to administration of euthanasia may be compromised by inadequate counseling on treatment alternatives and research, patient fear, family pressure, and the judgment of the physician that euthanasia is the proper course of action. In the civil proceeding against Dr. Kevorkian, for example, Judge Alice Walker made the following findings regarding a videotape of an interview between Dr. Kevorkian and Mrs. Adkins:

> The evidence surrounding Mrs. Adkins's desires is too sparse for this Court to factually find that Mrs. Adkins wanted to commit suicide. Mr. Adkins did most of the talking for his wife on the videotape. Dr. Kevorkian failed to probe Mrs. Adkins's limited responses of "wanting to get out" and "self-deliverance." At no time on the tape did Mrs. Adkins tell Dr. Kevorkian that she wanted to commit suicide or end her life, or that she wanted Dr. Kevorkian to immediately put her to death. Dr. Kevorkian appeared to be in a hurry on the tape, and exhibited little knowledge in understanding and communicating with an Alzheimer's patient. He also displayed a lack of knowledge and ability to obtain an informed consent by failing to explain the need for the procedure, the alternatives available, the risk involved, the implications of the procedure, the result if the procedure were not done and the benefits the patient would have from the procedure.

Finally, the Kevorkian case occurs at a time when some voices of organized medicine are indicating greater tolerance of physician participation in euthanasia and calling for open debate on the question. In March 1991, the *New England Journal of Medicine* published Dr. Timothy Quill's account of his decision to prescribe barbiturates for a terminally ill cancer patient, Diane, knowing that his patient intended to use the pills to commit suicide in the event that she "lost control of herself and her own dignity." Dr. Quill's case was presented to a New York grand jury, which refused to return an indictment. He said in the aftermath that he hoped the case will be used to stimulate further debate "about the options we allow for severely suffering persons."[20]

However, Dr. Quill's testament was not the first foray by a major medical publication into the subject. That honor belongs to the 1988 publication by the *Journal of American Medical Association* of "It's Over Debbie," an anonymous account of the euthanasia death of a twenty-year-old woman dying of ovarian cancer.[21] A study of that case, and the comparative reactions of the medical community and euthanasia advocates, demonstrates significant movement on the issue in the three years between the two articles. The author of "Debbie," a medical resident, had been called to the patient's bedside at 3:00 am to respond to her complaints of sleeplessness, vomiting, and discomfort. The patient's only words to the doctor were, "Let's get this over with." He ordered 20 mg. of morphine from the nurses' station, injected it by syringe, and watched the patient die. Critics, including proponents of legalized euthanasia, condemned the abrupt manner of the patient's death, the apparently unilateral decision of the physician to offer euthanasia, and the highly questionable manner of obtaining the patient's consent, as well as the physician's violation of the Hippocratic maxim.[22] However, accepting the account at face value, the patient did at least fit the classic narrow category of patients for whom euthanasia is often proposed: competent, conscious of pain, and terminally ill from incurable disease.

Janet Adkins, on the other hand, arguably fit only one of these criteria: competence. The purported ground for this mercy killing was to relieve her *fear* of suffering *in the future*. Furthermore, if she were suffering from Alzheimer's disease, her ability to consent to her own death might be questioned. In any event, the questions raised about "Debbie's" consent to euthanasia might likewise be raised about Dr. Kevorkian's manner of obtaining consent from Janet Adkins: he was not qualified to perform a physical examination of the patient, he refused the advice of the patient's attending physician against use of the suicide machine, and he has no specialized training in the type of disorder with which Mrs. Adkins was afflicted.

The killing of "Debbie" was an outrageous but spontaneous action, taken in a hard case, and not overtly calculated to challenge legal authorities. The death of Mrs. Adkins was virtually staged to incite legal action, and comes as close as any death could to exemplifying a public policy of euthanasia on demand. The fact should not be lost on anyone who believes that active euthanasia should, or can, be limited to cases of extreme suffering and terminal illness.

The Washington and California Proposals

Fifteen years after *Quinlan*, Initiative 119 appeared on a statewide referendum ballot in Washington in November 1991.[23] Proposition 119 would have amended the state's existing Natural Death Act to permit the administration, by a physician, of "aid-in-dying," defined as:

> the form of medical service provided in person by a physician that will end the life of a conscious and mentally competent qualified patient in a dignified, painless, and humane manner, when requested voluntarily by the patient through a written directive.

Ordinarily, the legislative condition that "aid in dying" can only take place with the consent of a competent patient could be expected to limit the practice to that category of patients. Courts would be loathe to ignore such an important component of the statutory scheme. Yet, as we have previously seen, the jurisprudence of autonomy spawned by *Quinlan* does not constitute an ordinary situation. These cases have proceeded from the assumption that competent patients enjoy a common-law right, if not a constitutional right, to refuse medical treatment. Through the vehicle of substituted judgment, they held, that right can be exercised even if the patient is not competent. If the law is now amended to give competent patients the right to request lethal measures from their physicians, would the same principles of "substituted judgment" permit third parties to request "aid in dying" for incompetent patients?

The case law strongly suggests that this will be so. Remember *Quinlan's* invocation of the popular consensus in favor of removing treatment in certain cases; if that consensus moves to embrace lethal injections, why should this "benefit" be denied those who cannot speak for themselves? A series of Washington Supreme Court opinions explicitly holds that the right to refuse treatment extends to patients who are permanently unconscious and left no advanced directive,[24] to patients who were never competent, and to patients who are not unconscious, but severely debilitated and terminally ill. And it is difficult to believe that the California courts, which protected Elizabeth Bouvia's right to starve herself to death, would, once "aid in dying" is endorsed by the populace, deny that "benefit" to an incompetent patient in similar circumstances.

If it were perfectly legal for a physician to kill a patient as long as that patient had made a written request, would not the physician be inclined to kill an identical patient who requested euthanasia, but had not signed a written form? What of a patient who is incompetent but clearly suffering?

Scores of judicial opinions and medico-legal commentaries reject the proposition that the refusal of medical treatment can be limited to circumstances where a living will or other directive is executed, or where a court has reviewed the case. Once public policy endorses active euthanasia as an acceptable option for the terminally ill, this same dynamic can be expected to operate.

Some physicians will test the boundaries of the law publicly; others may be expected to do so more quietly. In any event, the aid-in-dying law can not ensure that such "wildcat" euthanasia will not occur, and it is just as plausible to argue that such incidents will increase, as medicine and society become accustomed to the practice of active euthanasia as an alternative to the suffering and burdens imposed by terminal illness.

Although each of the previous points concerns the possible expansion of aid in dying beyond the scope specified in the initiative, they are not, technically, "slippery slope" arguments, if that metaphor is understood to mean what *might* happen once the barrier against killing by physicians is removed. Rather, most of these arguments stem from an analysis of what the law will, in fact, become if a statute such as those proposed in Washington and California is enacted.

CONCLUSION

Legalization of euthanasia in the United States will not occur in a vacuum. A complex jurisprudence of death and dying has been created over the past fifteen years, and it is this body of law that will guide the application, and probable extension, of the initial grants of legal authority to commit euthanasia. The circumstances in which euthanasia will be permitted will neither be limited to the terminally ill who are imminently dying, nor to those who are competent to give their consent. At the very least, legalization of euthanasia will include "advance directives" of the form now used to express a refusal of life-sustaining treatment. Most likely, it will also include "substituted judgments" by family members to permit direct killing of incompetent patients who are terminally ill or permanently unconscious. Finally, those who are competent may be able to obtain euthanasia, as did Janet Adkins, because they fear the ultimate consequences of a disease with which they are diagnosed. It is pointless to speculate how wide the euthanasia license may spread when measured in numbers of deaths. Such data is elusive even in the Netherlands, where active euthanasia has been allowed, despite formal legal prohibitions, for almost 20 years.[25] We must understand, however, that in granting a "right" to aid in dying, we would be embarking on a path of potentially far broader consequence than the Dutch approach of discretionary non-prosecution. "Rights" are powerful entities in American law and culture, and defy most attempts to circumscribe them. Before embracing the "right not to have rights," these consequences must be weighed. For once this right is embraced, it will be difficult to circumvent or control.

NOTES

1   M. Meade, quoted in M. Levine, *Psychiatry and Ethics* (G. Braziller, 1972):324-5.
2   Professor Karl Binding and Alfred Hoche proposed the "Release of life unworthy of life" in their seminal 1920 text, cited as a philosophical influence

upon those who later engineered the brutalities of Nazi euthanasia and human experimentation. A. Hoche and K. Binding, *Die Freigabe der Vernichtung lebensunwerten Leven: Ihr Mass und Ihre Form* (Leipzig, Germany: Felix Meiner, 1920). The title is translated as "The Permission for the Destruction of Life Unworthy of Life." See also F. Wertham, "The Geranium in the Window," from *A Sign for Cain*, reprinted in *Death, Dying, and Euthanasia*, eds. D.J. Horan and D. Mall (Frederick, MD: University Publications of America, 1980); R. Lifton, *The Nazi Doctors* (New York: Basic Books, 1986):45-48, 58. See also L. Alexander, "Medical Science Under Dictatorship," *New England Journal of Medicine* 39, no.47 (1949): "Whatever proportions the [Nazi] crimes finally assumed, it became evident of all who investigated that they had started from small beginnings. The beginnings at first were merely a subtle shift in emphasis in the basic attitude of the physicians. It started with the acceptance of the attitude, basic in the euthanasia movement, that there is such a thing as a life not worthy to be lived."

3   See generally A. Meisel, *The Right to Die* (New York: Wiley, 1989) and R.F. Weir, *Abating Treatment in Critically Ill Patients* (New York: Oxford Press, 1989); current statistics are complied by Concern for Dying, 250 W. 57th St., New York, NY 10107.

4   *Cruzan v. Director, Missouri Department of Health* 110 S. Ct. 2841 (1990).

5   Initiative 119 was sponsored by Washington Citizens for Death with Dignity, a political action committee of the Hemlock Society. Case, "Dying Made Easy," *National Review* (4 November 1919): 25-26. It was opposed by the members of the Washington State Medical Association (WSMA) by a vote of 562 to 543. "Physicians vote down euthanasia," *Spokesman-Review and Spokane Chronicle*, 23 March 1991, A10. The WSMA governing board also opposed the initiative. D. Glamser, "Washington state debates death with dignity," *USA Today*, 23 September 1991, 3A. The Washington Hospital Association also opposed the initiative. Proponents of Initiative 119 collected at least $1.11 million, six times more money than opponents. "Suicide, abortion backers way ahead in fund raising," *Spokesman-Review and Spokane Chronicle*, 11 September 1991, B2. Initiative 119 was defeated on 5 November 1991.

In the aftermath of the defeat of Initiative 119, a bill was passed in Washington in 1992 that would allow the withdrawal of food and fluids from incompetent patients. House Bill 1481 would allow third-party surrogates to order the removal of life-sustaining treatment, including food and fluids, from an incompetent patient without written or oral evidence of their intent. The bill would effectively overrule *In re Grant*, 109 WA 2d 545, 747 P.2d 445 (1988), modified, 757 P.2d 534 (1988). Initiative 119 was opposed by the Washington State Catholic Conference, but the conference supported HB 1481. "Initiative 119: questions and answers on issues of death and dying," *Inland Register*, 21 March 1991, 6.

6   See E. Grant and C. Cleaver, "A Line Less Reasonable: *Cruzan* and the Looming Debate Over Active Euthanasia," *Maryland Journal of Contemporary*

Legal Issues 2, no.2 (1991):100-03.

7   Y. Kamisar, "Some Non-Religious Views Against Proposed 'Mercy-Kill-ing,' " *Minnesota Law Review* 42, no.6 (1958):981-82.

8   E.D. Robertson, Jr., "Is 'Substituted Judgement' a Valid Legal Concept?" *Issues in Law & Medicine* 5 (1989):197-98.

9   Grant and Cleaver, "A Line Less Reasonable," 101 n. 4; 102-03 n. 10.

10   *Cruzan v. Director, Missouri Department of Health* 110 S.CT 2481, 2852 (1990).

11   *Rodas v. ErkenBrack* 87 CV 142 (Mesa Co., CO, filed 30 January 1987), published in "Complaint for Declaratory Relief in Rodas Case," *Issues in Law & Medicine* 2 (1987):481, 499.

12   *Bouvia v. Superior Court* 179 CA App. 3d, 225 *California Reporter* 297, 305 (1986).

13   *Ibid.*, 225 *California Reporter*, 307 (J. Compton concurring).

14   *Fosmire v. Nicoleau* 75 NY 2d at 218, 226, 551 NY 2d 876, 880, 551 NE 2d 76, 81 (1990).

15   *McKay v. Bergstedt* 801 P.2d 617 (NV 1990).

16   *Ibid.*, 624, 625.

17   P. Ramsey, *Ethics at the Edge of Life* (New Haven, CT: Yale University Press):294.

18   *In re Quinlan* 70 NJ at 41, 355 A.2d at 664.

19   Kamisar, "Some Non-Religious Views," 1013-29.

20   T. Quill, "Death and Dignity: A Case of Individual Decision Making," *New England Journal of Medicine* 324 (7 March 1991):691-94.

21   "It's Over, Debbie" (anonymous letter to the editor), *Journal of the American Medical Association* 259 (1988):272.

22   Letters, *Journal of the American Medical Association* 259 (1988):2094-98.

23   See generally A. Jonsen, "Initiative 119: What Is at Stake?" *Commonweal* (9 August 1991, special supplement):466; C. Gomez, "Euthanasia: Consider the Dutch," *Commonweal* (9 August 1991):469; F. Kass, "Why Doctors Must Not Kill," *Commonweal* (9 August 1991): 472; D. Callahan, " 'Aid-in-Dying': The Social Dimensions," *Commonweal* (9 August 1991):476. R.I. Misbin, "Physicians' Aid in Dying," *New England Journal of Medicine* 325 (1991):1307-11.

24   *In the Matter of the Welfare of Bertha Colyer* 99 WA 2d 114, 660 P2d 738 (1983).

25   C. Gomez, *Regulating Death: Euthanasia and the Case of the Netherlands* (New York: Free Press, 1991).

14

Sovereignty, Stewardship, and the Self: Religious Perspectives on Euthanasia

Courtney S. Campbell

The moral and political debate in our culture over physician-assisted suicide and voluntary active euthanasia[1] has evolved to the point that it has become a matter to be decided in the voting booth. In November of 1991, citizens of the state of Washington defeated (by 54 percent to 46 percent) the first public referendum ever held on the legalization of "aid in dying."[2] Proponents never-theless have seen, in the over 700,000 votes cast in favor of what was formally known as Initiative 119, mounting public support for such a practice. The public debate that preceded this vote illustrates two important themes that require acknowledgement at the outset in any discussion of religious perspectives on euthanasia.

First, there is no monolithic "religious" position on the question of the morality or legality of active euthanasia. As exemplified in the Washington context by, on the one hand, the strong support for Initiative 119 by the Unitarian Universalist Association, the Pacific Northwest Council of the United Method-ist Church, and the Interfaith Clergy Council, and on the other, by the strong opposition voiced by the Washington State Catholic Conference and the Evangelical Lutheran Church, a diversity of religious argumentation about euthanasia exists, a characteristic that reflects a more general pluralism of religiosity in our culture. In its most general terms, therefore, it is simply mistaken to portray the controversy over euthanasia as a clash of religious versus secular ethics. To ask whether public interest in the euthanasia question is a sign that this culture is a "godless" society is to distort both the religious and nonreligious parameters of the issue.

Secondly, public debate over legalized euthanasia will likely reflect our considerable cultural "dis-ease" over the civic role of religious discourse in a pluralistic society. That uneasiness is most commonly manifested in what I shall refer to as the "So what?" principle. This principle affirms that in a society constitutionally structured to require a secular rationale for public policy and legislation, religious appeals and arguments at best have limited relevance. Let me again draw on the Washington context to provide an illustration.

Human Life of Washington, an organization opposed to the "aid-in-dying" initiative, was routinely characterized by proponents as a group comprised of "religious fundamentalists." Human Life, however, declared that its opposition was "based not on religious convictions, but solely on grounds of public policy objections."[3] More revealing than the disparity over what "camp" the organization falls under is the assumption shared by both parties: appeals to religious values are misplaced in public-policy considerations. A religious historian once commented that "war is more humane when God is left out of it,"[4] and that attitude seems applicable as well to the context of euthanasia. A civil discussion of the question seems to require keeping appeals to religious convictions on the boundaries of public discourse.

This context of religious pluralism in a secular society needs to be borne in mind in considering specific religious perspectives on euthanasia. In the following, I will engage these perspectives at three levels: (1) a *descriptive and comparative* analysis of major US denominational positions on euthanasia; (2) the *normative* justification for these positions, as displayed in themes of sovereignty, stewardship, and the self; and (3) the *social policy* significance of these positions in public forums of debate.

DENOMINATIONAL DIVERSITY

In beginning this descriptive analysis, two qualifications are in order, both having to do with the moral authoritativeness of denominational positions. Such a position first may not fully represent the diversity of opinion on euthanasia within the denomination. One can no more infer from the Vatican *Declaration on Euthanasia* what the views of any given Roman Catholic might be than one can discern the views of individual medical practitioners from the resolutions on euthanasia adopted by the Council on Judicial and Ethical Affairs of the American Medical Association. Indeed, while the majority of US denominations oppose active euthanasia, general approval of the "right to die" among lay Jews, Roman Catholics, and moderate and liberal Protestants ranges from 70 to 85 percent.

Secondly, denominational positions are frequently offered less as authoritative and binding religious law and more as a set of guidelines or a framework for individual patients and caregivers to rely on in reaching a mutually acceptable decision about end-of-life choices. There is evident a pronounced concern that denominational committees not usurp the locus of moral authority residing in the patient-caregiver relationship.

The positions of US denominations on euthanasia (see Selected Denominational Perspectives on Euthanasia, below) can be differentiated according to ecclesiastical support, deference, silence, or opposition, both informal and formal. In this context, the emergence of the euthanasia debate is commonly seen as a sign of a deeper *crisis in moral values* in our culture, or a "crucible to test the spiritual sensitivities and ethical fiber of contemporary life."[5] A society that idealizes youth but is no longer capable of giving substantive content to questions of the human good seems equally impoverished when assessing the significance of suffering, dying, and death as part of a whole human life. In this void, the emergence of the individual asserting inviolable rights to self-determination becomes intelligible as a way to create meaning through a freely chosen style of life and an authentic manner of death. The denominational diversity reflects in part differences over whether euthanasia is an appropriate way to resolve this crisis in meaning.

Ecclesiastical Support

Advocacy of legislation permitting active legislation currently seems limited to the Unitarian Universalist Association (UUA), and the UUA played a prominent role in promoting Initiative 119 in Washington. The UUA's formal position, expressed in a 1988 General Assembly Resolution, "The Right to Die with Dignity," affirmed two normative values for end-of-life decisions, the "inherent dignity" of human life and the "inviolable right" of self-determination regarding medical treatment options in advance of compromised physiological or mental capacities. Based on these values, the resolution asserts "[t]hat Unitarian Universalists advocate the right to self-determination in dying and the release from civil or criminal penalties of those who, under proper safeguards, act to honor the right of terminally ill patients to select the time of their own deaths; . . ."[6] The values espoused by Unitarians can, of course, be defended on nonreligious grounds, and the resolution appears to ground these values in human nature rather than by appeal to some theistic referent. However, such criteria do not disqualify the Unitarian view from being considered a "religious" position on euthanasia.

Ecclesiastical Deference

A second perspective is reflected in denominations that have historically supported personal autonomy in a collaborative framework of decision making and which, while considering euthanasia a matter for ecclesiastical scrutiny, appear to defer to informed personal and professional choices rather than advance a formal policy on euthanasia. Such a stance is best illustrated in two major denominations, the United Church of Christ (UCC) and the Presbyterian Church (USA). The Eighteenth General Synod of the UCC adopted a resolution in July 1991 that affirms "individual freedom and responsibility to make choices in these matters. It is not claimed that euthanasia is the Christian position, but that the right to choose is a legitimate Christian decision," with euthanasia referring both to "putting to death the incurably ill and to the withdrawing or withholding of artificial means used mainly to prolong life."[7]

The 1990 Presbyterian General Assembly, meanwhile, authorized the preparation of "a study document . . . that examines all sides of both the technical issues and practical questions that theologically encompass euthanasia and assisted death." However, the assembly resolution clearly specifies that the intent of the document is to provide "a reliable resource to both clergy and lay people" who may confront such a decision, and "not . . . to seek a denominational position or policy. . . ."[8]

Ecclesiastical Silence

For many denominations, the articulation of substantive guidelines may await passage of a law making euthanasia a legal option. If a denomination's principal concern is to provide pastoral guidance to its congregants, and not to engage in the broader social policy debate, then the specific issue of euthanasia currently can be avoided by recommending that lay members confronting end-of-life decisions have recourse to a living will or durable power of attorney for health care. However, such an approach might well be reconsidered if such statutes were amended along the lines of an "aid-in-dying" initiative.

This speculation may be relevant for the numerous denominations that have yet to consider the question of euthanasia in any formal capacity, among them the Adventist Church; Assemblies of God; the majority of Baptist congregations, including the American Baptist Churches of the USA, the Baptist Bible Fellowship, and the Free Will Baptists; the Buddhist Churches of America; the Christian Church (Disciples); the Christian Reformed Church in North America; the Church of Christ; and the Pentecostal Church of God. In many instances, ecclesiastical silence on euthanasia is conditioned by prior convictions about ecclesiological structure, in which individual churches are presumed to be autonomous and self-sufficient, and there exists no coordinating superstructure or teaching magisterium to formulate an "official" policy. This would not preclude opposition to euthanasia at the local church level, grounded in appeals to scripture and the sanctity of human life, or support based on personal conscience. While most of these denominations feel no obligation to participate directly in the social policy debate, they may view their communal practices of care for the dying as a form of social witness.

Opposition of the Moral Tradition

A fourth perspective is comprised of denominations in which, while there may be no coordinating body to issue a formal policy statement on euthanasia, there is a historical tradition of moral teaching that would oppose euthanasia.

Representatives of this approach would include the First Church of Christ, Scientist (Christian Science); Jehovah's Witnesses; the Reformed, Conservative, and Orthodox congregations of Judaism; Orthodox denominations, including the Greek Orthodox Archdiocese and the Orthodox Church in America; and the United Pentecostal Church. I want to illustrate this perspective by devoting some attention to Jewish attitudes toward euthanasia.

Contemporary Jewish ethical discussion takes place against the background of the shadow of the Holocaust and is understandably influenced by the involuntary killing of Jews by Nazi doctors. While differences exist among the major Jewish traditions over terminating medical treatment, interdenominational consensus on opposition to active euthanasia is revealed in the following statement composed by scholars from each of the traditions: "The sanctity of human life prescribes that, in any situation short of self-defense or martyrdom, human life be treated as an end in itself. . . . Thus euthanasia may not be performed either in the interest of the patient or of anyone else. Even individual autonomy is secondary to the sanctity of human life and, therefore, a patient is not permitted to end his or her life or be assisted in such suicide by anyone else, be he or she a health care professional, family member, friend, or bystander."[9]

Moreover, rabbinic and medical discussion about euthanasia has been articulated within each branch of Judaism. Within Reformed Judaism, for example, the following responsum has attained substantial authoritativeness:

Q: "What is the Jewish attitude toward euthanasia?"
A: "Jewish tradition makes a clear distinction between, on the one hand, . . . positive steps which may hasten death, and on the other hand, avoiding matters which may hinder a peaceful death. . . . We would not endorse any positive steps leading toward death. We would recommend pain-killing drugs which would ease the remaining days of a patient's life. We would reject any general endorsement of euthanasia, but where all 'independent life' has ceased and where the [whole brain] criteria of death have been met, further medical support systems need not be continued."[10]

Within Conservative Judaism, the Committee on Jewish Law and Standards of the Rabbinical Assembly likewise affirms that medical decision making based on the best interest of the patient "would definitely not justify active euthanasia, even in cases where the homicide would clearly be a 'mercy killing'; absent the excuse of self-defense or a court order, we never in Jewish law, have the right actively to hasten our own death or that of another person." The dispute that emerged in 1990 within Conservative Judaism is whether withholding or withdrawing nutrition and hydration from an incurably ill person (terefah), including patients in persistent vegetative state, would contravene this prohibition of actively hastening the death of another.[11]

In Orthodox Judaism, there is no support whatsoever for active euthanasia and considerably more reluctance to withdraw medical life support, including nutrition and hydration. The prohibition of actively hastening death is held to apply to persons for whom dying is imminent *(goses)*; indeed, "A *goses* is considered as a living person in all respects." It may, however, be permissible to remove non-medical impediments to death (salt on a patient's tongue) during the final phase of dying, traditionally set at three days or less. For such reasons, the Orthodox tradition has frequently found "whole brain" criteria for death incompatible with Jewish law *(halakha)*, a point of divergence from the Reformed perspective cited above. The weight of Orthodox ethics therefore imposes a very strong presumption on the side of using all available medical means to prolong life and has commonly assessed procedures to remove or withhold treatment, such as do-not-resuscitate (DNR) orders, as violating obligations to a *goses*.[12]

Ecclesiastical Opposition

A last position is comprised of denominations that have articulated formal opposition to assisted suicide and euthanasia, including the Baha'i Faith, the Church of Jesus Christ of Latter-day Saints (Mormonism), the Church of the Nazarene, the Episcopal Church (USA), the Evangelical Lutheran Church, the Lutheran Church-Missouri Synod, the Reformed Church in America, the Roman Catholic Church, and the Christian Life Commission of the Southern Baptist Convention. Significantly, many of these traditions assume a social responsibility of public education and dialogue even on public policy issues as part of their ecclesiological identity. Among these several denominations, I shall focus briefly on the evaluation of euthanasia from within the Roman Catholic tradition, as it has played the most visible public role.

The core of Roman Catholic teaching on euthanasia is contained in the Vatican's 1980 *Declaration on Euthanasia*, wherein euthanasia is defined as "an action or an omission which of itself or by intention causes death, in order that all suffering may in this way be eliminated."[13] This definition is crucial to the Catholic critique of proposals like the Washington Initiative, which are suspect in part because they *redescribe* the act under scrutiny through such language as "aid in dying." Such language, even though it encompasses acts of assisted suicide and euthanasia, suggests an underlying motive of compassionate assistance, rather than an intention to cause death. My point here is that some religious opposition to euthanasia may be grounded in concerns that language can create a psychology of moral distance between a moral agent and his or her actions, and the consequences of those actions.

The *Declaration* proceeds to condemn an act of euthanasia as a "violation of the divine law, an offense against the dignity of the human person, a crime against life, and an attack on humanity," in that it violates the prohibition of directly killing innocent human life.[14] Yet, it is often overlooked that this vigorous condemnation of the act is coupled with a means to excuse the agent from responsibility through an appeal to the tradition's concept of "erroneous conscience." Thus, in cases of "prolonged and barely tolerable pain, . . . the guilt of the [suffering] individual may be *reduced* or *completely* absent. . . . [my emphasis]."[15] Such an argument has enormous policy ramifications, implying that flexibility and discretion ought to underlie legal enforcement of the law. This is not the complete exemption from prosecution under homicide statutes that proponents of euthanasia desire, to be sure, but it does suggest the practical policy positions of the two sides are much closer than the polarized moral assessments.

In this country, the perspective of the *Declaration* has been reiterated by the National Conference of Catholic Bishops and given perhaps its most articulate theological exposition in the "consistent ethics of life" of Joseph Cardinal Bernardin. Bernardin holds that this ethics is grounded in the sacred and social nature of human life, which generates positive (protect life) and negative (do not directly destroy or injure human life) obligations.[16]

This overview has illustrated that the picture of religious perspectives on euthanasia is much more complex and diverse than commonly conceived. We are now in a position to examine the normative and theological justifications and the public significance of these perspectives.

SOVEREIGNTY, STEWARDSHIP, AND THE SELF

While religious traditions certainly bear a burden of justification for their positions on euthanasia, that burden may not be either the most weighty or the most difficult to meet. Our culture is so steeped in individualism that it is easy to overlook that a right of self-determination (a negative right) does not automatically generate a claim for assistance (a positive right), let alone assistance in bringing about one's own death.

In the normative ethical discussion of euthanasia within religious communities, three appeals seem to be most prominent: An appeal to *sovereignty* that points to questions about ultimate authorization over the disposition of one's life and body; an appeal to *stewardship* that orients human responsibilities for other persons in a context of mutual dependence; and an appeal to an understanding of the human *self*. Collectively, these three claims bring a theological anthropology to bear on the issue of euthanasia.

Sovereignty

While much of the discussion of both termination of medical treatment and euthanasia has focused on the sovereignty and autonomy of the self to make end-of-life decisions, theistic religious traditions have been concerned to affirm that such choices are relativized by the ultimate sovereignty of God over human life. God is understood to be the origin and destiny of human life; our lives, therefore, assume the character of a "gift" or "trust" rather than personal "property."

Moreover, such an understanding invests human life with a sanctity that requires its protection, nurturance, and promotion. This perspective supports normative values, including what is often referred to as a "sanctity of human life" principle and the more specific prohibition against killing.

There is diversity among religious traditions over the stringency of the sanctity of life principle (is life an absolute good or a fundamental good required for the realization of other human goods?) and the bindingness of the prohibition against killing (is the prohibition virtually exceptionless or a presumption that can be overridden?), but it is important to emphasize a primary *common* assumption: the taking of human life is a violation or infringement of a basic human good. Human life has inherent worth, and is not to be treated casually, with indifference, or as holding solely instrumental value.

It is not simply perspectives about life that inform religious assessments of euthanasia, but also the significance of death. Within some communities, the biblical language of death as an "enemy," and a symbol of human alienation, is reiterated in discourse about euthanasia. For others, death is situated within the life processes created by God, and human beings have a responsibility to respect the integrity of these processes. Within either of these perspectives, however, there is little support for deliberately seeking death. Even among traditions that see in martyrdom the exemplary case of a higher good (integrity to faith) that might require sacrifice of life, death is accepted rather than sought after. In short, death, like life, is perceived as under the disposition and dominion of deity.

On such accounts, the deliberate and intentional choice of death for oneself or others through euthanasia can involve three kinds of wrongs. Most frequently such actions will be brought under the rule prohibiting killing and seen as violations of that rule (hence, the normative resistance to describing such acts as "aid in dying"). Secondly, the prohibition of assisted suicide or euthanasia may be connected with the sin of pride, in that such acts represent a wrongful usurpation of divine authority and prerogative over life and death; a sin of "playing God." Finally, such acts may be portrayed as a form of ingratitude for the gift of life.

For some critics, both within and outside of religious traditions, the appeal to sovereignty is misguided because it invokes a misleading normative paradigm, "killing," to evaluate acts of assisted suicide or euthanasia. The language of "aid in dying," whatever its conceptual inadequacies, suggests one morally relevant feature of such acts that differentiates them from those traditionally understood to violate the prohibition of killing, namely, that in this instance the agent *rationally consents* to his or her own death, rather than being deprived of life against his or her will. Thus, some have argued that the proper paradigm for assessing euthanasia is that of "respect" for the human person.[17]

A second critique of the appeal to sovereignty has focused on issues of internal coherence and suggested that the appeal inevitably leads to a "slippery-slope" problem. If human life and destiny are under the ultimate dominion of

God, it may then seem that defensible lines cannot be drawn between accepting medical treatment in the first instance, or subsequent refusals of life-prolonging medical treatment, and deliberate attempts to bring about one's death by medical means. The sovereignty appeal thus looks as though it pushes in the direction of either *fatalism* or a *vitalism* that requires an unrestricted use of medical technology.

The religious response to this critique has traditionally invoked claims about patterns of human responsibility. Most traditions, for example, acknowledge that culpability can be attributed for omissions as well as commissions. The failure to prevent a preventable death, as displayed in a fatalistic perspective, may be as blameworthy as directly inflicting a harm or injury that leads to death. It does not thereby follow that if the death is not preventable, one is obliged to expedite it. Nor has the appeal to sovereignty been understood to foreclose responsibility for moral choices, as though human beings were passive puppets. Thus, most traditions, some more successfully than others, have attempted to avoid vitalism by formulating criteria that differentiate "extraordinary" and "ordinary" treatment, to use language originally at home in the Roman Catholic tradition. The appeal to sovereignty provides a theological *context* for moral choices *made* by human beings. At this juncture, the stewardship appeal emerges as a complement to sovereignty.

Stewardship

The fundamental point of the stewardship appeal is that human beings are entrusted with caring for and respecting divine gifts that may come in the form of one's own life and body, or in the presence of others with whom we create relationships and covenants out of the equality of mutual dependence. The responsibilities of stewardship thus entail not only accountability before God but also before other persons. A responsible stewardship will involve a balance of care and respect, and a willingness to share in the burdens and the suffering of others, reflecting the virtue of "compassion." Care without respect can be insulting, while respect without care can express indifference.

Euthanasia may therefore be seen as an inadequate fulfillment or even betrayal of the trust invested by God: "Christian stewardship of life," affirms the Evangelical Lutheran Church, "mandates treasuring and preserving the life which God has given, be it our own life or the life of some other person.... To depart from this view by performing active euthanasia,... is contrary to Christian conscience."[18] Alternatively, the stewardship violated by euthanasia may be portrayed as encompassing accountability toward one's neighbor. Assisting in another's suicide or performing active euthanasia to fulfill the self-determined decision of another to choose death may err on the side of respect, and express indifference and apathy rather than care and compassion. Alternatively, when performed out of the motive of mercy, such acts may detach love from the awe and respect owed another person.

   The cogency of a stewardship appeal is, for many persons, undercut by the reality of protracted pain and intolerable suffering experienced by many terminally ill patients. Depriving these persons of any options by which they may alleviate such burdens seems, if anything, both uncaring and disrespectful.

   A religious response to this critique may well rely on two principal themes. Even within traditions that at times permit overriding the prohibition of killing (for example, self-defense, or a just war), the taking of human life is always understood to be a *last resort*, to be sought only after all other alternatives have been exhausted. Yet, as noted by a distinguished panel of medical professionals recently, there is a pervasive public perception that "physicians' efforts toward the relief of pain are sadly deficient."[19] Whether that perception is well-founded or not, all sides in this debate seem to agree that more effective pain therapy would substantially diminish the physiological and psychological burdens patients experience that make them request assisted suicide or euthanasia. A compelling case can be made that in this country we have not exhausted all measures to affirm the dignity of the dying and relieve their pain and suffering short of taking their lives.

   It should not be forgotten, moreover, that, particularly for Christian traditions, suffering has a stewardly and existential significance that is simply not accommodated by philosophical or professional perspectives on euthanasia. While no tradition sanctifies suffering in its own right, the suffering of a patient may be seen as an occasion for stewardly service and witness through visiting the ill or through prayer, or as a means by which "God can work the gift of grace for the one who suffers and for others."[20] According to the Vatican *Declaration*, "suffering during the last moments of life . . . is in fact a sharing in Christ's passion . . . ."[21] While it would be wrong to impose such a theology of suffering on terminally ill patients as a matter of public policy, it should nevertheless be recognized that one normative ground for religious opposition to euthanasia is that all suffering is not seen as an unmitigated evil that requires elimination. Instead, it may seen as a source of religious meaning and service.

Self

   Theological understandings of the human person also bear on the question of euthanasia in important respects. All the denominations that have emerged out of the Judeo-Christian ethos affirm that human beings are deserving of a fundamental reverence or respect because of their creation in the image of God. That respect encompasses decisions made in situations of practical moral choice, though it does not entail that all such choices are morally equal.

   At the same time, the self is comprised of a *social and relational* dimension that can constrain personal autonomy. Persons are not, as the presuppositions of liberal democratic theorists would have it, unencumbered individuals making rational choices based on self-interested preferences. We instead experience our lives in a web of relationships, with family, friends, colleagues, associates, congregations, and larger communities. The model of self-determined individuals freely choosing euthanasia in isolation from a semblance of human community seems, therefore, to present a truncated and distorted view of the self.

Moreover, the "slippery-slope" argument so frequently invoked in both religious and nonreligious opposition to euthanasia, that acts of voluntary euthanasia will proceed to practices of voluntary euthanasia, and acts of involuntary euthanasia will follow in course, are likewise religiously grounded in an understanding of the human self as *finite and fallible*. We have but limited abilities to predict, control, and assess the effects of courses of action once initiated. Put more theologically, human beings are simply not omniscient, omnipotent, or morally perfect. Moral principles and rules, including the principle of the sanctity of human life and the rule prohibiting killing generated by the appeal to sovereignty, are designed in part to compensate for persistent human tendencies to engage in rationalization and self-interested action.

"SO WHAT?": TRANSLATING RELIGION TO POLITICS

What, if any, significance does religious discourse contain for public policy debates on euthanasia? H. Tristram Engelhardt, Jr., suggests that invoking explicitly religious appeals in the public square amounts to bringing closure to a controversy through coercion: "Insofar as individuals do not share in the consensus of a common religious belief . . . appeals to religious consideration will appear to those without faith or with a different faith as an appeal simply to force in order to support private interests."[22] The problem is that a religious argument assumes or imposes a particular view of a good life that cannot be justified outside the religious tradition. Must religious traditions then be a-religious in public policy discussions? We can begin to address this issue by examining how prominent traditions have understood their role in public debate on euthanasia.

One might contend that denominational entry into public dialogue on euthanasia exhibits an attempt to enforce a biblically grounded vision of social order, on the model of a theocracy. While this view has often been advanced by critics of religious perspectives, with very few exceptions, this justification has not prevailed among the religious traditions themselves. Instead, for many traditions, discourse directed at a broad public audience will be justified by an appeal to a conception of citizenship in a democratic society, which assumes both rights and responsibilities toward the common good. The content of this responsibility of *citizenship* may involve a general pedagogical purpose--to educate or shape public opinion. Or, the civic responsibility may focus more specifically on influencing legislation or rulings by legal bodies. Thus, the Unitarian Universalist Association is resolved to "inform and petition legislators to support legislation that will create legal protection for the right to die with dignity."[23]

Suffice it to say that major religious traditions do not accept the proposition that the public policy dimension of the euthanasia debate forecloses their participation. At each level of discussion within the Roman Catholic tradition, for example, direct connections are made between moral norms and public policy. The Vatican *Declaration* was developed in part to "offer [Catholic bishops] elements for reflection that they can present to the civil authorities," and its contribution to the public debate over euthanasia appeals to the *universal* nature of the issues at stake: "... since it is a question here of fundamental rights inherent in every human person, it is obviously wrong to have recourse to arguments from political pluralism or religious freedom in order to deny the universal value of those rights."[24] Cardinal Bernardin, meanwhile, has maintained that the positive and negative obligations of the "consistent ethics of life" are already embedded in the common law tradition.

However, religious discourse on public policy about euthanasia may not always be recognizably "religious." As suggested by Bernardin's reasoning, the content of public policy argumentation from religious traditions will frequently appeal to an *embedded common morality* that is perceived as commanding fairly broad consensus in our culture, such as the distinctive dignity of human life, while theological themes that would be prominent in discourse within the community may play a background role. In many instances, this embedded ethos will be seen as rooted historically in the values of dominant Western religious faiths. This historical dependence does not entail any logical dependence, however; one can advocate the values of these traditions without affirming their faith convictions.

Two illustrations should convey the significance of this distinction. In 1989, the General Board of Church and Society of the United Methodist Church, acting in accord with its "prime responsibility ... to seek implementation of the Social Principles of the United Methodist Church through forthright witness on important social issues, educational programs, and efforts to influence the development of public policy and law," submitted an *amicus* brief to the US Supreme Court in support of terminating life-support to Nancy Cruzan. The *amicus* affirmed that as the constitutional notion of a "fundamental right" had to be consonant with the traditional values and collective conscience of a nation, the Court's decision "should be informed by our culture's traditional *moral* understandings." Moreover, the UMC's conviction that treatment could be discontinued was affirmed as "representative of a broad and deeply held traditional *moral* consensus [my emphasis]."[25] Similarly, in affirming the values Roman Catholics would bring to public discussion of euthanasia, the National Conference of Catholic Bishops asserts: "Although these principles have grown out of a specific religious tradition, they appeal to a *common* respect for the dignity of the human person rather than to any specific denominational stance [my emphasis]."[26]

Several important implications follow from this appeal to a common moral ethos. It will, first of all, be mistaken to claim that "religious" argumentation on euthanasia should not be given a public hearing because it involves appeals to values that are not generally accessible. Nor will it be valid to discredit denominational entry into the public fray on the grounds that this involves an attempt to "impose" a religious view as the social solution or a breach of church-state separation. In both instances, religious traditions will contend that the focus of public assessment of euthanasia will turn on whether it is seen as compatible with this common moral core (as in Unitarianism) or in violation of it (as in Roman Catholicism).

The problem with the common morality appeal, however, is that the argumentation ceases to express a distinctively religious perspective; it is, as the traditions recognize, a perspective that could equally be arrived at through nonreligious or professional ethics, or by reflection on the cultural ethos. Such an appeal, then, seems to concede the general a-religious nature of public policy discourse in a pluralistic society.

We might call this the "translation" problem for religious social ethics. In moving into the public square of the euthanasia debate, religious traditions need to translate concepts and values originally at home within a particular denominational community into language meaningful for those outside the tradition. As Cardinal Bernardin has maintained, "In my view, positions that are informed by particular religious beliefs or philosophical assumptions need to be translated into commonly agreed upon language, arguments, and categories before they can become the moral or ethical foundations for key public policy choices."[27] The consequence of this process is that something--typically the distinctively religious content--will get "lost" in the translation. Ironically, the discourse of religious traditions gains public relevance at the expense of its religious character.

The translation problem may seem to lend credibility to the "so what?" principle. Religious discussions of euthanasia seem to be meaningful only within a tradition; once translated for purposes of public debate, the religious influence seems at best indirect and perhaps dispensable. Yet, it is also important to recognize that there is not a "neutral" or "common" moral language that is independent of substantive assumptions. Thus, I concur with Bernardin's insistence that a full public discourse on euthanasia requires as well elucidation of the "philosophical assumptions" of arguments for and against euthanasia. For to see the parameters of the euthanasia debate in our society as exclusively a matter of the boundaries of public regulation of private choice is to adopt a rather superficial stance.

At a much deeper level, the debate reflects disagreements over the source of meaning and good in human life, the significance of suffering and death in human existence, the moral character of human relationships, and the nature of the human self. These are common questions of human meaning, identity, purpose, and destiny, which are at the core of religious reflection. Religious traditions may not, in our society, present satisfying answers to these issues, but they will raise unavoidable substantive questions. Only when public discussion of euthanasia comprehensively engages these questions will it be capable of moving beyond the current pretense of pluralism to the genuine pluralism toward which our culture aspires.

SELECTED DENOMINATIONAL PERSPECTIVES ON EUTHANASIA

American Baptist Churches

"American Baptist Churches . . . [should] familiarize themselves with the statutes within their states regarding living wills, durable power of attorneys, and natural death acts and where appropriate, [should] lobby for legislation that enhances and facilitates the individual's right to make his/her own decisions regarding life-sustaining treatment or measures."

Southern Baptist Convention (Christian Life Commission)

"Human life, from fertilization until natural death, is sacred and should be protected, not destroyed. . . . Efforts shall be undertaken . . . to oppose infanticide and active euthanasia, including efforts to discourage any designation of food and/or water as 'extraordinary' medical care for some patients."

The First Church of Christ, Scientist

"It is because of Christian Science teachings regarding life, death, and illness, and their century-long experience of healing, that approaches like euthanasia and assisted suicide would not be considered part of the genuine practice of our religion."

The United Church of Christ

"We affirm individual freedom and responsibility to make choices in these matters. It is not claimed that euthanasia is the Christian position, but that the right to choose is a legitimate Christian decision. It is contended that governmental powers and entrenched custom have made life and death decisions, closing off options which more properly belong to individuals and families."

Episcopal Church (USA)

"It is morally wrong and unacceptable to intentionally take a human life in order to relieve the suffering caused by incurable illness. This would include the intentional shortening of another person's life by the use of a lethal dose of medication or poison, the use of lethal weapons, homicidal acts, and other forms of active euthanasia."

Federation of Jewish Philanthropies (Committee on Medical Ethics)

"The sanctity of human life prescribes that, in any situation short of self-defense or martyrdom, human life be treated as an end in itself. It may thus not be terminated or shortened because of considerations of the patient's convenience or usefulness, or even our sympathy with the suffering of the patient. Thus euthanasia may not be performed either in the interest of the patient or of anyone else.... [A] patient is not permitted to end his or her life or be assisted in such suicide by anyone else, be he or she a health care professional, family member, friend, or bystander."

Union of American Hebrew Congregations (Reformed Judaism)

"We would not endorse any positive steps leading toward death. We would recommend pain-killing drugs which would ease the remaining days of a patient's life. We would reject any general endorsement of euthanasia, but where all 'independent life' has ceased and where the [whole brain] criteria of death have been met, further medical support systems need not be continued."

Evangelical Lutheran Church in America

"Christian stewardship of life . . . mandates treasuring and preserving the life which God has given, be it our own life or the life of some other person .... To depart from this view by performing active euthanasia, thereby deliberately destroying life created in the image of God, is contrary to Christian conscience."

Lutheran Church-Missouri Synod

"Euthanasia, in its proper sense, is a synonym for mercy killing, which involves suicide and/or murder. It is, therefore, contrary to God's law."

United Methodist Church

"[W]e assert the right of every person to die in dignity, with loving personal care and without efforts to prolong terminal illness merely because the technology is available to do so."

Church of Jesus Christ of Latter-Day Saints (Mormon)

"A person who participates in euthanasia--deliberately putting to death a person suffering from incurable conditions or diseases--violates the commandments of God."

Church of the Nazarene

"The Bioethics Commission categorically rejects euthanasia [an overt termination of the life of a patient for whom death is imminent] as an acceptable option for Christians."

Greek Orthodox Church

"The Orthodox Church has always taught that euthanasia constitutes the deliberate taking of human life and as such is to be condemned as murder. . . . [Euthanasia] does not constitute a viable alternative for the Orthodox physician or patient."

Orthodox Church in America

"The underlying guiding concern in selective non-treatment must be the welfare of the terminally ill patient. That welfare might be best served by removing life-support machinery; it cannot be served by deliberately causing death."

Presbyterian Church (USA)

The General Assembly authorizes a study document that "examines all sides of both the technical issues and practical questions that theologically encompass euthanasia and assisted death."

Roman Catholicism

"By euthanasia is understood an action or an omission which of itself or by intention causes death, in order that all suffering may in this way be eliminated. . . . [N]othing and no one can in any way permit the killing of an innocent human being, whether a fetus or an embryo, an infant or an adult, an old person, or one suffering from an incurable disease, or a person who is dying. Furthermore, no one is permitted to ask for this act of killing, either for himself or herself or for another person entrusted to his or her care, nor can he or she consent to it, either explicitly or implicitly. Nor can any authority legitimately recommend or permit such an action."

Unitarian Universalist Association

"Unitarian Universalists advocate the right to self-determination in dying, and the release from criminal or civil penalties of those who, under proper safeguards, act to honor the right of terminally ill patients to select the time of their own deaths."

This section was compiled from denominational resolutions or articles submitted by denominational representatives in response to the author's request for such information during the fall of 1990 and the spring of 1991. For additional discussion, see:

Hamel, R., ed., *Active Euthanasia, Religion, and the Public Debate*. Chicago: Park Ridge Center, 1991.

LaRue, G. *Euthanasia and Religion*. Los Angeles: Hemlock Society, 1985.

ACKNOWLEDGMENTS

The author wishes to express his gratitude to many denominational representatives for their invaluable assistance in providing position papers or resolutions, to Lois Summers for her assistance in manuscript preparation, and to Dr. Robert Misbin and Professor Margaret P. Battin for constructive substantive suggestions.

NOTES

1   For the sake of brevity, hereafter I will commonly use "euthanasia" to refer to both physician-assisted suicide and active euthanasia. The religious arguments I will consider typically do not distinguish the two kinds of acts.
2   Initiative 119, "A Voluntary Choice for Terminally Ill Persons;" R.I. Misbin, "Physician Aid in Dying," *New England Journal of Medicine* (21 October 1991); "Voters Turn Dowwn Mercy Killing Idea," *New York Times*, 7 November 1991, B16.
3   Personal interviews, Karen Cooper, Washington Citizens for Death with Dignity; Mary Jo Kahler, Human Life of Washington; October 1990.
4   R. Bainton, *Christian Attitudes Toward War and Peace* (Nashville: Abingdon Press, 1960):49.
5   Social Concerns Committee, the Lutheran Church-Missouri Synod, *Report on Euthanasia with Guiding Principles* (St. Louis, MO: Commission on Theology and Church Relations, 1979).
6   General Assembly of the Unitarian Universalist Association, "The Right to Die with Dignity--1988," *Resolutions and Resources*, eds. Catherine Devine and Mary Rosa (Boston, MA: UUA Department of Social Justice, 1990):74-75.
7   United Church of Christ, Eighteenth General Synod, *The Rights and Responsibilities of Christians Regarding Human Death*. (Cleveland, OH: United Church of Christ, 1991).
8   Presbyterian Church (USA), "On Studying All Sides of the Technical and Practical Questions Theologically that Encompass Euthanasia and Assisted Death" (overture 90-98), (Louisville, KY: Presbyterian Church (USA), 1990):787-88.

9   *Compendium on Medical Ethics*, 6th ed., eds. D.M. Feldman and F. Rosner (New York: Federation of Jewish Philanthropies of New York, 1984):106.

10   W. Jacob, *et al.* responsa 79, "Euthanasia," in *American Reform Responsa* (New York: Central Conference of American Rabbis, 1980).

11   E.N. Dorff, "A Jewish Approach to End-Stage Medical Care," and A.I. Reisher, "A Halakhic Ethic of Care for the Terminally Ill," adopted by the Committee on Jewish Law and Standards of the Rabbinical Assembly, 12 December 1990.

12   F. Rosner, "The Jewish Attitude Toward Euthanasia," and J.D. Bleich, "Neurological Death and Time of Death Statutes," in *Jewish Bioethics*, eds. F. Rosner and J.D. Bleich (New York: Sanhedrin Press, 1979):253-265, 303-316.

13   Sacred Congregation for the Doctrine of Faith, *Declaration on Euthanasia* (Boston, MA: Daughters of St. Paul, 1980).

14   *Ibid.*

15   *Ibid.*

16   J. Bernardin. "Euthanasia: Ethical and Legal Challenges," address to Center for Clinical Medical Ethics, University of Chicago Hospital, 26 May 1988.

17   L.S. Cahill. "A 'Natural Law' Reconsideration of Euthanasia," *Linacre Quarterly* 44 (1977): 47-63.

18   Lutheran Church in American (now the Evangelical Lutheran Church in America), *Death and Dying* (New York: Division for Mission in North America, 1982).

19   S.H. Wanzer, *et al.* "The Physician's Responsibility Towards Hopelessly Ill Patients: A Second Look," *New England Journal of Medicine* 320 (1989):844-849.

20   American Lutheran Church (now Evangelical Lutheran Church in America), *Health, Life, and Death: A Christian Perspective* (Minneapolis, MN: Office of Church and Society, 1977).

21   Sacred Congregation for the Doctrine of Faith, *Declaration on Euthanasia*.

22   H.T. Engelhardt, Jr. "Death by Free Choice: Modern Variations on an Antique Theme," *Suicide and Euthanasia* ed. B.A. Brody (Dordrecht, the Netherlands: Kluwer Academic Publishers, 1989):256.

23   General Assembly of the UUS, "The Right to Die with Dignity--1988."

24   Sacred Congregation for the Doctrine of Faith, *Declaration on Euthanasia*.

25   Brief of the General Board of Church and Society of the United Methodist Church as *amicus curiae* in Support of Petitioners, *Cruzan v. Director of Missouri Department of Health* (1989):1-5.

26   National Conference of Catholic Bishops, *Guidelines for Legislation on Life-Sustaining Treatment* (Washington, DC: NCCB Administrative Committee, 1984):2.

27   Bernadin, "Euthanasia: Ethical and Legal Changes."

15

The Historical and Religious Framework For Euthanasia in the Netherlands

Titia H.C. Bueller

The question why the practice of euthanasia has developed in the Netherlands cannot be easily answered. Some critics of this development will simply conclude that the Dutch society is a permissive one in which law and order are lacking. To enforce their criticism, they will point to the soft Dutch policy on people who break the law. They could illustrate their point of view with the story of the squatters in a huge building in the center of Amsterdam: a bunch of young people, who instead of being thrown out, were given renovated, fully-equipped apartments in the same building, courtesy of the city of Amsterdam.[1] They might also substantiate their claim with the apparently lenient Dutch attitude toward drug abusers, which is based on treatment rather than punishment. The Dutch free needle-exchange program and the idea of free heroin supplies for otherwise untreatable drug addicts might also be used to support their judgment, as would the liberal policy on abortion; or, to take a more mundane example, the Dutch beaches crowded with topless and nude sunbathers. They would condemn all these examples, including the practice of euthanasia, as symptoms of moral decline.

This moral condemnation of the Dutch society, however, might be based on a lack of understanding. Highlighting certain aspects of the Dutch society, and thus the climate in which the practice of euthanasia became permitted, might reverse this judgment.

First of all, Holland has a long tradition of tolerance. As early as the sixteenth and seventeenth centuries, the Dutch fought to secure their religious freedom. During the Eighty-Years War with Spain, many people fleeing from Roman Catholic oppression sought refuge in the Netherlands. At the same time, the Netherlands developed strength as a maritime power. A century-long seafaring tradition made the Dutch cosmopolitans. By sailing and trading all over the world, their awareness of different cultures increased. The Dutch tendency to look over borders and expand their view might have their roots in this era where the merchants, coming themselves from a small country, had to deal with many different peoples.

It was during a more recent part of history, however, that the conditions occurred for the practice of euthanasia. In 1973, a Dutch court permitted euthanasia for the first time, albeit under certain conditions.[2] This decision was, in part, a consequence of a revolutionary way of thinking that originated in the 1960s and had an enormous impact on society as a whole. The right to self-determination became a pivotal issue, both in political debates and in matters of medical ethics. The autonomous rights of women prevailed in the battle over abortion. A book called *Medical Power and Medical Ethics* stirred up a vigorous debate on the ethical limits of medical technology.[3]

In general, a strong desire for social change predominated. Authority, convention, and establishment were openly questioned. Even trade and industry were subject to democratization. The results are now institutionalized. These practical effects are sometimes collectively referred to as the "decolonization of the individual."[4]

The solidarity with the less fortunate in society found its expression in the creation of the welfare state. In criminal law, prison terms were shortened after surveys showed that prolonged detention did neither prisoners, nor society, any good.[5] The overall climate, in brief, was one of growing sensitivity to the human factor. In view of these developments, it does not seem surprising that the idea of granting the request of a suffering person to have his or her life terminated gained support.

The 1960s similarly influenced the role of churches in the Netherlands. To prevent young people from turning away, churches hastily tried to lure them with rock music services. At clerical conventions, church leaders took political stands. They summoned support for third-world countries and criticized the war in Vietnam. In those days, the Dutch Roman Catholic Church changed from the most authoritarian toward its flock and the most obedient to the Vatican, into the most progressive one. For example, the Dutch bishops commented on the Pope's encyclical on birth control, *Humanae Vitae,* by saying that while the encyclical should be considered with respect, its arguments were not entirely convincing. They also argued that it was necessary to respect the personal decisions of married couples about the "pill."[6]

The two most important protestant churches, the Dutch Reformed *(Neder-lands Hervormd)* and the Reformed *(Gereformeerden Kerken)* attempted to modernize, too.[7] They took part in the ecumenical movement and allowed women to become ministers. It is difficult, however, to generalize about the Protestant churches, because each separate congregation has always had a great degree of autonomy. Indeed, it would be false to imagine that the changes in the churches and in society were by any means total. Modernization was far more apparent in the "Randstad," a conurbation of separate, yet nearby towns, where nearly half of the population lives, than in the rest of the Netherlands.[8]

Although a great number of church-goers remained unaffected by these uproars, the secularization in the Netherlands increased. In surveys taken in 1960 and 1988, the number of people who said they did not belong to any church community rose from 18.4 percent to 32 percent.[9] In a survey in 1989, 39.7 percent said they did not believe in God.[10]

The three leading church communities are currently cautiously supporting the practice of euthanasia.[11] The Reformed Church concluded in a report on euthanasia in 1985, that euthanasia and assisted suicide are not necessarily irresponsible acts.[12] Such acts, it added, do not have to be met with outright refusal or disaproval beforehand. On the contrary, requests thereto should be openly considered and discussed for openness can only help the decision-making process.[13] This report was sent to the Dutch Reformed Church council with the remark that it was not a synodal standpoint. The Dutch Reformed Church concurred implicitly with the report, as might be inferred from its decision not to write a new report. It believed that the existing one provided enough issues for consideration.[14] The Dutch Roman Catholic Church, in its pastoral letter "Suffering and Dying of the Sick," leaves the door only slightly ajar for euthanasia:

> Many people are with us convinced that it is not permitted in this way to seek death or to terminate the life of the dying out of mercy. Respect for human life, also mutilated life, is a fundamental element of human and christian civilization. So from this conviction we neither can or may approve of deliberate termination of life in the dying process. On the contrary. It is a different matter that we can empathize with a personal decision of conscience on the part of a dying fellowman, even if we do feel it is contrary to the respect due to life.[15]

Apart from the changes which took place in religious thinking since the 1960s, another enormous influence on the Dutch attitude toward death and dying is the Dutch Calvinistic view on life and death. The prolonging of life by medical intervention, according to this view, is not always considered the realization of God's will. On the contrary, the use of medical technology during the process of dying is often felt to be a contradiction of the will of God, as it prevents His will from taking place. This Calvinistic way of thinking might be the cause of a greater acceptance of death as a part of life.

The idea of letting life and death take their natural courses may very well play a role in the sober attitude the Dutch have concerning home births as well. The Netherlands has the highest home birth rate in the world (33.4 percent).

Another fact noteworthy in this context is that the Netherlands, a country one-and-a-half times the size of Massachusetts, has some fifty different religions.[16] In part, this extraordinary number can be explained by schisms in the Protestant Church due to differences on minor and major issues, which caused, throughout history, a host of new congregations. A great variety of opinions is also expressed in the number of political parties that are active in the Netherlands (twenty-five political parties participated in the parliamentary elections in 1989).[17] The process of finding political solutions in the face of all those differences of opinion is called "pacification politics," that is a way of finding political compromises without leaving one's principles. This form of politics found its origin in the phenomenon of *verzuiling* (pillarization). *Verzuiling* divided the Dutch, both in politics and in religion, in to a Roman Catholic, a Protestant, and a neutral bloc. These blocs remained rigidly structured until the beginning of the seventies. *Verzuiling* kept members of each bloc at a safe distance from each other, but the leaders of each pillar were willing to transcend their respective frameworks in order to satisfy the demands of a dynamic society. Contrasts were sublimated for the sake of progress in the form of concrete policy decisions. It might be inferred from the variety of opinions that to tolerate ideas other than one's own was, and still is, a necessity in the Netherlands.

However, reaching a compromise on euthanasia legislation appeared to be impossible even after the revolutionary court decision in 1973, not in the least because of the opposition exerted by the ruling Christian-Democratic party. The indecision in the political arena forced the courts, confronted with the actual practice of euthanasia, to take matters into their own hands. That the courts could undertake such a role was made possible by the special position the judges hold in the Dutch legal system.

In contrast to the American judicial system, no jury takes part in the decision-making process in the Netherlands. In other words, legal decisions are purely the products of professionals. Furthermore, judges are appointed for life and not chosen democratically. Therefore, they are not restricted in any way, as, for example, their American counterparts are, by their electorate. The preference for an independent judge can be explained by the Dutch dislike of what is called in German *Gesundes Volksempfinden.* The "opinion of laymen" concerning legal issues is considered to be too impulsive and emotional. Specific provisions in the Dutch Constitution also contribute to the latitude judges enjoy. These provisions oblige the judges to give precedence to international law, that is, specific treaty obligations and decisions of international organizations. In other words, the role of the judge has exceeded the classical one of *la bouche de la loi.*

Apart from the legal profession, mention should be made of another group of professionals, the physicians who participate in the debate on death and dying issues. As the conditions under which euthanasia is permitted are mainly medical ones, their role is obviously significant.

Although the influence of public opinion should not be ignored, in the final analysis the decision to allow euthanasia is exclusively in the hands of experts. This phenomenon has unquestionably contributed to the rationality of the debate.

By way of conclusion it might be said that the different aspects of the Dutch society sketched above, the historical tradition of tolerance, the overall pluralism in politics as well as in religion, and the special position of judges in the Dutch legal system, have led to openness. The consequent necessity of debate to find solutions to difficult issues such as euthanasia, has had, as a side effect, the breakdown of taboos. As far as euthanasia is concerned, the debate thus far has been focused mainly on euthanasia on request in the case of competent patients. The debates on the life termination of the comatose, handicapped newborns, and psychiatric patients have only just begun.

The mere fact that in the Netherlands some people want to discuss the extension of the right to terminate life to include incompetents as well, is, to some, a sign that the Dutch are slipping down a slippery slope. In my opinion, they are mistaken. I would rather judge this development as a healthy one and one that gives the Dutch the opportunity to make rational choices based on substantial argumentation in which all possibilities, including excesses, are scrutinized and consequently, boundaries can be defined, delimited, and chosen.

NOTES

1   N.R.C. Handelsblad, 5 September 1990.
2   Nederlandse Jurisprudentie (Dutch Jurisprudence), 1973, no. 183.
3   J.H. van den Berg, *Medische Macht en Medische Ethiek* (Nijkerk, the Netherlands: Callenbach, 1969).
4   H.J.A Hofland, *Tegels Lichten* (Amsterdam: Contact, 1972).
5   H.J. Franke, *Twee Eeuwen Gevangen* (Misdaad en straf, the Netherlands: Spectrum, 1990).
6   F.E. Huggett, *The Modern Netherlands* (London: Pall Mall Press, 1971), 85.
7   Both *hervormd* and *gereformeerd* mean "reformed." To avoid confusion, I have called the main protestant church the Dutch Reformed Church, and the smaller, more orthodox church, the Reformed Church.
8   The main towns that make up the "Randstad" are the Hague, Amsterdam, Utrecht, and Rotterdam. Huggett, *The Modern Netherlands,* 93.
9   Central Bureau of Statistics, *Negentig jaar in tijdreeksen,* 1988.
10   Source: Central Bureau of Statistics, *Nationaal kiezersonderzoek* 1989.
11   In 1988 the Dutch population is 35.8 percent Roman Catholic, 18.6 percent Dutch Reformed, and 8 percent Reformed: Central Bureau of Statistics, *Negentig jaar in tijdreeksen.*
12   Reformed Church, *Euthanasie en Pastoraat,* no. 159 (March 1985), 8.
13   Reformed Church, *Euthanasie en Pastoraat,* no. 159 (March 1985), 11.

14   Letter to the *Moderamen* of the General Synod of the Dutch Reformed Church of June 1987.

15   Secretariate of the Roman Catholic Church in the Netherlands, *Pastoral Letter, Suffering and Dying of the Sick,* 1985.

16   Source: Central Bureau of Statistics, *Volkstellingen 1971.*

17   Source: Central Bureau of Statistics, *Statistiek der verkiezing 1989, 2e kamer der Staten Generaal, 6 September.*

16

Physician-Assisted Suicide and The Suicide Machine

Ronald F. White

INTRODUCTION

In recent years, the long-standing social stigma attached to suicide and laws forbidding suicide assistance have come under increasing public scrutiny. The macabre popularity of Derek Humphrey's best-selling book *Final Exit* and Washington state's Initiative 119 suggest that American attitudes toward death are indeed changing. Although Americans still regard death as a serious harm, approximately 28,000 adults kill themselves every year in the United States,[1] many of whom do so with the help of friends, relatives, and physicians.

Two areas of biotechnological advancement have been especially influential in reshaping modern perceptions of suicide: first, the development of technologies that enable medical professionals to sustain human life almost indefinitely; and second, a growing capacity for them to accurately diagnose and prognose many debilitating and fatal diseases. Hence, more than ever before, health-care providers have the capacity to knowingly preserve lives void of many of the attributes normally associated with "quality of life." Many physicians still feel ethically bound to preserve even the most marginal states of biological existence, while others argue that decisions relating to when, and under what conditions, a patient may die ought to be made by the patient, not the physician. This dialogue has spawned a national debate over what the media has called the "right to die."

In this chapter I will discuss the issue of suicide and suicide assistance via some of the recent cases involving Dr. Jack Kevorkian and his suicide machine. I will argue that given an accurate diagnosis of an incurable harmful disease (such as Alzheimer's) and a competent request, the choice of suicide can be morally permissible and that within certain restraints, so can physician assistance.

THE MERCITRON

On 12 June 1989, after a rigorous series of tests, Janet Adkins was diagnosed as having Alzheimer's disease. Although she could still play tennis well enough to beat her son, she discovered that she could no longer keep score. She also had increasing difficulty working with other numbers and reading. A devout member of the Hemlock Society, Janet decided that she would rather commit suicide under the guidance of a physician than suffer a prolonged death. However, in Oregon the task was complicated by laws against suicide assistance. After reading an article in *Newsweek*[2] she learned of a physician in Michigan who might be willing to help.

Dr. Jack Kevorkian, a retired pathologist, had become a nationally recognized defender of a terminally ill patient's right to commit suicide, and the proud inventor of the Mercitron or "suicide machine." The contraption consisted of an IV equipped with harmless saline solution, a pain killer (thiopental sodium), and a poison (potassium chloride). When he tried to advertise his invention in a medical journal he was bluntly rejected, an escapade which attracted national headlines and a personal appearance on the "Donahue Show."

Soon after he was initially contacted by Janet's husband Ron, Kevorkian obtained two medical opinions confirming the Alzheimer's diagnosis. He also encouraged Janet to enroll in an experimental trial at the University of Washington where she took the drug Tacrine from December 1989 to March 1990 with no improvement in her condition.[3] Then Janet, Ron, and a close friend traveled to Michigan to meet Kevorkian to plan and execute her suicide. Prior to their arrival, the doctor had been unable to convince a local hotel, church, or funeral parlor to provide a dignified place for Janet to die. So he set up a cot in the back of his 1968 Volkswagen, hooked Janet up to the machine, and drove to a park near Detroit where she pushed the large red button controlling the pain killer and poison. Less than five minutes later, on 4 June 1990, Janet Adkins died a painless death.[4]

Shortly thereafter, a judge ordered Kevorkian to stop using the suicide machine until prosecutors could decide the legal status of the machine and suicide assistance in the state of Michigan. In November, Kevorkian was indicted for second-degree murder, but a week later the case was thrown out of court. Since then, "Death" has assisted two other woman, Sherry Miller and Marjorie Wantz, in executing their suicides and is currently under indictment for murder in Michigan.[5]

The act of suicide assistance poses three interesting ethical questions. First, is suicide a rational and morally defensible act? Second, what are a physician's moral obligations to a patient wishing to commit suicide? And finally, if physician-assisted suicide is morally acceptable, how much causal involvement is appropriate for the physician?

SUICIDE, HARM, AND RATIONALITY

As is so often the case, philosophical debate must first wrestle with sticky problems of definition. At one level, the standard definition of suicide, "the intentional taking of one's own life," seems fairly clear. However, there are two major areas of ambiguity.

For example, how would one classify a soldier's decision to take his own life rather than divulge important information to the enemy that might endanger his comrades? By the standard definition, this act would seemingly qualify as a suicide, but there are obvious differences in the level of voluntariness that seem relevant. Therefore, some philosophers make a distinction between "self-regarding" and "other-regarding" (or sacrificial) suicides and claim that sacrificial deaths are not instances of genuine suicide.

There is also the conceptual puzzle of classifying persons who deliberately indulge in dangerous activities such as sky diving, race car driving, and smoking. In a sense, the chain smoker is, in effect, committing suicide when she "knows" that this activity will eventually take her life. But does the smoker really "intend" to kill herself? She may "intend" to enjoy the activity regardless of the consequences, or she may simply be unable or unwilling to quit. In light of these concerns, Tom L. Beauchamp has provided the following definition:

A person commits suicide if:
1. that person intentionally brings about his or her own death;
2. others do not coerce him or her to do the action; and
3. death is caused by conditions arranged by the person for the purpose of bringing about his or her own death.[6]

Despite the apparent plausibility of Beauchamp's three conditions, there probably is no simple definition of suicide.[7] The word "suicide" is not merely descriptive of an act, but also carries with it a negative connotation or stigma. Because its meaning is not simply descriptive but also valuative, in ordinary discourse the word is generally used to signify only unapproved instances of self-killing.[8] Hence, we wouldn't refer to the death of our self-sacrificing soldier as a "suicide" but rather as "giving up his life for his comrades." We might also predict that as long as smoking tobacco maintains an aura of social respectability, we will not label chain smokers as suicidal.

There are also significant conceptual relationships between "suicide," "suicide assistance," and "voluntary active euthanasia" based on the degree of involvement of other parties. The difference between physician-assisted suicide and voluntary active euthanasia hinges, in part, on comparative levels of causal involvement by the patient and the physician. *Physician-assisted suicide* occurs when the patient (primarily) and the physician (secondarily) contribute to the causal chain of events resulting in the patient's death. *Voluntary active euthanasia* occurs when the physician (primarily), or someone else, out of beneficence causes the death of a consenting patient. This distinction, unfortunately, is based on the naive belief that we can neatly assign primary causal responsibility to the individuals involved. Take, for example, the following hypothetical cases where five physicians assist in the suicide of five competent patients.

P1. Tells a patient where he/she can purchase a suicide machine.
P2. Explains in detail how to set up the machine.
P3. Lends a patient the money to purchase a suicide machine.
P4. Sets up the machine.
P5. Pushes the button.

Most would agree that P5 is indulging in active euthanasia and is not merely "assisting." It also seems evident that P1 is assisting to a very minor degree and P2 to a slightly greater degree. One might even conclude that providing information on how to commit suicide (as in P1 and P2) is generally less blameworthy than the other alternatives. Finally, P3 and P4 would seem to represent the most active levels of causal involvement, without crossing over the line to active euthanasia. But how clear are these lines of varying causal involvement? Consider the following possible scenarios:

Scenario A: P1's patient already knew how to assemble and operate a suicide machine and all he needed to know was where to purchase it.
Scenario B: P2's patient already bought the machine and knew how to use it, but didn't know how to set it up.
Scenario C: P3's patient knew where to purchase the machine, knew how to assemble and use it, but couldn't afford to purchase it.
Scenario D: P4's patient knew where to purchase the machine, could afford to purchase it, knew how to set it up, but was physically incapable of setting it up.
Scenario E: P5's patient purchased the machine, set it up, knew how to use it, but because of a subsequent stroke became physically incapable of pushing the button.

The question here is how much causal involvement is morally permissible under what circumstances? There seems to be a widely held, emotionally rooted belief that there is a morally significant difference between telling a patient where to purchase a suicide machine (speech), and actually setting up the machine (act). While it is true that in each of the five scenarios the physicians decided to assist in different ways, it is not at all clear that any one of them was less causally involved in the suicide. In each case, the patient was unable to execute a necessary condition. So the physician who pushed the button is not necessarily more causally involved than the other four.

This puzzle over causal involvement has a direct bearing on the drafting of laws regulating suicide assistance based on causal factors. Could a physician be justifiably indicted for merely providing information? Or, to cite a more common scenario, was Timothy Quill, MD, legally or morally culpable for knowingly prescribing barbiturates to a terminally ill cancer patient who had expressed her desire to commit suicide?[9]

There is another, rather puzzling aspect to suicide assistance involving the relationship between causal responsibility and blameworthiness. Blame can only be assessed when the effect of one's causal act is morally wrong: causal involvement by itself is an insufficient condition for blameworthiness. So, if we can agree that sometimes a well-executed suicide is preferable to a life dominated by excessive pain, disability, or the loss of pleasure or opportunity, then, too, suicide assistance cannot always be deemed blameworthy--but rather an act of beneficence. Of course, it would be absurd to say that one can be "blamed" for acting out of beneficence.

As an act of beneficence toward Janet, Kevorkian chose to lend her his van and set up the machine, but elected not to push the red button. He was, nevertheless, indicted for merely lending his van, providing the machine, drugs, and hooking her up. But is this level of causal involvement morally inferior to the more accepted medical practice where the physician provides the pills, a family member actually removes the pills from the bottle, and the patient voluntarily swallows the lethal dose? Who bears primary causal responsibility here? From a pragmatic standpoint, I would argue that given the fuzzy lines between levels of causal involvement, and the naive distinction between the causal efficacy of speech and acts respectively, and the concept of blameworthiness, any criteria intended to make moral distinctions down these lines will be unavoidably arbitrary. Therefore, only in the most extreme cases is the border between suicide assistance and active voluntary euthanasia fairly clear and relatively easy to maintain.[10]

One might argue, however, that in order to remain within the conceptual framework of suicide and not encroach upon the larger issue of euthanasia, policy makers might insist that the patient be the one to "flick the switch." After all, medical technologists are capable of designing switches that even the most feeble patients would be capable of flicking. But this will not do much for the thousands of Americans hopelessly trapped in permanent vegetative states, incapable of executing their own suicides.

The concept of "harm" also figures predominantly in philosophical discussions of suicide and the rationality of human action. Most contemporary accounts follow Aristotle and take rationality to be the primary datum of human action; that is, they assume that rationality can be identified and that all human actions either possess the attribute or not. From this view, there are two schools of thought. There are philosophers who argue that rational actions are those that maximize the satisfaction of one's desires and promote one's personal perception of pleasure. Other philosophers hold that rational actions are those based on true beliefs.

Bernard Gert has argued that any formal definition of rationality, including the ones cited above, asserts a "fictitious and misleading uniformity" common to all rational acts. After all, most of us have accurately observed that in any given situation there are often many alternative actions which might be equally rational. We have also grappled with situations where it is evident that there are more than one way to maximize our desires, or more than one rational course of action based on the same set of true beliefs. Gert, therefore, suggests that rationality that is the primary datum. Since we can discern positive characteristics common to all irrational actions, irrationality must be deemed the primary datum.

> People act irrationally when they act in ways that they know (justifiably believe), or should know, will significantly increase the probability that they, or those for whom they are concerned, will suffer any of the items on the following list: death, pain (including mental suffering), disability, loss of freedom, or loss of pleasure, and they do not have an adequate reason for so acting. A reason for acting is a conscious belief that one's action (or the rule or policy that requires the action) will significantly increase the probability either that someone will avoid suffering any of the items on the previous list or that they will gain greater ability, freedom, or pleasure. This belief must not conflict with the overwhelming number of other beliefs one has, such that this conflict is obvious to almost everyone else with similar knowledge and intelligence. A reason is adequate if any large group of otherwise rational persons regard what will be avoided or gained as at least as important as what will be suffered. All intentional actions that are not irrational count as rational.[11]

The issue from this point of view, then, is not whether it is rational for Janet to commit suicide, but is it irrational? Given her situation, would any rational, impartial person in the larger community accept her reasons to choose death in order to avoid Alzheimer's disease?

Because Alzheimer's eventually destroys the capacity to make competent decisions, the longer Janet waits, the greater the likelihood that she will not be able to make a rational (or non-irrational) choice on the matter. Nor will she be able to plan and execute her demise. Because active voluntary euthanasia is not now an option in the United States, if Alzheimer's patients are to choose suicide they must do so while they still have some quality of life remaining. This is unfortunate, but it does underscore the need to reexamine the widely held and mischievous distinction between physician-assisted suicide and voluntary euthanasia.

THE ARGUMENTS ON BOTH SIDES

There are two kinds of reasons that may be employed in justifying suicide: self-regarding and other-regarding.[12] *Self-regarding reasons* would include a patient's desire to die rather than suffer other more serious harms associated with continued existence. Some self-regarding reasons are irrational and are properly subject to paternalistic intervention. These are cases where patients choose to die rather than endure a manifestly less serious or temporary harm. In our society, teenage suicides over unrequited love fall neatly into this category. Without the benefit of any reliable public survey on the topic, I would venture to say that the presence of intolerable and intractable pain, life-shattering disability, or the presence of terminal disease would all constitute morally acceptable reasons for a rational suicide in our society.

Most of us can, at least, empathize with another person's desire to die quickly and painlessly, rather than die slowly and wither away from a debilitating disease. Because of Alzheimer's incurability, the resulting loss of personal identity, and the eventual need for institutionalization, living with the disease is surely a harmful experience. Most of us also recognize as harmful the loss of human dignity associated with long-term dependence upon others. This is not to say that Alzheimer's is logically incompatible with human dignity: only that it is not irrational to make that judgment and act upon it. So, while it may not be necessarily irrational to commit suicide, neither is it irrational to choose to live. Depending on how one values those human qualities devastated by the disease, some persons may rationally choose to continue their life, while others may rationally chose to end it.

Other-regarding reasons for committing suicide consider the impact that one's continued existence will have on other people. Strictly speaking, one might argue that these considerations often precipitate "sacrificial deaths" rather than genuine suicides. It is, nevertheless, undeniable that patients in the latter stages of Alzheimer's disease can be a burden to their caregivers requiring "around the clock" demands such as diapering, feeding, and bathing. Because many of these patients tend to wander off and get themselves lost, the family must often maintain twenty-four-hour vigilance.[13] The financial burdens can be equally devastating. Depending on the age of onset, the disease may persist from seven-to-nine years, although many survive beyond twenty years. Nursing homes currently cost about $20 thousand annually. Therefore, about two-thirds of all Alzheimer's patients are cared for at home, which costs the family an average of about $11 thousand a year in disease-related expenses alone. One might also cite the social cost of providing nursing home care for Alzheimer's patients. In the United States it is estimated that about half of the people in nursing homes have Alzheimer's or related disorders at a cost of about $13 billion annually.[14] It is the fourth leading cause of death for American adults after heart disease, cancer, and stroke, with disease-related costs of all Alzheimer's families at about $35 billion dollars. Within the next decade the number of Alzheimer's victims will double, which will contribute to already spiraling health care costs in the United States.

But as noted at the beginning of this paper, sacrificial suicides are not without moral uncertainty. First, some philosophers have questioned the "voluntariness" of sacrificial deaths on various levels. It has been argued, for example, that a person suffering from a debilitating or painful disease who is contemplating suicide would be acting out of a state of depression and, therefore, would be incapable of genuine consent. Indeed, psychiatrists argue that 90 to 100 percent of suicide victims die while they have a diagnosable psychiatric disorder and that suicide is not uncommon among elderly patients treated for affective illness.[15]

Secondly, many suicidal patients may fear that they may become a burden to their loved ones and choose suicide, despite an "authentic" desire to live. Procedurally, the first objection involving "voluntariness" can be easily eliminated by a rigorous psychiatric evaluation for competency and requiring a reasonable waiting period before acting on a suicide request. The second objection assumes that it is irrational to choose to die for the sake of others, which is simply untrue. In fact, our society generally regards such altruistic acts as heroic, if not saintly. This is not to say that Alzheimer's patients ought to commit suicide for the sake of their loved ones, but that it is not irrational to take other people into account.

The moral principle of autonomy, then, demands that we allow rational persons (more precisely non-irrational persons) to rank their own personal evils. Moral decisions involving the choice between life and death are indeed difficult, and, therefore, we ought to expect a certain degree of trepidation on the part of persons making these deliberations. But we surely ought not deprive these individuals of their right to choose death over life merely because of the inherent complexity and finality of the decision.

There are other arguments often presented in opposition to the social acceptance of suicide. Suicidologists and family counselors have long held that suicide is a family-centered activity, often signifying the resolution of a crisis for both the person attempting suicide and for the family members who contemplate assisting. On these grounds it is argued that true voluntariness becomes suspect for both suicidal patient and assisting family member. According to Joseph Richman, when a person is faced with the decision whether or not to assist:

The future assister feels trapped and sees no other recourse than the death of the one who is ill, disabled, in pain, or despair. A process is set in motion over which the participants eventually have no control and no choice but the assisting suicidal act. Behind this process are the four parameters which are found in all suicides: The exhaustion of the ego and emotional resources of the family and social network and especially the assister, the presence of a crisis which will not be resolved or go away, and the acceptance of suicide as a solution.[16]

Richman and others then conclude that what the family really needs is counseling.

But without disparaging the counseling industry, it is imperative that one recognize that this communitarian view of the relationship of the individual to society tends to erode the very concept of autonomy and personal liberty. If human beings are perceived as primarily social beings, most actions become "other regarding." This leaves very little theoretical room for personal liberty in the Millian tradition. Hence, by treating suicide as a social disease, we become locked into a mindset that denies *a priori* that suicide can ever be an autonomous and competent act. Indeed, it is often the case that if the patient and family are not swayed by their counselor to abandon their suicidal plans, then often the assumption is that they need a new counselor and more therapy until they are cured. But "cure" in this sense is often tantamount to a patient abandoning his/her own beliefs and values in favor of those of the counselor. From a Gertian perspective, however, community values rooted in real life experience would form the standard of whether a suicide is irrational, not the highly idealized therapeutic family that exists only in psychology and sociology textbooks. As Gert noted, no rational person would willingly accept a moral rule that would allow physicians to forcibly substitute their rankings of evils over the equally rational rankings of their patients.[17]

In her suicide note, Janet cited both self-regarding and other-regarding reasons. "I have Alzheimer's disease," she wrote, "and I do not want to let it progress any further. I do not want to put my family or myself through the agony of this terrible disease."[18] If it is true, as I have proposed, that it is not irrational or immoral for Janet Adkins to commit suicide, how do the principles of autonomy and beneficence apply to those who want to assist? The principle of autonomy asserts that we must, as far as possible, respect a person's right of self-direction. According to Mill, the domain of uncontestable personal liberty covers those actions which do not violate the interests of others. Self-inflicted harm by a competent person must be tolerated on Millian principles--even when in conflict with our obligation of beneficence.

Beneficence, according to Beauchamp and Childress, encompasses two principles: "The first principle requires the provision of benefits (including the prevention and removal of harm as well as the promotion of welfare), and the second requires a balancing of benefits and harms."[19] But if there are a number of alternative ways of fulfilling this obligation, how far are we morally compelled to go? How much hardship are we morally required to assume, and how can we respect a person's autonomy at the same time? Many philosophers, such as John Stuart Mill, classify beneficence as a "duty of imperfect obligation," which is to say that we may be obligated to act, but not at any specific time or in any particular way.[20] Mill, of course, concluded that these kinds of duties do not result in a corresponding right. Hence, we can not claim a "right to die" based on the principle of beneficence. Thus far in this essay it has been argued that the right to commit suicide is derived from a person's moral right not to suffer unwillingly one of the five major harms (death, pain, disability, loss of freedom, or loss of pleasure) as a consequence of the actions of other persons.

Duties of beneficence between Alzheimer's patients and their families, then, are imperfect in the sense that society ought not dictate that families adopt any one specific course of action on behalf of their Alzheimer's-stricken parents. For example, we ought not legally or morally force adult children to take their parents into their own homes regardless of their personal situation, nor should we absolutely require them to pay for the most expensive nursing care available. Similarly, Alzheimer's patients should never be morally required out of beneficence to commit suicide in order to benefit their children.

There are a several arguments that might be employed to undermine the proposed beneficence of a physician-assisted suicide for Alzheimer's patients. The matter of securing an accurate diagnosis is probably the most compelling. Diagnosis is currently made by eliminating other diseases or conditions that might present similar symptoms; a logical process that yields wrong answers about 30 percent of the time. Hence, brain-tissue biopsy, performed as part of an autopsy, remains the only means of securing a certain Alzheimer's diagnosis. Therefore, there is always the possibility of misdiagnosis. In response to this line of reasoning, one might say that a physician contemplating assisting in a suicide ought to make certain that the diagnosis is correct as part of the informed consent procedure. The law might, therefore, require that a physician contact other health-care professionals personally to confirm the diagnosis.

Published accounts of the Adkins case indicate that Kevorkian did make certain of the diagnosis. However, Kevorkian's public image, coupled with the demands of doctor-patient confidentiality, tended to obscure the details of the case. This fueled speculation and helped make Janet's suicide a focus of national debate. Physicians wishing to assist in a patient's suicide, however, may encounter other patients and other diagnosing physicians exhibiting varying levels of competence. So, as a matter of public policy, some regulation of physician-assisted suicide is probably desirable.

Critics have cited a litany of "slippery-slope" arguments, often referring to a gradual erosion of the central mission or goal of medicine. According to Leon

Kass, for example, the goal of medicine must be the preservation of health, and therefore society ought to guard against the pursuit of other "false goals" such as serving a patient's wants and desires. The prudent physician, Kass argues, must resist these socially mandated temptations and remain mindful of the true purpose of medicine. Given this perspective, suicide assistance turns out to be simply illogical. "Is it not self-contradictory," he exclaims, "for the healing art to be the killing art--even in those cases in which we might all agree that killing is not murder?"[21] But is this a plausible restriction upon the practice of medicine? Are physicians morally obligated to function in this narrow domain delineated by Kass? The mission of modern medicine has undoubtedly changed rather dramatically since the time of Hippocrates. Physicians of the twentieth century simply do not limit the practice of medicine to curing diseases, but also routinely perform socially mandated acts such as: easing pain and suffering, cosmetic surgery, fertility treatment, abortions, and weight reduction counseling. This is not to say that physicians necessarily ought to be involved in all these activities. Indeed, there may be strong reasons why physicians ought to refrain from some of these false goals. However, justification for such indictments must involve considerably more than adherence to a narrow teleology. After all, in the real world, policy decisions involving the "true function of medicine" must rely heavily on social and political considerations as well as on history.

Another slippery-slope argument refers to the "social drift" of empowering physicians with the right to kill. In our achievement-oriented society, they point out, it is vulnerable people (such as dying, disabled, or elderly patients) who are most likely to commit suicide. As Richard Doerflinger put it:

> Society's offer of death communicates the message to certain patients that they may continue to live if they wish but the rest of us have no strong interest in their survival. Indeed, once the choice of a quick and painless death is officially accepted as rational, resistance to this choice may be seen as eccentric or even selfish.[22]

But it is equally important to recognize that the dying, disabled, or elderly patients are also the most likely to have good reasons for wanting to die. By refusing to accept their life-and-death preferences, we communicate to them that we don't respect their life choices, which is to treat them with an utter disrespect that rational people find repugnant. Another slippery-slope argument predicts increasing social pressures upon physicians by the health-care industry to encourage indigent patients to commit suicide in order to control costs. If suicide becomes an acceptable option to expensive high-tech care, and if life-extending therapies become a matter of choice, society may tighten the purse strings and suicides will grow proportionately.[23] This view assumes that if physicians assist in suicides for their Alzheimer's patients now, they will eventually be involved in suicides for less serious diseases or those that can be cured only at great expense. These possibilities are certainly foreboding, but address an assortment of other moral problems with our health-care system beyond the suicide debate. An unjust health-care system may indeed cause a rise in the suicide rate, but outlawing suicide assistance will not make the system just.

Many physicians are willing to accept suicide assistance as a general principle, but still remain adamantly against physician-assisted suicide. But this sincere (if unsophisticated) view overlooks two facts. Physicians alone possess the technical knowledge necessary to insure a certain and painless death. While it is surely possible to train other professionals to acquire this knowledge,[24] the question of how society will regulate the practice becomes very relevant. Physicians are already accustomed to social and legal regulation through a variety of venues, where other professionals may not be. Moreover, most of the drugs that render suicide painless and effective are currently monopolized by physicians through prescriptions. The time may come when doctors will have to choose between providing lethal but painless drugs for their dying patients and relinquishing control of these substances to the "invisible drug economy." Like it or not, physicians are uniquely situated for suicide assistance. Ironically, by refusing to assist, they may unwittingly contribute to the pain and suffering of those who unsuccessfully attempt to commit the act on their own.

Indeed, given their dual roles of trusted repositories of medical knowledge and as pharmacological gatekeepers, it might be that physicians already have too much control over how we die.

CONCLUSION

It has been argued that suicide is sometimes a rational and morally acceptable alternative to intractable pain and suffering and that suicide assistance ought to be regarded as equally rational and morally acceptable. Suicide assistance, therefore, may be construed as a matter of fulfilling an imperfect obligation of beneficence. While it is true that physician-assisted suicide ought to be regulated by the state, there should be no laws compelling assistance, nor should there be laws absolutely prohibiting such involvement. Although the degree of causal involvement in suicide assistance is morally irrelevant and based on emotive rather than logical arguments, one virtue of the suicide machine is that a physician may choose from several different kinds of causal involvement as consistent with the needs of the patient and his\her own personal ethical standards. Finally, if suicide assistance is sometimes morally justifiable, and if the distinction between physician-assisted suicide and voluntary euthanasia is morally insignificant, we are probably on a slippery slope. However, as Rachels notes: "... if we went to the bottom of this particular slope, our attitudes towards suicide and euthanasia would have become not worse but better."[25]

PHYSICIAN-ASSISTED SUICIDE

ACKNOWLEDGMENT

The author would like to thank Valerie Marie Constance for her expert editorial assistance and critical remarks which substantially improved the final draft.

NOTES

1   T.L. Beauchamp, *Principles of Biomedical Ethics,* 3rd ed. (Oxford: Oxford University Press, 1989), 222.

2   T. Zeman, "Pushing the Button," *Newsweek,* 13 November 1989, 8.

3   Correspondence from Myriam Coppens, Hemlock Society (letter), *New England Journal of Medicine* 324 (16 May 1991):1435.

4   For a detailed account of Janet's death and other arguments in favor of physician-assisted suicide, see J. Kevorkian, *Prescription: Medicide: The Goodness of Planned Death* (Buffalo: Prometheus Books, 1991), especially chapters 15 and 16.

5   N. Gibbs, "Dr. Death Strikes Again," *Time,* 4 November 1991, 178.

6   T.L. Beauchamp, "Suicide," in *Matters of Life and Death,* ed. Tom Regan (New York: Random House, 1980), 77.

7   For an excellent discussion of the semantics of suicide, see: Beauchamp, "Suicide."

8   J. Rachels, *The End of Life: Euthanasia and Morality* (Oxford: Oxford University Press, 1986), 82-83.

9   See T. Quill, "Death and Dignity: A Case of Individualized Decision Making," *New England Journal of Medicine* 324 (7 March 1991):691-94.

10   For an outstanding summary of the issues involved in suicide assistance and euthanasia, see the "Dying Well? A Colloquy on Euthanasia and Assisted Suicide," *Hastings Center Report* 22 (March/April 1992). The entire issue contains articles by eminent scholars on the topic. Especially noteworthy are the opposing articles by Daniel Callahan ("When Self-Determination Runs Amok") and Dan Brock ("Voluntary Active Euthanasia").

11   B. Gert, "Rationality, Human Nature, and Lists," *Ethics* 100 (January 1990):280. For a detailed exposition of Gert's position, see B. Gert, *Morality: A New Justification of the Moral Rules* (New York: Oxford University Press, 1988) and C.M. Culver and B. Gert, *Philosophy in Medicine: Conceptual and Ethical Issues in Medicine and Psychiatry* (New York: Oxford University Press, 1982).

12   I have omitted another class of reasons often used against suicide, which we might call "God-regarding." These arguments are usually based on one or more of the following: the Sixth Commandment, "Thou shalt not kill"; the absolute "sanctity of life"; or the demand for noninterference in God's domain. Within

this class, I would also include arguments from natural law, which presuppose theological premisses. In a pluralistic society like the United States, there is very little consensus on theological issues--even within Christianity. On Gertian principles I suspect that these arguments would be treated as not irrational and worthy of respect; however, one could not interpret the failure to recognize these principles by an individual as irrational. For a detailed analysis of these kinds of arguments and others, see: T.L. Beauchamp, "Suicide," and R.B. Brandt, "The Morality and Rationality of Suicide," in *Moral Problems,* ed. J. Rachels, 2nd ed. (New York: Harper and Row, 1975). More sympathetic to the Roman Catholic tradition is G.D. Coleman, "Assisted Suicide: An Ethical Perspective," in *Euthanasia: The Moral Issues,* ed. R.M. Baird and S.E. Rosenbaum (Buffalo: Prometheus Books, 1989).

13   For an detailed and sobering portrayal of what it is like to care for an Alzheimer's patient at home, see N.L. Mace and P.V. Rabins, *The 36-Hour Day: A Family Guide to Caring for Persons with Alzheimer's Disease, and Related Dementing Illnesses and Memory Loss in Later Life* (New York: Warner Books, 1981).

14   Group for the Advancement of Psychiatry, *The Psychiatric Treatment of Alzheimer's Disease Report No. 125* (New York: Brunner/Mazel Publishers, 1988), 6.

15   Y. Conwell and E.D. Caine, "Rational Suicide and the Right to Die," *New England Journal of Medicine* 325 (10 October 1991):1101.

16   J. Richman, "Sanctioned Assisting Suicide: Impact on Family Relations," *Issues in Law & Medicine* 3 (1987):57.

17   Culver and Gert, *Philosophy in Medicine,* 171.

18   L. Belkin, "Doctor Tells of First Death Using His Suicide Device," *New York Times,* 8 June 1990, A1.

19   T.L. Beauchamp and J. Childress, *Principles of Biomedical Ethics,* 3rd ed. (New York: Oxford University Press, 1989), 195.

20   J.S. Mill, *Utilitarianism* (New York: Bobbs-Merrill), 61.

21   L. Kass, *Toward a More Natural Science: Biology and Human Affairs* (New York: Free Press, 1985), 234.

22   R. Doerflinger, "Assisted Suicide: Pro-Choice or Anti-Life" *Hastings Center Report* 19 (January/February 1989, special supplement):17.

23   *Ibid.*

24   It appears that the physician's monopoly on technical knowledge in this regard is already in jeopardy. On 18 August 1991 the *New York Times's* number one hardback best seller in the advice category was Derek Humphrey's *Final Exit: Self Deliverance and Assisted Suicide for the Dying* (Secaucus, NJ: Hemlock Society, 1991). Written by the executive director of the Hemlock Society, it is a manual on how to commit suicide and how to effectively assist suicide.

25   Rachels, *The End of Life,* 87.

17

Federal Policy Regarding End-of-Life Decisions

Mitchell M. Handelsman

Against human nature one cannot legislate. One can only try to educate it, and that is a slow process with only a distant hope of success.

Bernard Berenson

There's an old saying that there are two things that one should never see being made: sausage and legislation. The purpose of this chapter is to explore the federal government's involvement in death and dying issues by taking a look inside the "sausage factory." In 1990, Congress passed the Patient Self-Determination Act, which is the first piece of federal legislation that deals with end-of-life decisions. An exploration of the process of passage of the act will provide some perspective on the direction, and on the wisdom, of future congressional action in this area.

What should the federal government do about issues such as advance directives, active euthanasia, and others in the area of death and dying? Discussion of this question arouses much ambivalence. On one hand, many feel a need to create or clarify public policy in these areas, which are certainly growing in importance as medical technology advances. Legislation may be necessary to codify our collective moral reasoning and to help citizens make good decisions about their lives and deaths without undue manipulation by physicians, lawyers, and others with vested interests. Alternatively, many people react with horror to the thought of federal involvement in such sensitive areas. They remember the Baby Doe regulations,[1] the debates about abortion, and some of their own personal experiences with government agencies.

The ambivalence people feel about federal policy, and the lack of congressional action on many important questions, appears to be justified on a number of grounds. First, government's role in health care and the personal decisions involved is by no means clear:

> As the capacity of the medical system grows to sustain lives that would have been given up for lost a few years ago, the temptation for government to intervene to protect rights and contain costs grows too, generating new tensions between these objectives and between public authority and private prerogatives.[2]

Congress's experience with the Medicare Catastrophic Coverage Act,[3] in which a major bill of 1988 was repealed in 1989 after protest by senior citizens, has reinforced its tendency to wait until there is clear consensus before acting in controversial areas. In its search for workable solutions to complex problems, Congress runs the risk of producing compromises that please--and benefit--few. In the area of bioethics, Congress has contented itself with holding hearings and establishing commissions, committees, and task forces,[4] while eschewing the making of policy.

Second, Congress is subject to political pressures that often do not coincide with the thinking of those who are most familiar with the moral and technical issues involved in a given area, and, therefore, do not yield optimal public policy. For example, Congresspeople's stands on any moral issue will virtually always be assessed--especially by opponents--in relation to their stand on abortion, and their degree of support will depend heavily on who else is supporting it and how it will affect undecided voters back home.

Third, there is a tendency for members of Congress to act on a personal, human level. It is a myth that Congresspeople are removed from "the people," and respond only to issues rather than to individuals. Indeed, according to Vincent, "the human element is not just an integral part of the formation of public policy; I would argue that it is the primary element driving the development of federal policy."[5] Congresspeople respond on a very personal level to the influences of their own experiences, to the people and groups they represent, and to other members. Most members of Congress are not trained in sciences such as medicine--nor in fields such as philosophy--that would help them evaluate scientific and other available evidence. Rather, they are notoriously more responsive to stories in the popular media than to articles published in medical journals and law reviews.

The story of the Patient Self-Determination Act of 1990 highlights these pressures and tendencies of Congress. Even from before the decision to sponsor a bill, basic policy questions are subsumed in a web of personal and political concerns.

The primary justification for the Self-Determination Act were data showing that a huge majority of the public are in favor of the concept of advance directives, but that only 10-to-15 percent of them had prepared one.[6] The bill became law in November 1990 as part of the Omnibus Budget Reconciliation Act of 1990.[7] As passed, it covers all hospitals, home health agencies, nursing homes, health maintenance organizations, and hospices that receive Medicare or Medicaid funds, and contains the following major provisions: (A) Agencies must have policies to provide written information to adult patients concerning their "rights under State law (whether statutory or as recognized by the courts of the State) to make decisions concerning such medical care, including the right to accept or refuse medical or surgical treatment and the right to formulate advance directives . . . and the written policies of the provider or organization respecting the implementation of such rights." (B) Agencies must document whether or not patients have executed advance directives. (C) Agencies must not "condition the provision of care or otherwise discriminate against an individual based on whether or not the individual has executed an advance directive." (D) Agencies must follow state law. (E) Agencies must "provide (individually or with others) for education for staff and the community on issues concerning advance directives." The effective date of these provisions was December 1991.

In addition, the act requires the Secretary of Health and Human Services (HHS), within six months, to "develop and implement a national campaign to inform the public of the option to execute advance directives and of a patient's right to participate and direct health care decisions," to develop and distribute information, to assist states to develop their own information, and to "mail information to Social Security recipients, [and] add a page to the Medicare handbook with respect to the provisions of this section."

As passed, this bill represents a significant step in educating the public about advance directives and in assuring that people who create advance directives will have them honored. However, the original bill, sponsored in the Senate by John C. Danforth (R-MO) in October 1989, had much more ambitious goals, many of which will be discussed below. The process by which these ambitious (some would say grandiose) goals became streamlined (some would say diluted) is typical of congressional activity on controversial questions. Although the particulars described below will vary depending on the issue, any legislative initiative will face the same kinds of hurdles.

Having a bill introduced into both the House and Senate increases its chances for passage, partly because opponents cannot claim that their house did not have a chance to consider the bill. The major changes in, and influences on, the Self-Determination bill can be traced through the drafting of the House version of the bill, which was finally sponsored in April 1990 by Rep. Sander M. Levin (D-MI). Indeed, it took Rep. Levin a month to decide to sponsor the bill in the first place, and another several months to redraft the original Senate version in such a way as to ensure support and passage.

Rep. Levin's first concern when presented with the idea of sponsoring this legislation was a very personal one: what were the implications of associating himself with Sen. Danforth on this issue? Though Danforth--an ordained

Episcopal priest--has a reputation for integrity, he is a Republican; Levin, a Democrat. Although the policy was good, was it worth the association? For example, might it be a problem that Levin, who is Pro-Choice, sponsors a bill put forward by a staunch Pro-Lifer?

Although highly respected for his views, Danforth made some people nervous because those views could not be easily predicted or categorized. "He tends to arrive at positions after a moral inventory rather than a political calculus."[8] Sen. Danforth had opposed the previous year's catastrophic health-insurance plan, one that Rep. Levin strongly supported. Sen. Danforth's view was that too much health-care money is spent on the final days and weeks of life, that money could be better spent elsewhere. It was difficult to separate this view from the bill; the danger was that Danforth's motivation, although advertised to be the education of the public, would be perceived as being cost containment: more advance directives would save money by having people die a few days earlier. Even with these concerns, however, two factors came across clearly: the integrity and effectiveness of Sen. Danforth, and the soundness of the policy included in the bill.

The fuel of even the best policy needs the oxygen of political support, which was not immediately forthcoming for this bill. The major representative of the elderly, the American Association of Retired Persons, is a very powerful lobby, and has worked with its affiliates to get advance directive legislation passed in the states and has distributed literature on durable powers of attorney.[9] However, they refused to take a position on the bill. Many groups expressed early opposition or concern with the bill, including hospitals, doctors, Roman Catholics, Pro-Life organizations, and, indeed, the Health Care Financing Administration (HCFA) itself, which is the agency within HHS that is responsible for running Medicare and Medicaid. Provider groups were uniformly supportive of the concept of advance directives and uniformly opposed to those provisions in the bill that involved requirements of their members. For example, physicians argued that hospitals should be responsible for providing information and asking about advance directives, but that doctors would lose credibility by bringing up the issue of death with patients. Hospitals argued that because physicians were responsible for the care of patients, it should be the physicians' responsibility to handle these questions; hospitals would be put under too great a paperwork and administrative burden.

Those groups that did provide early support for the Senate bill were not the most powerful. For example, the American Medical Students Association was among the first to endorse the bill. However, the American Medical Association (AMA), whose support was considered very important for passage, opposed the bill or withheld support until very late in the process.

Religious and Pro-Life groups saw a dangerous precedent in federal government involvement in what has traditionally been a state issue. Both argued that they have negotiated successfully in the state legislatures, and that, in the fashion of the Supreme Court decision in *Webster v. Reproductive Health Services*,[10] these policy decisions should be handled on that level. The federal government should not make policy and should not force states to do so. They also made a slippery-slope argument: providing information and talking with patients about advance directives implicitly endorses and encourages their use. This, in turn, would surely lead to abuses of vulnerable populations and to active euthanasia.

In addition to the opposition Rep. Levin would have to address or withstand, he needed to think about the political capital he'd have to expend in order to get support for this measure. Was a small informational bill with no ardent supporters worth the effort, in light of the risk to his other initiatives and the support he might have to give to others in return for support? After much deliberation, Rep. Levin decided to sponsor a House version of the Patient Self-Determination Act. However, he decided to revise the original Senate bill and introduce his own version in the house. Even before introduction, the bill underwent several revisions to make it acceptable to enough Representatives and groups to have at least a chance of passage. The negotiations and revisions before the final introduction took over five months.

The original Senate version of the bill contained a requirement that states needed to have advance directive legislation--either living will or durable power of attorney--on the books. At the time, six states had no such laws and would have been forced to pass them. The first major change in the House version was the deletion of this state-law requirement. This deletion was accomplished by striking the entire section of the bill dealing with Medicaid, and leaving only the Medicare section.

Deletion of the state-law requirement was done primarily because Michigan, Rep. Levin's home state, had no advance directive law. State legislators were divided about the desirability of a federal mandate to pass such legislation. Although not legally recognized, advance directives were generally honored in Michigan. It was argued that this federal initiative would make people angry, and might spoil the way advance directives were working now, as well as negotiations that were going on to pass an advance directive law. The result might be a bill that was worse than nothing at all.

Deleting the state-law requirement by deleting the Medicaid provisions was also justified by jurisdictional concerns; "gaining jurisdiction over the most controversial and important issues is central to the power game in Congress."[11] Bills have the best chance of passage when they are referred to a committee on which the sponsor sits. Sen. Danforth had originally designed the bill to work through the requirements of participation in Medicare and Medicaid because those programs fall under the jurisdiction of the Finance Committee, of which he was a member. In the House, the situation was somewhat more complicated; bills can be referred to several committees for consideration. The Ways and Means Committee, on which Rep. Levin sits, has jurisdiction over Medicare. But the Energy and Commerce Committee, of which Rep. Levin is not a member, has jurisdiction over Medicaid. Stripping the Medicaid provisions increased the probability that Ways and Means would be the only committee to have jurisdiction, which would make passage easier.

The state-law requirement was the provision most vehemently opposed by Roman Catholic and right-to-life groups. They felt that they had worked hard in the states, and that states without laws did not have an absence of policy, but were making a positive statement about advance directives. Deleting the provision seemed to have the effect of softening and delaying their opposition to the entire bill. It was felt that retaining some ambiguity in six states was a price worth paying for obtaining good policy for the others.

With such good political reasons to delete the state-law requirement, substantive justifications were sure to follow. The major one was that there was case law in several of the states that supported the use of advance directives and that there was no law prohibiting their use.

The controversy surrounding the state-law requirement spread to a general issue that is sure to reemerge whenever Congress considers legislation concerning death and dying: should federal policy intrude in areas that have traditionally been left to the states? Several members of the Health Subcommittee wondered why Congress should pass this law at all. If people need to be educated about rights granted by the states, shouldn't the states require such education? The response to that argument was that empowering people by providing information about their rights was important enough to justify federal involvement.

In order for that argument to stick, the bill needed to be sold as a purely informational one; it was necessary to avoid overriding any state law. For example, the original Senate bill required agencies to "arrange for the prompt and orderly transfer of a patient to the care of others when as a matter of conscience the provider cannot implement the wishes of such patient." This was considered by many to be too close to making substantive law about transfers. After several revisions, it was finally replaced by a requirement for agencies to provide patients with "the written policies of the provider or organization respecting the implementation of such rights" to refuse treatment and create advance directives. The final law also stated that its provisions should not "be construed to prohibit the application of a State law which allows for an objection on the basis of conscience for any health-care provider or any agent of such provider which, as a matter of conscience, cannot implement an advance directives."

The changes discussed so far had several important benefits: they avoided trouble at home for Rep. Levin, they calmed the fears of those who were concerned about overriding--or simply getting involved in--state law, they muted some opposition to the bill and showed that Rep. Levin was willing to address concerns, they "bought" a couple of cosponsors, and they helped clarify the scope of the bill. It could be argued that the bill was already being shorn of some of its major impact and value by these changes. However, it was recognized that much policy does not come full-blown from the halls of the Capitol, but emerges over time in an incremental way. The decision was made to streamline the bill (make its goals more modest) in the hope that passage would represent the first step in such a process. The choice seemed to be between a modest bill that passed, versus a grandiose bill that failed.

The original Senate version of the bill required agencies to "inform any such patient of such patient's right to make decisions concerning such patient's medical care," including the right to do advance directives, and to "document the treatment wishes of such patient, and periodically review such wishes with the patient." As written, this would seem to achieve a very desirable goal: a conversation between patients and health-care professionals in which the wishes of the patient were made clear.

This broad goal was heartily endorsed by many, including those individuals who were already doing this kind of thing routinely and those who made their living as "ethics consultants" in hospitals. The opposition came from two quarters: from those who would feel too great a burden, such as hospitals and physicians, and from those--including some physicians and some ethicists--who believed it was premature to require such conversations when most providers are neither skilled nor comfortable with them.[12] The first version of the House bill[13] attempted to draw a fine line between asking patients what their treatment preferences were, and simply recording those preferences if they were voluntarily offered; in addition to the same language about informing people of their rights, the House version said that agencies needed "to inquire periodically (and to document in the individual's medical record) whether or not the individual has executed an advance directive and to document in such record the individual's wishes (if any) with respect to such medical care."

This compromise language still met with resistance. Gone was the requirement to ask patients specifically what their wishes were; the language required only that spontaneously expressed wishes be documented. However, there still seemed to be a requirement for an extended conversation with patients, and the *de facto* execution of an advance directive via patients expressing their wishes. The revised House bill[14] contained much more narrow language, which was included in the passed bill. It required agencies only "to provide written information" about rights to execute advance directives, and "to document in the individual's medical record whether or not the individual has executed an advance directive." Nobody was required to talk to patients anymore; nor was anybody required to listen to and document their wishes.

Now that it was clear that the information provided to patients needed to be written, the question of who produced that information emerged. There were those who wanted to leave it up to the individual agency. Others, especially those who were concerned about abuses, wanted HHS or the US Public Health Service to prepare information that would be distributed to all fifty states.

Two considerations influenced the compromise that was reached. First, there was some fear that HHS was not enthusiastic about advance directives, or was associated with those opposed to the bill, and therefore would not produce an optimal document. There was also resistance to a federal source for documents for all the states; state-specific sources might be better. The second consideration was a jurisdictional one: the bill could require the Public Health Service, or the Medicaid state agencies, to draft the information. However, these alternatives would fall under the jurisdiction of the Energy and Commerce Committee, not Ways and Means, and were therefore unacceptable. The compromise, enacted into law, states that "the Secretary [of HHS] shall assist appropriate State agencies, associations, or other private entities in developing the State-specific documents that would be distributed by providers."

Another rather grandiose goal of the original Senate bill was the requirement of ethics committees. Those who have been working with ethics committees for a long time and were familiar with their benefits were very supportive of the bill.[15] However, three major problems emerged. First, the literature on ethics committees is not conclusive.[16] Second, the goals of the committees required in the Senate bill went beyond the informational nature of the bill as it was developing on the House side. Third, many still had the bad taste in their mouths engendered by the Baby Doe debates of the mid-eighties.

The original Senate version of the bill required agencies to "implement an institutional ethics committee which would initiate educational programs for staff, patients, residents, and the community on ethical issues in health care, advise on particular cases, and serve as a forum on such issues." At the first negotiating session between staffers for Rep. Levin (the primary sponsor) and staffers for Henry Waxman (the chair of the Energy and Commerce subcommittee that would be handling the bill), it became clear that Rep. Waxman would not support such a broad mandate for ethics committees. He opposed anything close to having decision-making capacity taken from parties immediately involved. During the debates on the Baby Doe legislation in 1984, he argued strongly against "committees of bureaucrats and teams of lawyers to second-guess and overrule the informed decisions of parents and doctors and clergy."[17] He was not persuaded that ethics committees could remain advisory. In order to gain Rep. Waxman's cosponsorship of the bill (he was quite supportive of the major provisions), references to advice and providing discussion fora were deleted, and the difficulty smaller agencies would have in formulating committees was addressed: ". . . to provide (individually or with others) for educational programs for staff, individuals receiving medical care by or through the provider or organization, and the community on ethical issues concerning patient self-determination and concerning advance directives respecting such care."

This version was still unacceptable to many; what were "programs," what were "ethical issues concerning patient self-determination," and what would patients receive beyond the written information required by the other provisions of the bill? The final version: ". . . to provide (individually or with others) for education for staff and the community on issues concerning advance directives."

It was important to secure the cosponsorship of members of the Ways and Means Health Subcommittee. One influential member was very interested in the bill, but finally decided not to cosponsor, because the president of a major national right-to-life organization resided in his district. Another subcommittee member seemed to be significantly influenced by a recent personal experience. According to the rumor, his mother was hospitalized several months earlier, and had executed a living will. This member overrode his mother's directive and had treatment delivered. His mother died shortly before the Health Subcommittee began its deliberations; her death significantly influenced his approach to the legislation. One tactic he used for making passage difficult is typical of those who do not want to oppose a bill outright, but who do not want it passed. He offered a long list of amendments that he threatened to offer in committee, or on the House floor.

This episode highlights the difficulty Congresspeople face when weighing information that comes from personal experience, stories told to them by constituents, and scientifically derived data about large numbers of people. Congresspeople follow the general tendency to attend to vivid individual stories, and give less weight than they should to less vivid but more representative data about many people.[18]

In this case, which may be typical, there seemed to be an interesting interaction of the effects of various kinds of information. Members were moderately swayed by survey data suggesting strong support for advance directives. However, that moderate response was significantly strengthened by three news stories that conveniently hit the papers during consideration of the bill. The most important was the June 1990 Supreme Court Decision in *Cruzan v. Director Missouri Department of Health*.[19] The dramatic circumstances of this case, and the explicit endorsement of advance directives by Justice O'Connor and others, made Congresspeople take notice and recognize the importance of the issues--although the bill was only tangentially relevant to the case. The second story was about a New York nursing home that was held liable for $100 thousand worth of treatment to a woman whose family had decided on an alternative course of treatment.[20] The third was the story of Edward Winter, whose do-not-resuscitate order (DNR) was not honored by a Cincinnati hospital. His heirs sued the hospital.[21]

One news story threatened to undo much of the work of the previous six months. This was the Kevorkian "death machine" story, which came from Rep. Levin's own Michigan district.[22] The "damage control" for this took the form of a memo distributed to the Health Subcommittee members, detailing the distinctions between Kevorkian's actions and the issues addressed in the bill. "In fact," the memo read in part, "the Self-Determination Act may serve to *sharpen and strengthen* the line that Dr. Kevorkian obviously crossed, by heightening the awareness of all the issues surrounding end-of-life treatment decisions. It seemed as though the damage control worked. Indeed, the Kevorkian story may have made some members more willing to read about the bill, and to understand the issues a bit better.

It is too soon to tell the long-term impact of the Patient Self-Determination Act. There have been a plethora of articles in the popular press[23] and professional literature[24] that have expressed grave concerns about the act. However, many of these concerns seem to be contradictory. For example, some have argued that the act, as passed, will have no significant effect: paragraphs in the Medicare manual and in admission materials will not be read and will not lead to conversations about end-of-life decisions.[25] At the same time, worry is expressed that admission to a hospital is not the best time to offer information to patients because of the significant negative impact the information will have on them. Another example of seemingly contradictory arguments concerns who should provide information. The AMA lobbied strongly for hospitals to be responsible for providing information, but physicians are now arguing that hospitals "must not commit the clinical ethical error of making an admissions clerk do the physician's work."[26] How well-founded these concerns are is an issue that awaits empirical research.

Some concerns are expressed under the guise of discussions of the new law; in reality, they highlight weaknesses of current advance directive laws. For example, it has been argued that state law is vague and is difficult to communicate to patients. But this vagueness has always existed, and has hindered the proper handling of advance directives. A related concern is the difficulty in educating staff and the community. The need to educate staff about advance directives has existed since their development; the new law merely mandates what should have been going on anyway. It has also spurred a variety of ideas for educating the community, including showing videotapes in waiting rooms, presenting public service announcements in the media, holding community workshops, and forming consortia to coordinate the efforts of individual agencies.[27]

This is not to say that there are not problems with the implementation of the act. Perhaps the major impediment to implementation was HCFA's delay in publishing regulations. As of December 1991, the date the act took effect, HCFA had not issued regulations, nor had the national education campaign, mandated by the act to be initiated in 1991, taken place. HCFA can continue to communicate its original opposition to the act by not generating an educational campaign and not enforcing the provisions of the act.

In the absence of regulations, agencies must answer questions[28] including the following: Who should convey information to patients, and who should be available to answer specific questions patients may have at the time of admission? What are the exceptions to informing patients on admission? What effect will this law have on our existing policies regarding the implementation of advance directives? If patients are being transferred from other facilities that have already informed them about advance directives, do we have to do it again? What role do nurses and other professionals have? As with any new policy, it will take some time before the details are worked out. In addition, implementation will vary across different types of agencies. For example, the needs and processes of nursing homes are different from those of hospitals.[29]

Although there are concerns and problems to be anticipated, there are signs that the act is being taken very seriously by health-care agencies, and is already having significant and lasting effects. There is no shortage of information agencies can use; producing materials for agencies and patients has become a thriving business,[30] and workshops are being held throughout the country. Many health-care agencies and organizations, while concerned about the specifics of implementation, are seeing the act as an opportunity to improve the knowledge of health-care professionals and the relationships between professionals and patients.[31]

The act may heighten awareness of advance directives among patients and lead to more advance directives being written; however, there is evidence that such information alone will not accomplish this end.[32] Even if no new advance directives are written, however, the act has achieved an important purpose by raising consciousness among the public and professionals. Health-care agencies are becoming more clear about how to implement those advance directives that already exist.[33] In addition, the act has stimulated a broader and deeper discussion of advance directives, including the reliance on statutes versus constitutional and common-law rights for their justification.[34]

Another potential benefit of the act is that it will be a "foot in the door" of Congress, which may be more willing to involve itself in "right-to-die" issues. It is important to understand that policy is not made by 535 members of Congress, but by a much smaller number of Congresspeople who serve on the relevant subcommittees (along with their staff members[35]). The Self-Determination Act exposed many of these Congresspeople, in a personally and politically important way, to one type of problem regarding end-of-life decisions. Of course, the policy provided in the act still leaves many issues totally untouched. For example, the act does not come close to proposing a national advance directive law. Nor does it consider the issue, raised by many supporters of the bill, of portability of advance directives, to ensure that advance directives produced in one state would be honored in other states. Passage of the act, in the context of increased concern about issues such as health-care rationing and care of the poor and elderly, makes it more likely that Congress will consider many end-of-life issues in the future.

The question remains: *Should* Congress consider these issues in the future? As advances in medical technology continues, and discussions of physician-assisted suicide and euthanasia become more common in the popular media, Congress will be pushed more and more to enter the arena of end-of-life decisions. Indeed, Congress can potentially play a major role by providing a forum for extended and informed debate, and by creating much needed consistency. Many of us would feel much more comfortable with a national policy, rather than leaving such important decisions up to the seemingly more capricious state legislatures. At the same time, however, as the issues become more controversial, political considerations--many of which are outlined above --will become that much greater. It is hard to oppose notions such as greater information for citizens or greater participation in decision making. It will take much more energy and courage to discuss issues and policies for which there are no handy slogans that are politically neutral. Those of us who favor increased Congressional action must be sensitive to the political and personal contexts of Congressional debate and action, lest we find that the resulting "sausage" is to nobody's liking.

ACKNOWLEDGMENT

I thank Margie Krest for her valuable comments on earlier versions of this manuscript.

NOTES

1   L.D. Brown, "Civil Rights and Regulatory Wrongs: The Reagan Admini-
stration and the Medical Treatment of Handicapped Infants," *Journal of Health, Politics, Policy and Law* 11 (1986):231-54; R. Gustaitis and E.W.D. Young, *A Time to Be Born, a Time to Die: Conflicts and Ethics in an Intensive Care Nursery* (Reading, MA: Addison-Wesley, 1986):181-208.
2   L.D. Brown, "Civil Rights and Regulatory Wrongs," 233.
3   Medicaid Catastrophic Coverage Act, Public Law no. 100-360.
4   A.M. Capron, "Bioethics on the Congressional Agenda," *Hastings Center Report* 19 (March/April):22-23; Office of Technology Assessment, *Life-Sustaining Technologies and the Elderly* (Washington, DC: Government Printing Office, 1987); Senate Special Committee on Aging, *A Matter of Choice: Planning Ahead for Health Care Decisions* (Washington, DC: Government Printing Office, 1987).
5   T.A. Vincent, "A View from the Hill: The Human Element in Policy Making on Capital Hill," *American Psychology* 45 (1960):61-64.
6   S.V. McCrary and J.R. Botkin, Jr., "Hospital Policy on Advance Directives: Do Institutions Ask Patients About Living Wills?" *Journal of the American Medical Association* 262 (1989):2411-14.
7   Omnibus Budget Reconciliation Act of 1990, Public Law no. 101-508.

8   M. Garone and G. Ujifusa, *The Almanac of American Politics 1988* (Washington, DC: National Journal, 1987), 665-66.

9   C.P. Sabatino, *Health Care Powers of Attorney: An Introduction and Sample Form* (Washington, DC: American Bar Association, 1990).

10   *Webster v. Reproductive Health Services,* 109 S. Ct. 3040 (1989).

11   H. Smith, *The Power Game: How Washington Works* (New York: Ballantine Books, 1988), 285.

12   A.M. Capron, "The Patient Self-Determination Act: Not Now," *Hastings Center Report* 20 (September/October 1990):35-36.

13   H.R. 4449.

14   H.R. 5067.

15   J.C. Fletcher, "The Patient Self-Determination Act: Yes," *Hastings Center Report* 20 (September/October 1990):33-35.

16   B. Lo, "Behind Closed Doors: Promises and Pitfalls of Ethics Committees," *New England Journal of Medicine* 317 (1987):46-50; F. Rosner, "Hospital Medical Ethics Committees: A Review of their Development," *Journal of the American Medical Association* 253 (1987):2693-97.

17   H. Waxman, Floor Debate, *Congressional Record* 130 (2 February 1984): H 396.

18   R.E. Nisbett and L. Ross, *Human Interference: Strategies and Shortcomings of Social Judgement* (Englewood Cliffs, NJ: Prentice-Hall, 1985).

19   *Cruzan v. Director Missouri Department of Health,* 58 USLW 4916.

20   H. Meyer, "Nursing Home Cannot Collect Fees in Right-to-Die Case," *American Medical News* (16 February 1990):8.

21   D. Margolick, "Patient's Lawsuit Says Saving Life Ruined It," *New York Times,* 18 March 1990, 1, 24.

22   L. Belkin, "Doctor Tells of First Death Using His Suicide Machine," *New York Times,* 6 June 1990, A1, B6.

23   W. Booth, "U.S. 'Living Will' Rule Creates Confusion," *Washington Post,* 17 July 1991, A1, A5.

24   A.M. Capron, "The Patient Self-Determination Act," 35-36; C.C. Obade, "The Patient Self-Determination Act: Right Church, Wrong Pew," *The Journal of Clinical Ethics* 1 (1990):320-22; J. La Puma, D. Orentlicher, and R.J. Moss, "Advance Directives on Admission: Clinical Implications and Analysis of the Patient Self-Determination Act of 1990," *Journal of the American Medical Association* 266 (1991):402-05.

25   Capron, "The Patient Self-Determination Act," 35-36.

26   Puma, Orentlicher, and Moss, "Advance Directives on Admission," 405.

27   M. Mezey, "Community Education," *Hastings Center Report* 21 (September/October 1991, special supplement):S11-S12.

28   R.B. Purtilo, "Institutional Quandries," *Hastings Center Report* 21 (September/October 1991, special supplement):S13-S14.

29   S. Johnson, "PSDA in the Nursing Home," *Hastings Center Report* 21 (September/October 1991, special supplement):S3-S4.

30   *Advance Directive Protocols and the Patient Self-Determination Act* (New York: Concern for Dying, 1990); "Practicing the PSDA," *Hastings Center Report* 21 (September/October 1991, special supplement):S1-S16.

31   J.M. Riley, "Living Wills: Making Life and Death Decisions," *Provider* (February 1991):15-23.

32   La Puma, Orentlicher, and Moss, "Advance Directives on Admission," 402-405.

33   S. Okie, "Living Wills and Dying Wishes: The Pain of Deciding When Enough Is Enough," *Washington Post* (National Weekly Edition), 1-7 July 1991, 11-12.

34   S.M. Wolf, "Honoring Broader Directives," *Hastings Center Report* 21 (September/October 1991, special supplement):S8-S9.

35   H. Smith, *The Power Game.*

Appendix

Appendix

Summary of California Proposition 161, Physician-Assisted Death, Included on State of California Ballot 3 November 1992

Summary

- Authorizes mentally competent adult to request "aid in dying" in the event a terminal condition is diagnosed. The patient must first execute a directive, which is written and witnessed. When the patient has been diagnosed as having a terminal illness, has determined that the time for aid in dying has arrived, and has made an enduring request, the patient will communicate that determination directly to the attending physician who will administer aid in dying in accordance with the act.

- Authorizes physician to terminate life in "painless, humane, and dignified manner" if request is made by the dying patient as described in the act.

- Provides immunity from civil and criminal liability for health-care professionals and facilities who provide aid in dying when properly requested; however, no one is forced to provide aid in dying who objects on religious, moral, or ethical grounds.

- Prohibits existence of directive from affecting terms of insurance policies. Death would be considered to result from the terminal illness and not from suicide.

- Requires health-care providers to keep records and report to the California State Department of Health Services the patient's age, type of illness, and date that aid in dying was carried out.

Voluntary Directive to Physicians

Notice to Patient:

This document will exist until it is revoked by you. This document revokes any prior Directive to administer aid in dying but does not revoke a durable power of attorney for health care or a living will. You must follow the witnessing procedure described at the end of this form or the document will not be valid. You may wish to give your doctor a signed copy.

This Directive will not be valid unless it is signed by two qualified witnesses who are present when you sign or acknowledge your signature. The witnesses must not be related to you by blood, marriage, or adoption; they must not be entitled to any part of your estate or at the time of execution of the Directive have no claim against any portion of your estate, nor anticipate making such claim against any portion of your estate; and they must not include: your attending physician, an employee of the attending physician; a health care provider; an employee of a health care provider; the operator of the community care facility or an employee of an operator of a community care facility.

If you have attached any additional pages to this form, you must sign and date each of the additional pages at the same time you date and sign this Directive.

Administration of a Medical Procedure to End My Life in a
Painless, Humane, and Dignified Manner

This Directive is made this _____ day of _____ (month)_____ (year).

I, _____, being of sound mind, do voluntarily make known my desire that my life shall be ended with the aid of a physician in a painless, humane, and dignified manner when I have a terminal condition or illness, certified to be terminal by two physicians, and they determine that my death will occur within six months or less.

When the terminal diagnosis is made and confirmed, and this Directive is in effect, I may then ask my attending physician for aid in dying. I trust and hope that he or she will comply. If he or she refuses to comply, which is his or her right, then I urge that he or she assist in locating a colleague who will comply.

Determining the time and place of my death shall be at my sole discretion. The manner of my death shall be determined jointly by my attending physician and myself.

This Directive shall remain valid until revoked by me. I may revoke this Directive at any time.

I recognize that a physician's judgment is not always certain, and that medical science continues to make progress in extending life, but in spite of these facts, I nevertheless wish aid in dying rather than letting my terminal condition take its natural course.

I will endeavor to inform my family of this Directive, and my intention to request the aid of my physician to help me to die when I am in a terminal condition, and take those opinions into consideration. But the final decision remains mine. I acknowledge that it is solely my responsibility to inform my family of my intentions.

I have given full consideration to and understand the full import of this Directive, and I am emotionally and mentally competent to make this Directive. I accept the moral and legal responsibility for receiving aid in dying.

Signed: _____

_____

City, County, and State of Residence

Statement of Witnesses

I declare under penalty of perjury under the laws of California that the person who signed or acknowledged this document is personally known to me (or proved to me on the basis of satisfactory evidence) to be the declarant of this Directive; that he or she signed and acknowledged this Directive in my presence, that he or she appears to be of sound mind and under no duress, fraud, or undue influence; that I am not the attending physician, an employee of the attending physician, a health-care provider, an employee of a health-care provider, the operator of a community care facility, or an employee of an operator of a community care facility.

I further declare under penalty of perjury under the laws of California that I am not related to the declarant by blood, marriage, or adoption, and, to the best of my knowledge, I am not entitled to any part of the estate of the principal upon the death of the principal under a will not existing or by operation of law, and have no claim nor anticipate making a claim against any portion of the estate of the declarant upon his or her death.

Dated: _____

Witness's Signature: _____

Print Name: _____

Residence Address: _____

Dated: _____

Witness's Signature: _____

Print Name: _____

Residence Address: _____

Statement of Patient Advocate or Ombudsman

(If you are a patient in a skilled nursing facility, one of the witnesses must be a Patient Advocate or Ombudsman. The following statement is required only if you are a patient in a skilled nursing facility, a health-care facility that provides the following basic services: skilled nursing care and supportive care to patients whose primary need is for availability of skilled nursing care on an extended basis. The Patient Advocate or Ombudsman must sign the "Statement of Witnesses" above *and* must also sign the following statement.)

I further declare under penalty of perjury under the laws of California that I am a Patient Advocate or Ombudsman as designated by the State Department of Aging and that I am serving as a witness as required by Section 2525.4 of the California Civil Code.

Signed: ——————————————————————————————————————